I Belong to No One

I Belong to No One

Abused, afraid and alone. The shocking true story of a young girl forced to make the ultimate sacrifice for her survival.

GWEN WILSON

The events that occur in this book are factual. Most names have been changed to protect the privacy of individuals, and the timing of some events has been compressed.

This edition first published in Great Britain in 2015
by Orion
an imprint of the Orion Publishing Group Ltd
Carmelite House, 50 Victoria Embankment
London EC4Y 0DZ
An Hachette UK Company

5 7 9 10 8 6

A CIP catalogue record for this book is available from the British Library.

ISBN: 978 1 4091 6489 0

Printed by CPI Group (UK) Ltd, Croydon, CR0 4YY

The Orion Publishing Group's policy is to use papers that are natural, renewable and recyclable and made from wood grown in sustainable forests. The logging and manufacturing processes are expected to conform to the environmental regulations of the country of origin.

www.orionbooks.co.uk

To Bill

Thank you for having the faith to go with me into the unknown.
May we belong to each other for the rest of time.

PART ONE

Motherless Daughter

1955–1971

1

I feel myself drift away from my body, in that space between wakefulness and sleep. I drift up to the ceiling and I float, unable to control my path, bumping into walls and ceiling and corners of the room. Disconnected from what I see below, I am just an observer. Interested, but not involved. My tiny body is curled in the bed below, and I know it is mine, but in that moment I feel as if I'm somewhere else. Mum steps into the room, arms cradling some freshly ironed clothes, and passes soundlessly to the baby-sized wardrobe wedged in the niche between the fireplace and the wall. I watch her as she opens a drawer and carefully places the folded items inside, smoothing them down and sliding the drawer closed again with methodical movements.

So there *you are, Mum.*

So, there was *a time when I knew you. In that time before I could talk, maybe before I was three years old. You wrote to my father that I didn't speak until that age. You were worried for me, but I didn't know it then. It was something revealed to me much, much later when you gave me Dad's replies.*

Before I could talk I often left my body, but I never left the room that held my bed – perhaps I couldn't. Up there I had no strength, no use of my arms and legs. I couldn't walk or crawl through the air, or choose in which direction to go. I surrendered to hovering, never straying too far from my form lying motionless in the bed below.

My rational mind tells me this must be a false memory. It sounds weird even to me. I know it shouldn't be possible, and yet it persists there in the recesses of my mind. Something from long ago, something that was true then, and is still true to me today.

•

This narrative is one part of the tapestry of my life. I have told it as factually as possible, yet I know that not every detail will be precise. It is recorded in the way I remember it in the fibres of my being. Those who wove my threads may remember an event or a conversation in a different time and place, or have a different interpretation of their meaning or significance.

•

It smells of damp earth underneath the house. The odour permeates my skin and invades my nostrils. I like it down here. I like the secret nature of it. Underneath the house is an otherworldly place, a house within a house, sealed from the outside world by its bricked-in walls and sagging wooden doors tugged shut behind me.

Above, the house is quiet. There are no sounds of television or people.

There is *Mum.*

Mum, lying in a motionless trance on her bed in the front room. She seems so far away. Even if I crawled commando-style, I could not reach the underneath of her room. There, at the front of the house, the floor is almost level with the ground. Here, at the back, I stand upright, to my full six-year-old height, and I can breathe in the smell. I stand in the gloom and soak up the mustiness around me. The silence, only broken by my breath echoing in a rhythmic timelessness, presses against my ears. Waiting, listening, being.

•

Memories of my mother are always like this, perceived from a distance and loaded with a sense of detachment and inertia, even though I know she was once a busy, functioning person. Before me. In the days before my existence. In the days when she lived at Lavender Bay with her mother and her sister, and with my brother Steve and his cousins. 'Our cousins,' I correct myself. In the days before we came to live in Old Guildford. In the days before she was cast adrift to the isolated nothingness of her new location, burdened with a nine-year-old son, a baby daughter and a shabby old house she couldn't possibly look after.

'She has a lot on her plate,' the neighbours used to say. 'Imagine bringing up two children on your own and the girl just a baby? How she copes in that old house, what with going to work and all . . .'

They said the house was jerry-built. I knew what it meant. The house was cobbled together from scraps of timber, fibro and Masonite – bits other people threw away. Our roof was not terracotta tiles like the others in the street. It was tin. Corrugated iron, they called it. When the sun beat down, the heat spread through each room like an oven. We gasped and baked and prayed for a Southerly Buster. We knew it would come in the evening: we could smell its approach. It roared up the hill from the bottom of the street, and found us perched at the corner, wilting. As it rushed towards the south-facing window, I ran to open the front door opposite. The wind raged through, dragging the accumulated hot air away with it.

'Hot air rises, cool air drops,' Steve told me. 'That's why they put in sash windows. They open at the top and bottom and drag the air in and out, around and around.'

That was hard for me to understand. My brother was nine years older, and he knew so much more than I did.

Winter felt different. The tin roof carried cold air into every corner of the house. Draughts whipped around the gaps in the walls and the windows, and out of the holes in the skirting board where the mice had eaten through. Steve stuffed the holes with steel wool. He said the mice would eat it and the steel would kill them; that way, we wouldn't have to lay so many traps. I hated finding little grey mice lying stiff and strangled in the traps when we woke each morning. Sometimes their tiny tongues were sticking out and their eyes were wide and staring. It made me sad that they died in pain. Of course I didn't realise it might have been just as painful to die with a belly full of steel wool.

I liked our tin roof best when it rained, and best of all when it rained hard at night and I was tucked in bed. I imagined a team of wild horses above me, or a chariot being pulled at full gallop. The horses would be charging this way and that, and as their thudding feet came nearer I imagined they would fall through onto my bed beside me.

It was never horses that fell through, though, it was the rain. Seeking out every crack and opening where gutters had rusted away, or where sheets of iron had torn loose and lifted in the wind, the rain seeped into the house, drip by drip, slowly at times and like the popping of a machine gun at others. We ran to collect all the buckets and saucepans we could find and lined them up under the drips. We didn't want our clothes and books or our few bits of furniture to get wet. It didn't matter about the floor – we only had linoleum, not carpet like our neighbours. If we didn't catch the leaks in time, the water ran in rivulets to the central room. The roof supports had given way, leaving the house crumpling and sagging like an old man tired of life.

The house was sad, just like us: Steve, Mum and me.

Three lonely castaways marooned together.

2

I was luckier than Steve, because I had another mother. Our neighbour Kulpie had been my carer since I was a babe in arms and Mum had to work to support us.

'Lynn,' she would tell me, 'your mother bundled you up in your bunny rug and walked you down here that first morning, and by the time she got here all she had in her arms was the rug. You were hanging by your chin from the crook of her arm. It was lucky I rescued you. You were nearly strangled.'

Lynn isn't my real name. It is Gwendoline. Some call me Gwen or Gwenny, but Kulpie didn't like any of those names. She thought Gwen was too short and sharp and not a suitable name for a little girl. She preferred to call me Lynn: it was softer and prettier, she said. She chose it as her special name for me the day I came into her care, just as if I were *her* baby to name.

She was Mrs Kulper, but I called her Kulpie. I could hardly call my mother 'Mrs'. Nor could she be 'Mummy', because that was for my real mother.

If I ever asked anything of my mother, it wasn't enough to ask politely, 'Please, Mummy, may I . . . ?' It could never be a simple request. She demanded I dress it up. She coached me in dreary, insincere superlatives: 'Please Mummy, darling', or 'Mummy dearest' or '*Best* Mummy in the whole wide world.'

Kulpie never made me go through that. Kulpie was just Kulpie and no frills about it. Her house was warm and busy; neighbours came in and out asking to borrow a cup of sugar, then stayed for a glass of pilsener and a cigarette. Kulpie bragged about me and showed me off to her friends and neighbours. The older I grew, the prouder she became. 'Mrs P, listen to this poem she can recite,' she would say. Or she might ask me to do a little dance, or just to show off how my thumb could double over backwards. Her visitors were always agreeing what a bright girl I was and fussed over me and wrote clever things in the autograph book she bought me. Kulpie drew in it, teams of horses with wild, flowing manes racing across the page, or she would write something smart such as, 'Don't tell the world all you know – 'cos then they'll know that's *all* you know!' People laughed when I showed it to them. Whenever I was with Kulpie, I felt I was the centre of her world. A world where even being naughty was treated with tolerance and gentle guidance.

'She's a mischief maker, Mrs M. Remember the dead goldfish? Well, I got to the bottom of that. Caught her the other day with the new ones in her hands. Turning 'em over and over and then droppin' them back in the bowl one at a time. Watching 'em sink to the bottom, she was.'

'Oh you are a one, Lynn!' said Mrs Mahboub, tossing her head back and slapping her hands together.

'I just wanted a closer look. I thought they'd swim away.'

'Thinks too much for her own good if you ask me, Mrs M. Last week it was the lolly jar. Took out all the toffees and caramels and stashed them under the lounge cushions. Told me she thought she'd miss out if she didn't hide them. Middle of summer! Didn't know they were there 'til the cushions stuck together. I was picking off bits of toffee for days.'

'Cheeky monkey.'

'Sure is. Sooner she starts school, sooner we'll both be better off.' Kulpie threw me an affectionate wink, so I knew she was just teasing me.

•

It was a happy day when at four years old I came down with measles, because Mum said she couldn't look after me and sent me to live with Kulpie full time until I recovered. I was in heaven – except for the eggnog, Kulpie's cure for sick children. She had little time for my squirming over the stink of raw eggs.

'Lynn,' she said. 'I've nursed four kids through the measles, and this fixed them up every time. Stop screwing up your nose and get it into you. Swallow it in one go. That'll do the trick.'

I wasn't the only one Kulpie was nursing. The district nurse came every day to see her mother, a fragile ghost who never left her room. I rarely saw or spoke to her. When the nurse knocked at the front door on the first morning of my illness I leapt off the sofa and ran to the door.

'She's come for *me,*' I thought. 'I *knew* I was dying.'

Kulpie rushed to the door and elbowed me out of the way.

'The *real* patient is up the hall,' she said with a laugh, and she and the nurse smiled in my direction. 'Lynn, get back on the couch, I'll see to you shortly.'

The nurse felt my forehead and looked down my throat. 'Oh yes,' she said, 'you must lie very, very still until you get better.' So each day from then on I lay straight and stiff like a dead mouse whenever the nurse was around.

Kulpie was always ready to take me in suddenly, even if her house was full, making room for me in the double bed she shared with her husband, topping and tailing so our legs tangled and our heads stuck out at opposite ends. Everything about her routine became familiar to me, starting from when she got up in the morning and pulled on her pink chenille dressing gown, put a few curlers in her blonde hair and walked into the kitchen to down a Vincent APC powder. It can't have tasted very nice, because she screwed up her face when she did it, but she said it helped her start the day. When the worst of the measles had passed, Kulpie often sent me to the corner store to buy powders and cigarettes; she liked Capstan or Craven A. She wrote what I was to fetch on a note she wrapped around some coins and tied into the corner of a handkerchief, which she then pinned to my dress with a safety pin. The man in the shop tied the change back into my hankie and put the shopping into the string bag Kulpie had given me, and sometimes there was a penny's worth of lollies for me.

It felt normal to have a life split between two homes, and to belong to two families at once. I cannot remember a time when it was different.

'Grant John, Graaaant Joohhhhhn,' Kulpie would sing from her porch as the end of day drew in. The sound would float up the street, catching our house with its fading lilt, echoing into the gloomy recesses of our musty underworld, where Grant and Steve were absorbed in schoolboys' games, hidden far away from the prying reach of a baby sister. It was the signal for Kulpie's youngest to come home for dinner, and for Steve to fetch me home to ours. I was always disappointed to leave Kulpie's house of light and warmth and cosiness and talk and laughter, and return to our house of silence.

If I had been given a choice, I would have said I wanted to live with Kulpie forever.

3

So this is where my early memories find me. A little girl not yet school age, living with my mother and older brother Steve in a small weatherboard cottage rammed into the corner of Springfield and Crawford streets in a suburb called Old Guildford in Sydney's west. We were doing it tough in the nuclear family ideal of Australia's post-war utopia.

There were no rich people in Old Guildford. Any semblance of refinement had died with the Misses MacDonald, two ancient sisters who drifted on a waft of lavender, their gloved hands proffering gifts of welcome to each newcomer. Their mansion was set back from the main road at a discreet distance on a huge block of land, its two storeys bland and square from the outside, its treasures of carved cedar staircases and intricate fireplaces known only to the rare and privileged guest. We were linked by the understanding the core of our house had once belonged to them, the benevolent offering of a two-roomed cottage originally built for a long-vanished estate worker.

No, there were no rich people in Old Guildford, not now the Misses MacDonald were dead and gone, without heirs. Now there were only the poor, the poorer and the poorest.

When we bought the house, we had enabled the 'new Australians' – old Mr and Mrs Pellarin – to move up a level on the social scale. When they arrived from Italy years before, the cottage was only two rooms with a veranda on the front. They added a room that served as kitchen, living room and bathhouse. Time passed, and they tacked on another bedroom and a separate kitchen. The old fuel stove with its ivory and green enamelled oven door emblazoned with 'Metters' was their legacy to us. It sulked in a wall of our living room, useless and smoke-blackened. The stove shared the only chimney in the house, backing on to the delicate fireplace of the original cottage. That fireplace was the only pretty thing in the house, framed by a semi-circle of beaten metal and fronted by exquisite cream and rose patterned tiles. Neither the fireplace nor the stove worked properly, the chimney having long since blocked up. We never fixed it. We didn't know how. We knew nothing – how could we? It took all of Mum's time, effort and money to go to work, to shop and to feed us.

The tragedy for the Pellarins, who moved next door to a house they had designed and built, was watching us let their years of sweat and 'doing without' in their original home disintegrate in front of their eyes. We had no idea how to raise chooks, keep fruit fly from infesting ripening peaches and nectarines, or stop flyscreens from disintegrating and shredding away at the windows. Crikey! We couldn't even cut the grass, and there was almost two blocks of that.

Across the road, the secrets of the MacDonalds' mansion were thrown open when it was subdivided into flats and rented to Australia's 'new chums', the Ten Pound Poms, fresh off the boat from England. Among them was a boy of my age named Paul, giving me my first experience of childhood in my world of adults.

Paul and I weren't the first children to discover the expansive grounds were dense with mulberry trees, but to us the experience was fresh and new. We shared the joy of scrambling into them, skinning our knees and scrabbling for the rich, ripe fruit, stuffing handfuls of lusciousness into our mouths and abandoning ourselves to the silky dripping of the juice.

We collected silkworms from the trees, nesting them in a shoebox filled with mulberry leaves to eat, and holes punched in the lid so they could breathe. We were confused when the worms turned themselves into cocoons, hiding their furry grubbiness in a shell wound round and round with a soft down. Then came the disappointing day when we opened the lid to find our cocoons empty husks, and in their place were moths fluttering for freedom.

Paul wasn't at my side on my first day of school when a gaggle of giggling girls surrounded me and one of them shrieked, 'The hairs on your legs are long enough to plait!' Then she bent down and showed the others she could do it.

From then on, though, Paul and I walked to school together. There he was, a scrawny blond kid with see-through skin and blue eyes that were too big for his head, dressed to the nines in a grey school uniform and long socks which kept dropping down around his ankles. There I was, a solid, dark-haired girl with olive skin and big hazel eyes, wearing a pretty cotton dress Aunty Myra, my mother's sister, had made me. In one hand we each held our Globite school cases containing nothing more than a sandwich wrapped in greaseproof paper, and with our free hands we clutched tightly to each other as we bravely set off to face the day together. We walked hand-in-hand down the length of Crawford Street, past the vacant blocks which were still part of the mansion's grounds, past the first of the Housing Commission homes, past Mrs Mahboub's cheery yellow fibro home with the kelpie dog which had just had pups, past Kulpie's and a half-dozen more, and on to the end of the street and across the drainage ditch at the bottom. The ditch was dry at the start of the school year, and lay deep below us. Three wooden planks formed a rough bridge, and if we fell we would have to climb out of the dusty, gravelly hole, with no hope of staying clean. We would giggle with relief when we reached the other side. In reality it was only four steps, but in our Lilliputian world, it was as if we had crossed a great river.

As we opened our silkworm box and let the moths fly away, any more memory of Paul flew away with them. His family moved on to better things in their new life in Australia, and they took with them their gentle son with the peculiar accent and the hair so blond it shone golden in an Aussie summer.

I was left to battle those early days of school on my own.

'You started early because of your special circumstances, Lynn,' Kulpie explained to me years later. 'There were no other children who didn't have a father at home. Your mum had no choice but to work. How else were you and Steve to live? Most mothers with young children only worked outside the home if there was a grandmother or aunty to look after them. There was no such thing as preschools. So, for you, it was school or me. You could read already, and you were bright, so the school let you start even though you were only four and a half.'

Well, I can't have been as bright as she believed, because when I got to the end of the kindergarten year, they made me do it all over again. I tell everyone it was the three-piece jigsaws. I could get the first two pieces in place all right, but I'll be darned if I could work out where that third piece belonged.

•

I often felt confused about the concept of a 'father' when I was young.

My friend Doreen lived across the road. We were the same age and went to school together, and I played at her place from time to time. I was around five when I began to notice that every afternoon a man came to the house, and he hadn't gone by the time I went home.

Eventually curiosity overcame me.

'Who is this man?' I asked Doreen.

'Huh? My father, stupid,' she replied.

'Hmmm . . .' I was struggling to make sense of this. 'So why does he come here every day?'

Doreen gave me a look. ''Cos he lives here.' Her voice went up at the end. 'Are you an idiot or something?'

Well, that was curious. My father was a hero. He had been a World War I flying ace and I thought he was so brave, going into battle against the German Hun in a flimsy aircraft held together with string and a prayer. That's how he lost the tops of three fingers, mangled in the machine gun in the frenzy of a dogfight. I was so proud of him, I kept his photo beside my bed. There was never a man more debonair. He was up close to the camera, looking straight at me with clear, open eyes, pencil moustache outlining his top lip, his thinning hair slicked back with Brylcreem. The photo was only of his head and shoulders, but it seemed to me he was wearing a well-cut suit. He looked just like a movie star.

But my father didn't live with us. He lived somewhere else – I didn't know where, and it didn't occur to me to ask where. I had no idea mothers and fathers might live together. My father visited twice a year, once at Christmas and the other time for Steve's birthday, and I didn't expect to see him at any other time. He always brought Steve fabulous presents, but nothing for me. That made sense. After all, Steve was a boy and I was a girl, and I understood intuitively that was the way of things. Boys mattered more than girls.

4

'They're pretty, Aunty Myra.' I eyed the beads she was clipping around her neck. Their pearlised finish glistened back at us in the bathroom mirror. Shiny and sparkling, just the way I thought of her. I caught a glimpse of the scar running across her throat. She noticed my stare.

'They slit it, Gwenny. The surgeons – when I had my op. They cut it from one side to the other so they could take the thyroid out. It was going too fast.'

Her bright eyes twinkled at me in the reflection. They protruded, making it seem as if there was pent-up energy waiting to burst out of her body.

Aunty Myra was my mother's sister, five years older than Mum, and she was used to being the 'grown-up', not in a bossy way, but in a caring, 'stick with me and I'll show you how it works' kind of way.

Both Aunty Myra and my mother, Joyce, were brunettes, of average height, slender build and fair skin. Both kept their hair short: Myra in a stylish cut; Mum in a permanent wave. Both had round, pale blue eyes – Myra's wide and eager; Mum's hooded and guarded. That's where any similarity ended. Aunty Myra's square face was always ready to break into a wide smile, while Mum's rare smile was apprehensive, tightly locked into her oval face with a receding chin. Aunty Myra was an outdoors woman who loved bushwalking and gardening, while Mum sheltered in introspective hobbies of reading and knitting. Aunty Myra was animated and bubbly, energetic and enthusiastic, her whole being swelling with the joy of life. Mum was silent and withdrawn. Aunty Myra was day; Mum was night.

Until 1956, less than a year after I was born, Aunty Myra and her husband and three sons had lived together with Mum, Steve and my grandmother in a house in the harbourside suburb of Lavender Bay. Then my grandmother died and everyone scattered. Uncle Bill, Myra's husband, lived long enough to build a two-bedroom cottage at Tascott. It was a simple house, with a rainwater tank and a fuel stove, set amid the beautiful bushland of the Central Coast. I lived there every school holidays.

Aunty Myra had three sons, but Chris, the youngest and still in school, was the only one who lived at Tascott. The older two were working and living in Sydney. Whenever the three were together, she couldn't get their names straight unless she called them in the order of their birth.

'Phillip, Brian – I mean Christopher!'

She would sound annoyed when she did it, as if it was their fault she couldn't remember what she had named them. It was so funny, and her nature so sunny, that within moments she would be laughing along with us.

I was the daughter Aunty Myra never had. I knew if anything were to happen to my mother, Mum's will declared Myra was to be my guardian.

That was fine by me. Mum never spoke about her younger years, or even ours, but Aunty Myra prattled on, darting from one lively story to the next with hardly a pause in between. The double-time bopping of her thyroid may have been why her conversation jumped around at such a startling rate, hurtling from one story to the next, twisting from the past to the present and back again so that I never knew quite which tale I was following.

'There were thirteen in my grandma's family back in England, and every other child had to learn a skill and teach it to the one below them,' mixed up with, 'Gee Gwenny, I've got some pretty material for your next dress . . . did I show you . . . ?' and, 'Daddy had a beautiful copperplate . . . but he drank too much and didn't work too regularly.'

For all her chatty nature, there was one subject Aunty Myra would not dwell on. She and Mum lived at the Burnside Presbyterian Orphan Homes in Parramatta in the 1920s. She always dismissed those five years by saying, 'It was a bit grim, Gwenny.'

Aunty Myra was scarred by the lack of education she received in the orphanage.

'Three years they left me in sixth class,' she said. 'Can you imagine, me so big with all those littl'uns?'

'Why, Aunty Myra?'

'My eyesight. Couldn't follow the lessons.'

The story stuck with me.

'Why didn't the orphanage notice your blindness?' I asked her years later.

'I don't know, Gwenny. They didn't take much notice of us. I don't suppose they should have.' The dismissive wave of her hand signified to move off orphanage questions.

Aunty Myra was twenty when she got her first pair of glasses. The world of words was opened to her, and she embraced it. She read voraciously, and she never lost her reverence for the written word, as if ink and paper were too precious to be wasted on trifling piffle. She drew her own conclusions from the scientific evidence.

'Gwenny, love. We need vitamin D, it makes strong bones, and it comes from the sun. So what we need to do, when we hang out our clothes, is to turn them inside out. So the sun will shine on them, and when we wear them, our bodies will absorb the vitamin D. Okay?'

Often, people couldn't understand the bizarre twists and turns of her mind as it skipped along a few beats ahead of the others.

'What! Us rabbits? Do something?' she replied to a neighbour who was complaining they should get together to protest some change in local regulations. The neighbour looked baffled but I knew she was referring to the rabbits in *Wind in the Willows,* the ones who had failed to come to the aid of Mole when he ran into trouble at Toad Hall.

'That's *ridukuluss,*' she growled as she mulled over what the neighbour wanted her to do, 'that's what it is Gwenny. It's just *ridukuluss!*' I knew she was letting off steam, giving way to a moment of rare contempt. Then she caught my eye and laughed, her frustration spent as quickly as it had built up.

It wasn't in Aunty Myra's nature to dwell on the injustices life dealt her, even though there were plenty of those. She rolled with the punches, accepting adversity was her lot in life – and she made light of negative situations. I think it is thanks to her I learned to look for the positive in every situation. She made cheerfulness look so easy, I had no chance to sit around feeling sorry for myself. I didn't even know I had a reason to feel down in the mouth.

'The world's a funny old place, Gwenny love, mmph?' she would say as she shrugged up both shoulders, lifted her eyebrows, and screwed her mouth into an expression which said, 'not much we can do about it – best resign yourself to it'.

In her mind, the workings of world order were a mystery, known only to those with greater intelligence than either of us possessed. Best not to dwell on things. Just go with the flow, get on with it, and try to remain cheerful. As Lord Tennyson said, and Aunty Myra re-modelled, 'Ours is not to reason why, ours is just to do and die.'

5

Mr van den Avoort was bent over the sink, his long, lanky body spotlighted in the sun streaming through the kitchen window above.

'Crowd around, you three. You'll need to be watching closely to see how this is done.'

We clustered up tightly, straining around to the left and right of him, each of us anxious for a good view of the magic that was about to happen. Joanne and Adrian were used to their father's experiments, yet they never tired of them. He could always be relied upon to come up with one quirky idea after another; he had a brain that never shut down, moving restlessly from one project to the next. Most of the time there didn't seem to be any urgent purpose; it seemed to me his tinkering was primarily for our fun and enjoyment, and his, too. Recently he had taken an old cocktail cabinet to pieces and transformed it into a three-in-one stereo system. He had installed a television sideways where the drink bottles should have been, and covered the television with a hinged wooden lid. He showed us a mirror inside the lid, and with it set at the right angle, we could watch the television from the reflection in the mirror.

'When the object is inverted, the reflection will be seen the right way up.'

At least, I think he said something like that. I couldn't always understand what he was explaining to us, and he was forever taking things apart and turning them into something they had never been before, so there was plenty for us to get our heads around.

This time he had promised to show us how to turn a raw egg into a jet boat.

Time dragged by as he dribbled water into the sink, measuring the depth with a finger joint, and carefully laying the egg on its side. The egg floated on top of the water. I had expected it to sink. He took up a pin and gently worked it into one end of the egg. Nothing happened. I broke the silence with a slight sneer.

'This is stupid. This experiment is *never* going to work.'

'Gwendoline! If you have nothing good to say, then please leave!' Mrs van den Avoort rounded on me smartly. I bit my lip. It hadn't been so long since she'd sent me home 'quick sticks' when I'd told Adrian there was no such person as Santa Claus.

Joanne squeezed my arm.

'Look,' she whispered.

The egg wobbled, still floating on the surface of the water, then suddenly it whooshed around in a circle.

'There. See how that works? Did you notice I pricked the blunt end of the egg? There's an air sac there, a little space between the white and the shell; it's a breathing hole for the baby chicks. When I pierced through the shell and then pulled the pin out, the air escaped and the force pushed the egg around. Understand?'

Mr van den Avoort was a fascinating man to be around, but it wasn't on his account that I spent so much time in his household. It was his daughter who drew me there. Joanne was as fair as I was dark, her light skin tone and freckles reflecting her Dutch heritage. We had been joined at the hip since we'd met earlier that year in kindergarten. She lived one block from me in a modest fibro tile home with an enormous backyard and a weeping willow smack in the centre of its grassed area. We spent hours in that tree, weaving magic with the stories we made up for each other, engrossed in each other's imagination.

The two of us were class 'nerds' before the name was invented. We shared common interests outside the normal scope of five- and six-year-olds. In the narrow-mindedness of 1960s Australia with its stereotypical roles for males and females, we were stimulated – by the scientific mind of her father, and most of all by the dominant force of her mother – to think and be aware.

Mrs van den Avoort was a powerful influence in our young lives, moulding us as if we were lumps of clay. She was kind and motherly, but also strict and an upholder of standards. She brooked no nonsense from us, and she expected us to use our faculties to their utmost, making no allowances that we may be 'only babies' in the eyes of some people. She was an educated, cultured woman who tried her best to pass her knowledge on to us, and this extended to formally instructing us in elocution. Her offer sparked my mother into action, and she mysteriously scraped up the two shillings a week so I could have regular lessons. There was a touch of delusion of grandeur about my mother, as if she had descended from royalty only to fall on hard times along the way. She was all for my learning to speak with a plum in my mouth.

'Girls! Again! Pe-ar-no. Pe-ar-no. Round those vowels. I don't want to hear pee-yan-o. Open your mouths.'

'Not ow-er. OU then soft a in the throat. Shape your lips. Repeat, "Fools! For I also had my hour." Ou-a.'

If Joanne and I weren't already outsiders, we were now certain to be. Speaking so differently from our working-class schoolmates was sure to mark us out. But I didn't care. Adults loved the way we spoke and the words we could use, and that meant they would listen to my chatter and indulge my recitals.

'Girls, now you've had plenty of practice for "The Serial Story". We are going to act it out as you recite it today. Gwendoline, start with the announcer.'

I put on my best BBC radio announcer voice.

There's a popular and paying kind of story,
which is really quite exciting on the whole.
It is either most mysterious and gory,
Or else, 'tis full of sentiment and soul.
Its principal and most important feature
is just – to be continued in our next –
For example – The Ghost Story.

'Good. Now, the narrator. Remember to emphasise those words with sound effects. Boom. Rustle. Groan. Use the voice to make the sound effect. And I want to hear the "p" in enwrapped. En-wrrappd. Push off from the "r".'

He stood at night within the haunted tower
Enwrapped in silence, frightened and alone.
The solemn bell boomed forth the fatal hour.
What's that?!! – the sound of rustling and a groan.

'Now the ghost. Old raspy voice. Crackly. Scratchy. Thin. Then back to the narrator.'

Fly, fly rash youth, thy fatal quest abandon
For little of its consequence thou wreckest –

'Narrator. Sound urgent . . .'

His shoulder – something lays its icy hand on –
He turns – and there, in the moonlight –
His eyes darting from their rockets, pockets, I mean sockets.
His brow wet with damp, he sees before him –

'Rising inflection!'

Oh heaven, this agony is too great to be borne any longer . . .

'Panic. Draw it out. Scream with the ahh.'

It is . . . ahh . . . it is . . .

'Sweetly now . . .'

TO BE CONTINUED IN OUR NEXT . . .

6

There came a day in March 1962, when I was six years and nine months old, that Mum took me with her to do business in the city. To the offices of J Stuart Thom & Co, Solicitors, to see a man called Mr Cotter. I remember the place. I remember because it was called Merino House, and I knew a board game based on sheep stations.

'Mrs George. It's good to see you again. How are you?'

Mr Cotter beamed at Mum, shaking her hand as he greeted her. 'And is this Gwendoline? You were just a baby the last time I saw you. My – aren't you pretty as a picture!'

His cheeks were chubby in his genial face and his manner towards me was kind. 'Isn't that a charming dress?' he was beaming at *me* now.

'Mmmm,' I glowed back at him, giving a little twirl so the skirt flowed out around me. 'My aunty made it.' I was proud, and I puffed my chest out.

'Ahhh – that would be your Aunty Myra,' Mr Cotter responded.

I didn't know then just how much Adrian Cotter knew about our family. I didn't know he had been our family solicitor for years, or that he knew our secrets better than we did ourselves. Nor did I have any idea of why we were visiting him that day. Mum sat across from him at his enormous wooden desk piled high with papers wrapped in red and green ribbons. While the two of them were deep in conversation – all gobbledygook to my six-year-old ears – I frittered away the time with my face and hands plastered against an enormous picture window. Its high vantage point gave me a bird's-eye view of Sydney sprawled below us. Directly in front of me I could see the Harbour Bridge and the harbour itself, busy with ferries in the middle of a working day. The sun glinted on sparkling water. Bright and blue and busy. It was a long way from suburban Old Guildford.

'So!' he was finishing up. 'The next thing you need to do is take her back to the hospital at Annandale. Queen Victoria Maternity, wasn't it?'

Mum had been busy with her own thoughts ever since we had started out early that morning, hurrying me to the bus that connected with Granville rail station, and during the hour-long train journey she had little to say. Even now she didn't waste any time explaining to me what was going on. Suddenly we were on the busy city street, surrounded by people in suits and hats hurrying this way and that. I scuttled along beside Mum, a tiny figure battered by the crowd, and as my eyes fixed on the uneven pavement I noticed dust filming on my shiny black patent leather shoes. I hoped the lace frill on my white ankle socks wouldn't get dirty; Mr Cotter wouldn't think I looked so pretty if that happened. A tram clanged up; the step up was so high I could barely manage, and as I struggled to get on board Mum gave me a little shove from behind to hurry me along.

I couldn't imagine why I was going to hospital – I didn't feel at all sick. I was desperate to ask but it was clear Mum was not in a talkative mood. She was deep in thought, and saving her words for her business on arrival. More talking, more papers, and again I was left to my own devices, wandering around the hospital corridors, poking my nose in places I had no business. There seemed to be a need for me to appear every so often. I was called to join Mum and whomever she was talking with at the time; then that person would look me over and ask her a few questions. It seemed there was something wrong with me, but I couldn't understand what, and Mum gave me no chance to interrupt.

Still without explanation, we went back into the city, to a large sandstone building near Hyde Park, where Mum had to fill out more forms and shuffle more papers.

It was a long day full of unfamiliar places and faces, and it seemed to me as if we had spent the whole time going from one place to another; what had started out as an exciting adventure had gradually dragged on until I was tired and confused by it all. What on earth was it about?

The answer came fifteen years later, quite out of the blue, when I had long since put that day to the back of my mind. Focused on applying for my first-ever passport, and excited at the thought of my upcoming overseas trip, I applied for my birth certificate.

I wasn't looking for anything in particular when I opened the envelope, so it came as a shock when I smoothed out the long paper. Springing off the page were two straight bold lines where information should be. My father's name and the details of my parents' marriage were blank, and the columns allowed for them were struck through with thick black lines. They may as well have stamped *illegitimate* in big red print. No father, no marriage – and I was born and recorded as a bastard for the entire world to see. No wonder Mum never kept a copy.

This birth certificate held more surprises in store. It was as clear as day. Mum had waited until I was almost seven years old before she registered my birth. Legally speaking, I did not exist for the first six years of my life. It's a strange feeling, to think how much of those years and of the people in my life I remember, and yet to know officially . . . I did not exist.

The details of that day in the city in March 1962 came flooding back to me. As I put the pieces of the puzzle together, I realised even though everyone I knew called my mother Joyce George, her real name was Joyce *Clark*, right up until that day in March when she changed it by deed poll. At least, I *assume* she changed it legally. It was an alias she had been using for years, so surely she would have had to make it legitimate if she was to register us with the surname of George? Until she had done so, Steve and I were also Clarks, but everyone had always called us George. We were the George family that wasn't. We had a double identity without even knowing it. It was as if we were a family on the run, without ever having committed or witnessed a crime – it was all extremely disorienting.

There was the proof of it, stamped across my birth certificate: *Evidence has been furnished that the surname of the within-mentioned Gwendoline Marie Clark is GEORGE. Deputy Registrar General, 6th March 1962.*

Above that, another endorsement: *This registration has been made by the written authority of the Registrar General.*

Of course I can understand why Mum didn't explain to me at the time why we were in the city that day; why she had to take me to the hospital to prove my existence; and why she had to recover the records of my birth. Hospitals keep birth records for seventy years, so it was just as well this one only had ten beds. They 'found' me quickly enough for us to get back to the registry office on the same day.

I can imagine what would have happened if she had tried to explain. I wasn't even seven. It would have been beyond anything I could understand. I would have plagued her with questions and blabbed the story to anyone who would listen.

I can even understand why Mum never discussed any of it with me once I was older; in those days families kept their secrets close, and didn't speak much of the past.

I would have liked to have known the reasons for her actions, though, first in *not* registering me, and then in choosing *that* particular time to do so. I can theorise – but it is all conjecture, with many unanswerable questions. I know, even though I cannot remember the moment of my first knowing, that if she had waited until my seventh birthday, I would have had to appear in court to prove I was a living, breathing person. So, time was running out for her to act. I know of the *Marriage Act* of 1961, which determined for the first time that children born out of wedlock could be legitimised if the parents later married. Did she hold out hope for a belated marriage? I know the man whose name she took, the man I understood was my father – named George George – was in failing health. Did she know he was sick? Did she know he was dying? Did she need his agreement to use the George surname? Why? When I know even that name was an alias – *his* real name was George Cook. All the theories in the world will never enlighten me as to what drove Mum's decisions and actions.

Knowing what I know now as a mature woman, I can make a deductive guess – but this story belongs way back in 1962, when I was that compliant six-year-old, a little girl who thought she knew who she was, and who her mummy and daddy were.

7

It started with the letterbox. It was such an ordinary letterbox. Just a square box of battered tin, with a latch that never locked, hanging lopsidedly from a crooked post that never held the fence up.

Sometimes there was mail. A letter, or a bill, or maybe a birthday card, or, better still, a cheery note from Aunty Myra in her loopy writing galloping across the page. Every week or two there was a small brown envelope. A little packet with lines and boxes printed on the outside, exactly the same as the ones men brought home from work and put on the kitchen table for their wives to open.

No one ever told me how the brown envelope got into our letterbox, who sent it, or who put it there, but just like the other women in the street, when Mum opened hers, she would find a few pound notes folded inside.

Except her packet hadn't arrived for a very long time.

I cannot remember when the brown envelopes stopped, or when Mum's obsession with the letterbox began. The two things seemed to go hand-in-hand, and they seemed to belong with that big day in the city three months before, the day we met the solicitor.

Now I watched as Mum walked to the box for the third time that day. She walked out the front door and up the cement path, leaned across the empty flowerbed, and stretched to open the tin box. She'd been doing this for weeks now, back and forth, back and forth, back and forth. The same mechanical, obsessive, repetitive routine – again, and again, and again.

Each time she flicked the latch, creaked open the lid and stared inside as if willing the brown envelope to appear, but it never did. And still she walked up the path, repetitively, compulsively. She couldn't stop.

It didn't matter how many times she made this trip, the brown envelope was never there. And it never would be again.

•

My father died on 15 June 1962, one week before my seventh birthday. No one sat me down and explained what had happened. Why should they? No one had even told Mum. Steve says it was Kulpie who found out first. She saw his name in the death notices of her daily newspaper. He said she scurried up the road with the newspaper stuffed under her arm and rushed to show it to Mum.

'Do you think this is your man?'

It certainly was.

I knew about dying. Aunty Myra nursed her mother right up to the end.

'I was sitting on the end of her bed, and she sat bolt upright and shouted *"Look!"* I turned around to look where she pointed and when I turned back she'd collapsed on her pillow. Dead . . . just like that!' Aunty Myra clicked her fingers at me.

I knew everyone died sometime. It wasn't something to be afraid of. My grandmother had died when it was her turn, and now it was my father's turn.

No one spoke about a funeral. I didn't know much about funerals, so I didn't think to ask why we weren't going to one. No one knew our father's body was sent to the medical school at Sydney University. That was something we learned about years later. The university kept him for more than a year before they buried him, and it was on my brother's seventeenth birthday, which was strange, because that's the day my father would have normally come to visit us. We didn't go to see his body placed in the ground, because none of us knew it was happening.

The next school holidays, Mum packed a few things and took me up to Tascott. The first night I lay curled up on the *chaise longue* at the foot of Aunty Myra's bed, waiting for sleep. I could hear the television murmuring in the next room. We didn't have one at home and I found the disembodied voices and music comforting, the sounds wrapping around me as I drifted in and out of consciousness.

'Last night, thieves stole twenty thousand pounds worth of liquorice allsorts. They're still on the run.' Aunty Myra laughed out loud – she was a fan of English comedy.

The program finished.

'Cup of tea, Joycie?' I heard them move into the kitchen. The television was still running; the low volume was soporific.

I was almost asleep when my mother's voice jolted me awake.

'His photo . . . beside the bed . . .'

'But, Joycie . . . you have to tell her . . .'

'No. I can't. Not yet.'

'Joycie . . . she'll find out some day. Better you tell her now.'

'No. She's just a baby. Not yet.'

'I don't know that's such a good idea, little sister.'

'She believes it. Just leave it at that.'

'Well Joycie,' Aunty Myra sighed, 'if that's what you want.'

'You have to promise you won't say anything.'

'All right.'

'Tell her nothing. Promise me. Swear it, Mydee.'

'All right, Joycie . . . I swear.'

•

No one ever spoke directly to me about my father: not when he was alive, and not after his death. Never. I'd only overhear a snippet here and there, or notice a whispered conversation which included a furtive glance in my direction. Conversations that ceased when I entered the room. I knew to ask no questions. Mum wouldn't have answered them anyway.

When the brown envelopes disappeared, my father disappeared with them.

I tucked away my memory of the war hero with the chopped-off fingers, kept his photo beside my bed and went on living.

When my father died, all I thought about was my seventh birthday. Mrs van den Avoort was making a fuss of me for my special day. We were off to the park in Guildford, the four of them and me, just as if I were part of their family, which I was in a way. A bag full of party hats and lollies, sandwiches, chocolate cake and cordial were all in the picnic basket. Joanne and I gobbled our lunch and rushed to the merry-go-round with Adrian. Clinging hard to its metal rails, we ran alongside to get the speed up, and then threw ourselves on board in a tangled heap of legs and sandshoes. We wanted it to spin as fast as possible, despite the danger of one of us throwing up. We spun it faster and faster, bracing ourselves against being thrown off by the *centrifugal* force. Mr van den Avoort taught me that word – *centrifugal*. I liked it almost as much as Mrs van den Avoort's word – *procrastinate*. She used it when she wanted me to hurry up and get on with something: my recital, or making a decision. It always had '*don't!*' in front of it.

Well, she didn't need to say it that day because there was nothing we were hesitating over. We ran around like madcaps, laughing and shrieking and singing happy birthday and trying to blow out sparklers that wouldn't go out until that last obstinate splutter. Nothing spoiled the excitement. Even now I can feel the bare boards of the park bench under my buttocks, and picture who sat where as we stuffed our faces with food I never had at home. All of us were happy and carefree and I didn't spare a thought for my poor dead father, or for what life might look like now through my mother's eyes. I didn't even spare a thought for why Mum and Steve weren't with us at the park. It was normal for me to have a life that was separate from the people I lived with, and this was just one of those days.

•

A few years later in the schoolyard, a classmate asked me, 'What does your father do?'

'Mmmm. I don't have a father. He's dead.'

'Ow! I'm sorry.' She flushed with embarrassment.

'Ohhhhh don't be!' I said airily, summoning up all the wisdom of my ten years on earth. '*You can't miss what you never had.*'

Could I really have felt so callous about something as significant as the death of my father? Have the passing of time and the discoveries and knowledge that came later obscured the grief I felt then? Or was I just too young to be affected by what was happening? Or had I inherited Aunty Myra's gene that enabled her to take the hits life dishes out and come up smiling? Or was he such an absent figure in my life that his death merely brought to an end any expectation of further absences? He was, after all, a man I had met maybe ten times in my life, and half of those I was too young to remember.

I missed having *a* father – but I didn't miss *mine* in particular. If I had a father maybe the roof wouldn't leak, and the paspalum wouldn't grow so high it stuck to my legs and broke the skin into irritated sores, and we'd have picnics from time to time. We might have even had a car and gone on drives. But if I had a father, he might have been a drunk like Mum's was, or a bully or a womaniser, or worse still, a man who interfered with his children. Or he may have been both protector and tyrant in one, which would have been more frightening than having no father at all.

8

As the winter of 1962 merged into spring, the tension in our household was building. It wasn't something obvious. It was more like electricity in the air, a spark triggered at unexpected moments. Not the kind of tension you know you've caused by being naughty or rude. Nor the kind that comes after an argument. Maybe I shouldn't even call it tension. It was like something was stirring the air, changing our rhythm.

Everything looked normal from the outside: every weekday Mum dressed in a black skirt and blouse and rode the bus to her job as a sales assistant at David Jones department store in Parramatta. Steve packed his schoolbag with exercise books and rode his bike to Guildford station to go by train to Warwick Farm. I got up in the morning, dressed, had breakfast at Kulpie's and walked to school. I was in first class at Old Guildford Infants School. When school finished at 3.30pm I went to Joanne's house or walked 'home' to Kulpie, where we chatted or I watched some television. By dinnertime, I was back in my own home, eating with Mum and Steve. I fought with Steve over the washing up, had a bath, did my homework, listened to the radio and went to bed with a book.

The other children at school had another reality – their mums behaved differently. Not many of them went out to work and some of them helped at school, running the canteen and baking and sewing for school fêtes. All the other children had fathers who lived at home and went to work, and after dinner the children put on their pyjamas and the family watched television together in a room with comfortable furniture and carpet on the floor. When they had a birthday, it was *their* parents who gave them a party and bought them presents *as well*. I knew their home lives were dissimilar to mine, but despite this, in my eyes my reality was just as normal as theirs.

Now in this ordinary world, Mum was acting strangely. Ever since the envelopes stopped and we found out Dad had died, she started doing things that were out of character. There was an energy building inside her – plans and schemes were popping into her head as first one thing and then another grabbed her attention.

Mum had always been reluctant to embrace new technology or to change the way she did things or the order in which she did them. We were the only people I knew who didn't use a washing machine. Our washing day was a laborious process which started days before with the delivery of the load of wood we needed to make the fire to boil our clothes in the copper.

Mum would not be persuaded from this routine even though she knew Kulpie and Aunty Myra had long since bought themselves a Wilkins Service wringer washer. The mere mention of updating brought terror to her face and a solid opposition to change, even if Aunty Myra would pay for it. Aunty Myra had already insisted we stop boiling our bathwater in the copper, and had arranged and paid for a hot water element to be installed above our bathtub, which was housed in the room next to the laundry, away from the house.

So it was completely out of character for Mum to buy a refrigerator, even if Kulpie's daughter had just started work at the factory and could get us one cheaply. We'd never had a refrigerator, only the ice-box, and it seemed to do the job of keeping what little food we had fresh. As much as I hated our old-fashioned way of washing, I didn't mind the ice-box – perhaps because it didn't look much different to a fridge. Or maybe because I liked the ice-man. He was all rolled-up sleeves and bulging muscles, with an ice pick in each hand, heaving a block of ice up the eight stairs at the back of our house and flinging himself into the kitchen.

'Orright Missus?' was his cheery greeting as he dropped the large cube into our ice-box, and, 'See ya in a coupla days,' as he skipped back down the stairs.

I wondered where the water went when the ice melted? I never thought to ask Steve, and I never thought to ask him where the ice-man had gone after we got our refrigerator, even though I missed him filling up our kitchen with his heartiness and the smell of his leather apron, dripping water onto our lino floor. My attention was distracted. There it stood against the only spare wall in the kitchen, beside the only powerpoint, a gleaming white Kelvinator refrigerator with an insignia on its door: a man wearing a helmet, like the winged Mercury, bearing messages from the gods.

I was so excited it didn't occur to me buying a refrigerator could be a signal of trouble on the horizon, and I don't think it occurred to Steve, either. It almost seemed a *normal* thing to do, and maybe it was. Just not a normal thing for *our Mum* to do.

•

Around this time, Mum developed an interest in religion and becoming friends with God, even though we had never been churchgoers. God and Mum started talking to each other regularly. He gave her a hotline, and took her call on the first ring. Perhaps it was God who reminded her Steve hadn't been baptised, because it seemed as though divine intervention enabled it to happen so quickly!

The next thing we knew, we were standing inside a church, gathered close to the font with other parents and babies. Steve looked uncomfortable; he was probably willing it to be over. I doubt any almost sixteen-year-old youth would welcome being put in the spotlight in that way, but I was enthralled with the process. We were dressed in our Sunday best, a neighbour had driven us to church, and Steve was going through a mystical ceremony I had never seen before. I was fascinated.

A well-wisher gave Steve a friendly thump as he turned away from the font.

'Do you want your nappy changed now?' he joked.

The laughter exploded out of me. I thought it was the funniest thing that had taken place that day. There had been plenty of funny things happening in our household, but most of them were strange funny, not laughing funny. Now I couldn't stop laughing. I laughed until I hiccupped. I laughed so hard I didn't see Steve cringe under the weight of the well-meant slap on the back or the dark, embarrassed look on his face, but I could feel his awkwardness. While he was going along with Mum's ideas because he didn't have any other choice, he was reluctant. Why was she suddenly so proactive? He must have felt so bewildered and even more confused than I was.

•

For several years, Mum had been renting out our garage for a token amount – two pounds or so a week. We weren't the only family doing it tough financially, even though 1960s Australia was supposed to be enjoying an economic boom. Each family came to us as tenants after some disaster had left them homeless: fire, flood, or something equally dramatic. Our single-width garage stood at the bottom of a sloping driveway, some distance from the house. It had an annexe, one small room where we stored the firewood. Our bathroom, laundry and toilet were part of this out-building. We had no use for the garage; we had no car or garden tools or mower, and the wood annexe could be made to serve as a child's bedroom. The families who came to live there each stayed long term, making the space as habitable as they could. Having people living in our garage and sharing the bathroom and laundry was just another of the off-beat arrangements that made us stand out from the neighbours, and yet it had gone on for those years in a routine enough manner.

A couple of months after Dad's death, I noticed Mum spying on them from our kitchen window. She was ranting under her breath. 'Tenants!' she spat the word loud enough for me to hear. She rocked from foot to foot, and as soon as they were out of sight, she darted down to the toilet. It caught my attention, and as I watched Mum over the next week, I realised something about them was agitating her. She was avoiding contact with them, spying on them and dashing to the bathroom or toilet whenever they were out of sight.

Then they were gone. Maybe they had an argument with Mum. Maybe Mum threw them out. Maybe they just found somewhere else to live. I had no idea where they went or why, but their leaving set the stage for the next project to catch my mother's attention.

•

'Muuuummmm!' I was hollering from the bathtub, down in the garage, away from the house. She came running.

'Sssshhh, Gwenny, ssssshhhhh. You can't scream out like that anymore. Soon we are going to have Bruce and Jutta living next door. When the woodshed is knocked down, they'll start building. You have to learn some modesty! They'll hear you over the fence.'

I knew all about this plan, and I was looking forward to it as much as Mum was. I had been tuned into the vibes of excitement at Kulpie's house for weeks. It was about her eldest son, Bruce. He was marrying Jutta, his glamorous German girlfriend, she of the long, long legs with long blonde hair swept on top of her head in a permanent beehive. What a perfect combination of fate and good luck that they planned to build their own home and we owned a double block of land. The second block was clear, except for the fruit trees and the woodshed annexe. Mum's brain had worked overtime ever since she had heard they were looking for land. It seemed the garage tenants were hardly out the door before she hit on the idea to sell Bruce and Jutta our block of land. How perfect. Mum knew and liked Bruce and it would be as if she and Kulpie were living next door to each other. No more strangers invading her world, only people she knew and trusted.

What a dream! All of us as one big happy family. To Mum, the plan seemed flawless, and she executed it immediately, selling the land to Bruce at the affordable price of 170 pounds. He paid her a deposit of thirty pounds, with the rest to be paid in small weekly instalments. The garage tenants had not even been gone a month when Mum wrote Bruce his first receipt.

•

These things sound rational. The actions of a woman putting her life in order after the death of her husband: buying appliances, kicking out the tenants, selling our land, finding solace in religion. It wasn't like Mum to be *so* active, however, nor to do things in such a hurry. It wasn't her standard way of going about things, and until you live with someone who is grounded in routine and reticence, it's difficult to grasp how weird her behaviour was becoming. She was out of her normal rhythm, and she was sweeping us along with her. Our lives were out of kilter. If we had been older and had more experience – as we came to have – we would have recognised Steve's baptism as a warning sign.

Then Mum had visitations from spiritual beings who took over her dreams. I cannot remember who came first. Perhaps it was the soul of her dear, dead husband, imparting one final word of advice. Before long, though, God had chosen Mum as his messenger on earth, using her as his mouthpiece to quote random texts from the Bible. Her interpretation was literal and personal. 'Go ye into all the world and preach the Gospel,' she erupted. The voices in her head had invaded even her waking moments.

One day Mum became agitated, grabbing Steve by the arm and shaking him. 'Alan Walker, you must find a way to contact him,' she said. 'There is a message.' Alan Walker was a Methodist minister who was prominent in the media. 'What I tell you in darkness, that speak ye in light; and what ye hear in the ear, that preach ye upon the housetops! He must be informed! Steve!

'Steve! How shall we do it, Steve! Steve, go to the phone box! Call Alan Walker – you must find a way. God has spoken. Reverend Walker must broadcast the message! Down the airwaves, Steve. People must listen.'

Our neighbours, the Spearmans, were dedicated Christians, with fervent evangelical beliefs, and Mum's religious conviction was infectious. They recognised their teachings in her, and she reached out to them as the kindred souls who understood her message, who understood she had been chosen as one of God's intermediaries. They started to visit often, and sat with Mum, reading passages from the Bible. Texts such as 'How beautiful are the feet of those who preach the Good News!' (Romans 10:15) fanned our mother's religious fervour.

'I have been chosen to receive the message of God,' she cried as she paced the floor nervously after one visit. The pacing went on all night, with Mum babbling increasingly incoherent snippets from the Bible.

Steve was at his wits' end when he saw the Spearmans coming across the road the next day. He stood in their way at the front gate, his elbows jutting out to block off their entrance.

'I'm sorry,' he said, 'but I just don't think any of this is helping Mum at all. It's not doing her any good. We can't get any sense out of her. You have to stop visiting.' It was a brave and desperate stand, but Steve was way out of his depth, and powerless to stop what was about to happen.

I was no help. At seven, I was focused on where the next slab of chocolate cake might come from, or the home-made ice-cream Steve was conjuring out of our new fridge. Just like a dog who loves any master who feeds it, I was happy to respond to any source of food, shelter or love and I didn't concern myself with much outside of that. So long as my support network of family and neighbours remained in place, my life was as normal as it had ever been. My oblivion had only another week or two to run.

•

As I came around the corner of our house, I was startled to find Steve sitting on the front fence. He shouldn't have been at home in the middle of the afternoon. He was staring into his hands, and when he saw me he dropped off the fence and turned to face me.

I looked at him, puzzled. 'What's up?'

'Something's happened to Mum.'

'What?'

'Something happened at work. She had to be taken away from there. She's in hospital.'

'Why? What happened?'

'Well, I don't know exactly. There was some kind of scene. She was out of control. She wasn't herself. They call it a nervous breakdown. She's gone to a special hospital for rest. They say life's all a bit too much for her right now.'

The weeks of uncharacteristic activity had brought us to this moment. It was only a month since Mum had sold the land, two months since the tenants left, three months since Dad died. The woman who detested change couldn't bear the chaos of it all. She had crumpled, and she disappeared from my life, just as Dad had disappeared. Just as Paul, my first childhood friend, had before them.

I can't remember much of that night; it all passed in a blur. No one from the hospital or any social worker came to see if anyone was with us at the house. Steve and I got by as best we could. He tried to cook us a meal, even though he had no idea how to go about it. Even today he is hard-pressed to cook a simple meal. How must he have felt then? Just about to turn sixteen, his father dead, his mother in hospital, and his seven-year-old sister looking to him for guidance. He stood in the kitchen looking at a loss where to begin. The leaky, rusting Kookaburra gas stove must have seemed his enemy at that moment.

9

Christian Broadcasting Association
October 25th, 1962

Mrs Joyce George
North Ryde Psychiatric Hospital

Dear Mrs George,
The fact of your illness was brought to my attention just today so I thought I would send you a word of greeting.

I am sorry you were admitted to hospital on October 11th, and want you to know that we of the Christian Broadcasting Association are remembering you in prayer and trust that the Lord will give you his peace and comfort in the weeks ahead.

The letter continued for several more paragraphs, going into great detail about how Christ died for our sins; and while life wouldn't suddenly become a 'bed of roses', if Mum would just put her faith in Christ then she could have confidence God would become a 'friend that sticketh closer than a brother'. She was urged to read the several pamphlets enclosed and to gain strength from them.

I *am* grateful strangers were concerned enough for my mother's welfare to take the time to write, and I do appreciate religion brings comfort to many in times of distress. All the same, I cringed when I read the letter. Harsh as it may seem, October 1962 was not the time for Mum to be aspiring to be any closer to God than she already believed she was. According to the voices in her head, she was already his chosen messenger on earth. The letter was sincere and well meaning, but just at that precise moment – not helpful. Not helpful at all.

10

Our twenty-something cousin Phillip came to look after Steve, and I was sent to stay with Uncle Jack and Aunty Nan. Uncle Jack was my mother's brother. Born in 1909, he was ten years older than her. Mum was only three when she was sent to the orphanage, so they hadn't grown up together. Nevertheless, he looked out for his baby sister's interests. He was a regular visitor to our house, and ever since I was a toddler I spent weekends with him and Aunty Nan and their grown-up children: Esther, Pat, Bruce and Ron.

Kulpie warned me to behave myself while I was away from her. An occasional weekend visit was one thing. Living there full-time, as I sometimes did with Kulpie, was something else altogether.

'Lynn – tables are made for glasses, not arses. You best be remembering that while you're living at your Aunty Nan's.' Kulpie poked a face at my legs swinging back and forth.

I had just come in from my last afternoon at Old Guildford School and made myself comfortable on the table in her tiny dining room while she bustled around her even tinier kitchen.

'She'd kill me,' I grimaced, rolling my eyes.

I tried to imagine Aunty Nan saying 'arse'. I couldn't, but then I couldn't picture her killing me, either. I couldn't think of a time when she would even slap me. Aunty Nan was too much of a lady to let anything upset her calm. I wouldn't dream of sitting on her dining room table, or even the utility table in her kitchen. Aunty Nan liked to do things in a proper manner. She had a proper time for meals, and at *her* dining table, everything was set in its proper place. When she entertained at lunch, after a proper time, she served her guests a home-baked afternoon tea on delicate china plates. After another proper time had passed, the guests said their thank-yous and left, and it would be time to do the washing up. There was no scope in that formality for parking my 'arse' on *her* dining room table.

If Uncle Jack was home from his shift work, we washed up together, with him wearing an apron and me standing at his side, tea-towel at the ready.

'Well, girl,' he'd wink, 'must be time for a song?'

'Oh yes! The pinky-dinky one!'

Mademoiselle from Armentieres,
She hasn't been kissed in forty years,
Hinky, pinky, parley-voo.

'Jack, don't teach her those songs!'

This from Aunty Nan, taking a break in the loungeroom, sipping on a 'nice' cup of tea.

Uncle Jack clattered cutlery in the sink and banged around pots and pans to cover us as we switched to the 'Drunken Sailor'.

Shave his belly with a rusty razor,
Earli in the morning.

We'd finish on a deep-voiced flourish and a growl,

and that's what you do with the drunken sailor . . .

'Really – Jack!' said Aunty Nan in exasperation, bringing in her teacup. 'They're not the *proper* songs for a young girl to learn.'

•

I adored Uncle Jack. He was handsome, smart and lively. He looked like the actor Kirk Douglas, with the same chiselled face and a cleft chin. Uncle Jack spoke well, read widely and understood things about literature, but most of all he was an outdoors man. He had medals for lifesaving in the 1930s. He played tennis every week, and kept up a bit of boxing sparring. He could fell a fly on the wing, letting go a quick left jab as it buzzed past.

Uncle Jack was the closest thing I had to a father, apart from Steve.

I loved Aunty Nan, too, even though she had quite a different personality. She was straight and conservative, the type of woman who wore a corset every day of her life. Aunty Nan had a certain way of doing things, and she didn't have a great sense of humour – or if she did she sheltered it behind a well-behaved reserve – but she took me on without question, and cared for me as if I were another one of her brood.

I was ecstatic living with them. Their three-bedroom Federation home at Concord was as familiar to me as my own. I preferred it to ours, not only because it had tiles on the roof and carpet on the floor and an inside bathroom. Everything about living at Concord seemed grand to me, as if only sedate, refined, well-bred people could live there. Directly opposite the house was a large expanse of greenery with a cricket pitch and a children's playground. At the end of the street was Queen Elizabeth Park, a much larger park with tree-lined walks and the war memorial. All around me seemed green and fresh and bright with roses. Such majestic names for their streets and parks, such an abundance of trees and greenery, so much order and gentility everywhere the eye could see. The full-brick houses and the well-tended neighbourhood spoke to me of comfort and stability. I loved living there; I felt like a lady, and I was warm and well-fed and protected.

•

I was used to walking to school on my own, but back in Old Guildford it was a straight line from home to school gate. This was going to be a different matter, up and down and across several streets snaking their way to Concord Public School on Burwood Road. Aunty Nan was going to show me two or three times, and from then on I would be expected to do it on my own, as was expected of all other young schoolchildren.

As we walked down one wide tree-lined street and turned into another, Aunty Nan issued instructions. 'Be very careful of the traffic. Cross the road here, look left, look right, and then look left again. Be sure there's not a tree in the way. Only step out when you're certain there's no car coming.

'When the bell rings, take your lunch bag and sit on one of the wooden benches under the trees in the schoolyard to eat your sandwich. I'll come for you this afternoon when school finishes.'

I was a quick learner; I must have convinced Aunty Nan I was taking it all in. A few hours later the bell rang through the classrooms with a strident call; it was a different sound to the one at Old Guildford. I knew this one was my call to action, but perhaps it was the urgency in this bell that disoriented me. I picked up my things and walked out of the room. Then I walked out of the grounds, down the road and around the corner, just as Aunty Nan had shown me, until I ended up on the porch of their house on Majors Bay Road and rang the front door bell.

Aunty Nan answered the door and looked at me in alarm. 'What are you doing here?' she said. 'Are you all right?'

I looked at her in confusion. 'Don't I live here now?'

'Of course you do. But why are you here *now*? It's lunchtime.'

I felt a flush of embarrassment flood through my body. When the school bell rang I had just assumed it was the end of the day and had walked home. How stupid of me! I could feel the tears welling up inside, pricking at the back of my eyes. I stood on the doorstep feeling hot and flustered and ashamed. Only my first day and already I had made a mistake.

'There now. Don't get upset. There's no harm done. Come inside and eat your lunch, and when you're all settled I'll take you back to school.'

Aunty Nan spoke briskly, rushing to cut off any impending scene. Aunty Nan did not like scenes.

•

I never settled at the Burwood Road school. I don't remember any of the names of my classmates, nor even my teacher. It was already late in the year by the time I joined them, and since it was coming up to Christmas the teacher invited us each to sing a carol. At home I had a little prayer book which included hymns and carols, and my favourite was 'O Little Town of Bethlehem'. I knew all the words, and with the benefit of my elocution lessons, I was able to get my tongue around all of them. I stood up at the front of the class and sang my way through this carol, anxious to please. I love its dreamy, tranquil quality, and perhaps I put a bit of heart into it as well.

O little town of Bethlehem,
How still we see thee lie!
Above thy deep and dreamless sleep
The silent stars go by . . .

I closed my eyes and swayed as I pictured the little town of Bethlehem, lit by the full moon, its beam concentrated on the stable, and the little baby Jesus lying in a manger.

The teacher was delighted, saying, '*Well done*, Gwendoline!', clapping enthusiastically and turning to the class. 'Wasn't *that* splendid!' Thirty sulky faces stared back at me. I was marked as a show-off and no one wanted much to do with me after that.

In the long run it didn't matter. We were nearing the end of the year, and the six-week summer holidays loomed. By the time school resumed in early February, Mum was home from hospital and I was back at Old Guildford Infants School, ready to start second class.

•

All this time Steve had been left behind at the house with Phillip. At sixteen, he was considered too adult to need farming out. Also, as he was due to sit his Leaving Certificate the next year, it wasn't a good idea to change schools at the time. He and Phillip muddled along together, making the best of a bad situation.

No hospital social workers or other bureaucrats had come anywhere near us, and they never did. Welfare for the families left behind as a result of mental illness wasn't considered. I doubt whether any authorities even asked who was left behind. They concentrated on treating the patient, and some of that treatment was scary stuff – including electric shock therapy administered without anaesthetic. It's a mercy the treatment induces memory loss. Mum knew she was treated in this way on many occasions, but had no memory of the actual event, and seemed to have no idea of what it involved. It was left to Steve and me to imagine what she must have gone through, and how alone and frightened she must have felt. It had no noticeable therapeutic effect, and it alarms me to hear it is a treatment regaining favour, albeit now with anaesthesia.

Most people think hospitals are where you go to be cured of an illness. If you can't be cured, then you might die. It's a kind of 'either-or' situation.

Psychiatric hospitals aren't like that. For the most part, psychiatric doctors can't cure a patient of mental illness. Usually, but not always, the patient doesn't die because they can't be cured. Psychiatric hospitals concentrate on treating an 'episode', the doctors try to stabilise the patient to the extent they can return to something approaching their pre-episodic 'normal' life, until such time as they have another episode and the cycle begins again.

Our problem was no one explained this to Steve and me, so the first time Mum came home from hospital, we expected her to be cured. It came as quite a surprise to us when she was re-admitted to hospital only a few weeks later.

•

Some disappearances were easier to accept than others. At the end of 1962, while I was living in Concord with Uncle Jack and Aunty Nan, my best friend Joanne disappeared. It was to be another forty years before we reunited.

Even as a seven-year-old, I knew it was a special achievement for Mr van den Avoort to be promoted. His firm transferred the family to Western Australia. I knew we were supposed to be proud and happy for him, but it was hard for me to feel good about it. It was as if all the fun, laughter and light had been stripped from my life. For the first time in my mixed-up life, I felt a real sense of loss. Not only was my best friend gone, but so was one of my stand-in families. I took it hard, but I later learned Joanne took it even harder.

Perth! It was the other side of the country. For all I knew it could be the other side of the world. It amounted to the same thing: Joanne and I were never going to see each other again. No more clambering into the weeping willow to invent stories as we hid under its trailing leafy fronds. No more prancing around the house acting out parts and projecting our voices from one room to another. No more huddling on her bed sharing our whispered secrets, heads pressed close together, the gold of Joanne's fair hair contrasting with the darkness of my mop. No more stealing glances at each other in anticipation of her father's latest experiment, wondering . . . *Will it work or will it blow up?* No more steady guidance from her mother, stretching our imaginations, encouraging our inquisitiveness. No more trips to the park, running around like madcap children, with her brother Adrian in tow. No more elocution lessons, the two of us standing beside each other, bolt upright and stiff, concentrating on her mother's instructions, filling our diaphragms with air, contorting our mouths and tongues to achieve just the right sound. No more hours watching Joanne at her piano practice, trying to match her timing to the steady beat of the metronome's *tick-tock* as the pendulum swished back and forth. No more drifting in the daydream that those were *my* hands trilling out the scales on the keyboard.

Ebony and ivory – that's who we were. We belonged together just like the keys on that piano. Except now the piano, and everything that went with it, was dragged as far away from me as was possible.

Joanne felt the trauma deeply, and it was left to Mrs van den Avoort to write and explain her silence.

> *'Gwen she misses you very very much, & she has started to write a few times, but bursts into tears and can't finish. You are really Joanne's best friend.'*

Then it was my turn to burst into tears as I read Mrs van den Avoort's closing words,

> *'Remember, Gwennie, I love you almost as if you were my little girl.'*

11

Mum's two hospitalisations at the end of 1962, when I was seven, were just the beginning. Over the next five years, her life was a revolving door of relapses. Name *any* 1960s Sydney psychiatric hospital and Mum's name will be on the admission register. She was in and out of hospital so regularly, and for such intermittent durations, it was impractical for me to change schools again.

I went wherever I was sent, to a narrow band of trusted neighbours and family: Kulpie, Aunty Myra every school holiday, Nan and Jack some weekends and to other neighbours in an emergency. I didn't mind being passed around, and there was nothing to be homesick about. Every place was an improvement on what I left behind. I thought of each as my alternative home, and considered all the women as my alternative mothers.

Even today, Steve remarks how I took it all in my stride. It was a different story for him. Apart from when Cousin Phillip lived with us, he received no substitute care. It must have been so difficult for him – a young man on the threshold of his change from schoolboy, to youth, to manhood – living with this chaos. Steve sits on the periphery of my memories, trying to salvage a life for himself. He finished school at the end of 1963, and, with hopes for Teachers' College swept aside in the bedlam, started as a junior clerk at a nearby aluminium rolling mill. Then he joined the Citizen Military Forces (CMF), a forerunner of the Army Reserve, and fashioned a social life based on male mateship.

My birthdays came and went, not marked by parties or presents, merely measured by the events around me, and whether Mum was home or in hospital. Memories telescope and draw together. In March 1963 – six months after the first breakdown – I was Cousin Esther's seven-year-old flower girl. Mum was there for some of the dress fittings, and for the wedding, but it was a brief moment of respite. The next year, when I was eight, I was savaged by Kulpie's corgi dog while I was living with her. I spent a day in the emergency department of the local hospital, and when Mum was discharged from *her* hospital, I was bursting with excitement to show her my scars and tell her my story. The following year, just as I was turning nine, Beatlemania gripped Australia. Kulpie helped me stick up posters on the wall of what I now considered as *my* bedroom – even though it was in her house.

Nine months later, in early 1965, Mum's latest hospitalisation co-incided with Kulpie breaking her leg, so this time my salvation came in the form of the Spearmans. They had visited and supported Mum during her first hospitalisation, and now, with Mum in hospital again, they took me across the road to live with them. Steve may have had qualms about whether their encouragement of Mum's spiritual messages had contributed to her illness in the first place, but he couldn't deny that it was charitable of them to offer me sanctuary.

Ken Spearman was a builder and his wife, Jean, had been a Red Cross nurse during the war. They owned a solid, pleasant house, but it wasn't huge or luxurious, even though Mr Spearman was a builder. Their three boys made room for me. At the back of the house was a large room which had the appearance of an enclosed veranda, and Daniel, Lance and Peter squeezed in out there, with their beds lined up as if in a boarding school dormitory. If they resented this, they never showed it to me. The boys were good with me. They didn't pick on me, make fun of me, tease me or call me names. Dan was the eldest, followed by Lance, me, then Peter. We had an easy friendship, almost as if I was their sister. They seemed to like having me around, that is, after we got over the first night.

At dinnertime, Mr Spearman sat down in his place at the head of the table. Through the gap between the kitchen bench and overhead cupboards, I could see Mrs Spearman's body twisting as she ladled food from the pressure cooker onto dinner plates. She gave one a wipe with the edge of her apron.

'Dan, take this one into Grandma please. Make sure she's sitting up and has a serviette.' As he headed for her bedroom the scent of the meal wafted my way. I didn't recognise the smell, but my mouth started to water. I was ready to eat.

'So!' Mr Spearman's gaze bore down on me. 'How has your first day with us been?'

'Fine, thank you.' I replied meekly, summoning my politest rounded vowels, my eyes meeting his for an awkward moment. I wouldn't admit it to anyone, but I was a little afraid of Mr Spearman. I slid my eyes away; he seemed to be waiting for me to say something more, but I couldn't think of anything. I was desperate to find something I could say to shift his focus from me, and as I felt my eyeballs flitting around under my drooping lashes, they came to rest on a frame with gold-lettered text: *Christ is the Unseen Guest at this table.*

I sneaked a look at Lance opposite me. He hadn't seemed to notice the sign, he was just sitting there, fidgeting a little under the table and avoiding eye contact with his father. I counted the chairs, one each for Mr and Mrs Spearman, one each for the three boys and one for me. Where was Christ going to sit? Six of us were already jammed together in this alcove between the kitchen and loungeroom, and there was no spare chair.

Mrs Spearman was pushing loaded plates through the serving hatch, issuing instructions for them to be passed around – this for Dad, this for Dan and so on, until the one I was hanging out for, *this for Gwendoline.* I devoured the contents with my eyes, a rich brown sauce with morsels of meat, piled on a hill of mashed potatoes, carrots and beans on the side. It was a relief when she joined us moments later, and as she settled in to her place at the foot of the table, she cast a look at her husband. A silent message passed between them.

'We'll say Grace,' he announced.

I reached for my knife and fork. From the moment that plate was put in front of me, I was focused on the aroma, carried on a fog of steam lifting from the mound of meat and potato. It had my full attention, and I was bursting to tuck in. I had only held back because Aunty Nan had taught me to wait until the hostess sat down.

'Gwendoline, we say Grace in this house. Please clasp your hands together and bow your head.'

I looked around and saw the boys were already in position. Mrs Spearman gave me a little nod, indicating with her eyes that I was to do as they had. I dropped my knife and fork and copied them.

'Heavenly Father, we thank you for your goodness and bounty, and for the food . . .' words drifted over my head, '. . . all those in the world . . . without food tonight . . . mercy upon them . . . blessing upon this meal . . . and upon us . . . make us truly grateful.'

That seemed to be the end of it. I looked up, but Mr Spearman went on.

'We thank you Father for delivering Gwendoline into our care and protection and we pray you will give us strength and guidance in our task.' That gave me a jolt, but still he went on . . . 'We ask you to bring your compassion on her mother and restore her to health.'

Finally, in a burst of passion, he said, 'In the name of Jesus Christ, our Lord. Amen.'

'AMEN!' It was a hearty chorus from the boys as they lunged

for their knives and forks. I was right behind them. The food was getting cold.

Mrs Spearman smiled at me. 'Do you like it, Gwendoline?'

'Oh yes! It's delicious. What is it?'

'Why . . . savoury mince. Don't you have it at home?'

'Nuh, uh. I don't think I've eaten this before.'

'Really. What do you have?'

'Well,' I took a deep breath, I would need it for what I was about to recite. 'Mondays it's sausages, Tuesdays it's lamb chops, Wednesdays it's steak, then Thursdays chops again and on Fridays we have steak again.' The words tumbled out – I was anxious to make a good impression on my ally Mrs Spearman.

'Goodness! That must be expensive. But surely you don't have the same thing every week?' Mrs Spearman looked at me with a teasing expression on her face. I could read her unspoken words: *'Now come on, Gwendoline, don't exaggerate.'*

'Yes we do.' There was a stubborn edge to my voice.

'Now, Gwendoline, I'm sure your mother cooks other things. You just don't remember.' Mrs Spearman was being tolerant now, jollying me along to change my story. The problem was it was the scout's-honour truth. She just didn't understand my mother's need for order and regularity in her life. That . . . and her extremely limited cooking skills. I was on the defensive now.

'No. It's the same thing every week. Mum says she doesn't know how to cook anything else – except roast dinner. We have that on Saturdays, lamb roast one week and rolled roast beef the other . . . and . . . and on Sundays we have the leftover meat boiled in a pot with tomatoes. Oh that is *awful*! It's the worst thing. The tomatoes squidge around and around in my stomach and lamb smells disgusting when it's been cooked twice and the rolled roast is mostly fat.'

I rushed on. 'Mum gives Steve *all* the meaty bits and I just get the fat. It's not fair. It's all spongy and see-through when it's boiled, and sometimes I think I'll throw up.'

I shoved a forkful of food in my mouth.

'Boiled fat and tomato is the worst.' I talked around the side of my mouth. 'I feel sick for ages. It tastes *so* disgusting.' Gulping down the mouthful, 'Not like this mince. This is really good! Mum's a terrible cook. She can only grill meat and it's always cooked in the centre and still raw on the outside. She calls it the pink bits. She always cuts them off and gives them to me. She says I like the pink bits, but I don't really. She saves the best bits for Steve. It's just not fair.'

I finished on a rush of gulping air.

As I jammed another forkful in my mouth I realised everyone had become quiet. Dan and Lance stared wide-eyed at me as if I'd gone insane, until my eyes met theirs and they focused on their plates, concentrating on forking up mouthfuls of food one after the other. Mr Spearman stared at Mrs Spearman, who stirred uncomfortably in her chair. The only one who didn't seem shocked was Peter. Sitting beside me, I could feel his shoulders shaking as he tried not to laugh. Mrs Spearman folded her hands in her lap, as if about to say something, and then thought better of it. Mr Spearman glared at the top of Peter's bent head.

What had I said? I rushed on, anxious to fill the gap of silence. I could make it better again if I kept talking, if I just tried to explain myself more. I gathered up my best elocution voice.

'We don't have carrots at home. These are delicious. And we don't mash potatoes either. Mum just boils them until you can see through them. And we have peas one day and beans the next.'

The silence lengthened.

'I help,' I said in a small voice. 'It's a lot of work to shell peas and string beans, don't you think?'

'I certainly do.' Mrs Spearman sighed as she looked around at the men gathered at her table. All the plates were empty now.

'Jelly and ice-cream all round?'

'Yes please, Mum.' The boys were almost too quick to answer.

As we scraped our spoons around the bowl, fishing for the last piece of slippery jelly, I turned to Mrs Spearman in triumph.

'You're right! I just remembered. Sometimes Mum makes a rice pudding.'

Mrs Spearman beamed comfortingly at me. Daniel and Lance rolled their eyes; Peter was still giggling under his breath. They were not used to having the evening meal turned into a circus by little girls who talked too much and shoved food in their mouth at the same time. I dared not look at Mr Spearman. He must have been thinking, Oh why, Lord? Why are you testing me so?

•

On the whole, I enjoyed living there and it was a happy time – except for Mr Spearman's religious fervour. His faith was so stern it frightened me. The entire family were regular churchgoers and practising Christians. They lived and breathed their belief in the Lord and the Bible, and behaved in a caring and tolerant manner every day of the week, not just when they went to church. If believing in Christ made people act nicely towards each other, and take care of little girls who didn't have a father or mother, and feed them great-tasting food and lots of it, then Christ must be a good man, but I wasn't always sure of that. Look what he had done to my mother.

Billy Graham was not Christ – I knew that much, but he thundered through the house every day of the week. I don't know how his voice got to be everywhere, huffing and puffing down the airwaves, railing at everyone to believe in the Lord. I knew he had come to Australia on a crusade. I wasn't sure what a crusade was, but Mr Spearman was happy he had come, and couldn't listen to him enough. I wanted to be happy, too, but I was scared of that big voice. I think he told me I was going to hell, and I didn't like the sound of that at all.

I didn't go to hell, but my stay with the Spearmans wasn't all plain sailing. One day I was hit in the mouth with a softball bat and was sent home from school with a mashed-up tongue. I ran away and hid under our house when I heard Mrs Spearman talking on the telephone to the doctor. They were planning to stitch my tongue and I couldn't imagine anything worse.

I became cold and hungry, shivering as I sat hunched on the cement floor of the storage room the Italians had built under our house, but no one came looking for me; at least I heard no one. It was dark by the time I crawled out of my hidey-hole and went back to Mrs Spearman. I hung my head as I confessed what I had done to repay her kindness.

'Well,' she said, examining my mouth again. 'It's far too swollen now to get the stitches in, and besides, the doctor went home long ago. I guess we'll just get you into bed and see how you are in the morning.'

My tongue healed itself but with lumps and bumps here and there, and that's why it doesn't fit inside my mouth properly, which is why I have to talk so much, because it's at its most comfortable when it's moving around. At least, that's the story I told my mother when she came home from hospital the next time. I was still young and naïve enough to look forward to her homecomings, and to be excited to tell her of the adventures I'd had while she was away.

I never seemed to be at home for long before she went back to hospital, though. It seemed no time at all before I grew used to her disappearing and reappearing. By the time I was ten, I lost interest in telling her about any of my adventures.

12

Screaming, struggling, snarling, spitting, growling, howling! Here and there I caught a word, mixed up within the animal sounds, 'Fall! Metal plate! Horse! Head!' My mother was thrashing her head from side to side, as if trying to shake out something stuck inside there. Two men were wrestling her out to a waiting van. She broke loose and, driving her body forward, closed fist outstretched, punched one straight in the eye.

'Shit! Grab her! Get hold of both arms. I'll get the jacket.'

He ran to the back of the van and grabbed a bundle of white cloth. I watched in horror as they struggled to get Mum into a straitjacket, her body twisting and turning, spitting disconnected words and sounds through her bared teeth.

A child shouldn't have to see her mother taken away like that, and it's a mercy most of my mother's breakdowns happened while I was at school. Even that occasion is a faint memory, one that is better left buried, but the horse was often with us whenever Mum was manic, the horse and the metal plate, residing side by side in her head, creating pain and hysteria. The plate pressed in, crushing her brain, the plate they had inserted after a fall from a horse. Except there was no plate. There may have been a horse, and there may have been a fall, but there was *no* plate.

Over the years, Steve and I tired of hearing about the metal plate. We couldn't persuade her it wasn't true, and we couldn't do anything to alleviate her pain. Years later, when she was in care, it even became a habit, dropping her head in her hands and moaning about the horse.

Steve leaned forward one day, stilling her hands in his. 'Did this horse have a name?'

'No name, no name, no name,' she repeated.

Steve sat back in frustration, 'Did it ride through the desert?'

I burst out laughing. On the drive home, the America tune that Steve was referring to rolled around and around in my head.

It was cruel of me to laugh. Years of living with my mother's mental illness had robbed me of sensitivity.

•

I lived with my mother for sixteen years, but I cannot say I knew her. I learned her routines, I learned how to interpret her unspoken words, I learned how to recognise her body language, but I cannot say I knew the person who dwelt inside that body.

I want to focus on the positives, the good things she did for us, but the hurt and confusion is never far away. Mum housed, clothed and fed us, and she never put us into debt. 'If you can't pay cash, you can't afford it,' was her motto. Excessive and reckless spending is a characteristic of many mania sufferers but Mum did not overspend. In her case, the mania would show itself in unrealistic projects or hyperactivity, a short phase that preceded hospitalisation.

'I want to start a school for unmarried mothers to learn to knit,' she told a local church minister. 'They can sell the garments and raise money for themselves.' It was a great idea, but it would have come to Mum when she was already manic. That's how it would have sounded in her head, but it's not what the minister would have heard. When she was manic, the words tumbled out so fast, he would have had no idea what she was saying. The minister was polite and charming at first, feigning interest, but as Mum pestered him more and more, his patience waned and he avoided her. Mum became more and more agitated because he wasn't recognising the genius of what she had to offer. Before long, she was stomping up and down in the house all night, opening drawers and flinging out needles and wool, ravelling clumps in her hands as she ranted, 'Suffer them . . . he spoke! Come to the party. Gather them in . . . Needles! All good men. We must have needles! . . . Suffer the unfortunates to come to thee. He commands us. Find wool! All good men must come to the party.'

Except when manic, it was unusual for my mother to display any violence. Occasional outbursts were caused by an instinct for self-preservation rather than aggression. Her reaction was triggered only when her security was threatened by someone stepping into her imaginary safe space.

One day when we had been shopping for what seemed like hours, I was hot and tired and I was desperate to go home and read my book. Mum didn't want to be there, either. We were about to leave . . . and she was heading for the stairs.

'Muuuuuum,' I whined at her back, reaching out to tug her. 'Can't we take the lift?'

'No.'

'Oh Mum! This is stupid. It's just a lift.'

'I don't like lifts.'

I rolled my eyes. 'You don't like lifts, you don't like escalators. It's just soooo stupid. They're just machines, Mum. Come oooooonnnnnn.'

Mum was starting to back away from me.

'Mum! Why can't we take the lift? Why Mum? Why?' I was strident now.

Her hands were coming together. Any moment now she would be wringing them.

'Muuuuum. I'm tired. I want to take the lift.'

My whining was reaching a higher pitch. I was fed up with this phobia she had developed. Whenever she was confronted with an escalator, she came to a sudden halt near the top, frantically looking for the stairs. The lifts weren't any better.

Her hands were together now, jerkily wrapping around each other, crushing together, wringing compulsively. She was backing into the nearest corner. I knew this signal. This was the frightened, cornered animal. This was my hint to back off and give her breathing room. She needed time to deal with this confronting situation and time to process whatever images and messages she was receiving. Thinking back, I suppose it was the sense of being enclosed and the feeling of losing control that caused this fear. As a ten-year-old, I was too young to work that out – I was focused on myself and the only message I wanted her to hear right at that moment was, *TAKE THE LIFT!*

I stepped towards her, into the invisible semi-circle of her safe zone. I saw her arm lift and, caught off-guard, didn't think to duck as it swung in a wide arc. *Thwack!* I felt it strike the side of my head as I was knocked to the ground. Through my yelp of surprise and hurt I was aware of Mum flashing past me down the stairs. She must have raced right out of the store, down to the bus stop, and ridden all the way home, leaving me dazed and bewildered where I had fallen.

An hour or so later the store detectives arrived at our home with me in their car. Mum acted as if she didn't remember the event, greeting them pleasantly and appearing surprised to see me on the doorstep, rather than curled up on my bed with a book. They declined her offer of a cup of tea, and left shaking their heads.

•

Although my mother rallied a little in my first three years of high school, she never overcame her mental illness, and was never well again. My main memory of living with her, however, is not of violence and ranting, but of silence and lethargy. The sense of inertia that hung in the house rendered my mother as insensible as a hibernating animal. Torpor hung in the air, silent and invisible, and it felt like a weight, bearing down on us, physically heavy, drowning us in its mass. Nothing happened. There was no energy in the house. 'I remember how strange it was whenever I visited you,' said a school friend from those years, 'we always spoke in whispers.'

It was even more disturbing if there *was* any energy in the air. That was a warning sign something awful was about to happen.

It followed a pattern, this repetitive cycle. Mum existed in a trance-like state, doing what was necessary to keep us functioning – shopping, cooking and washing, all reduced to their basic level, everything performed methodically, each task sapping her limited reserves of energy. Then from nowhere an interest would emerge, a fixation on a theme which built up until it fanned into frenetic energy, her dreams and schemes becoming more ambitious by the day, her words tumbling out faster than her brain could form them, until those dreams, schemes and words spiralled so high and so fast they disconnected with any reality. They became so fantastic that there was no hope of achieving any of them, and then finally Mum's hopes and plans disintegrated and lay shattered around her, leaving her feeling a deep sense of betrayal. She felt the world was deliberately thwarting her, refusing to recognise her unique insight and vision. She would catapult into mania, spitting savage words and ranting about the metal plate in her head, her body movements agitated, unable to recognise friend from foe, reality from fantasy.

Next would come the spiriting away to the hospital – sometimes for weeks, sometimes for months, and then the return of a shadow, which slipped into her bedroom and lay cocooned there for long periods, emerging only to do the most necessary tasks.

I blame prescription drugs for stealing my mother's personality. Of course I understand that she was mentally ill, and without the drugs she would have spiralled even further between mania and depression – but I wonder whether there may have been moments in between when she could have given me a glimmer of the woman hiding underneath. I knew she was intelligent, observant, and, by copying what she read in Victorian novels, capable of conducting herself with grace and dignity. She was occasionally witty. She knitted superbly and diligently, creating many beautiful items as gifts for young mothers. Yet for the main part these characteristics remained dulled and hidden under the barrage of drugs. There were so many drugs. So, so many drugs. Pill bottles lined alongside each other on the old oak sideboard, like soldiers shoulder to shoulder waiting their call to arms. Pills to wake her up in the morning, pills to settle her at night, pills to keep her functioning in the day. Pills to stop the voices in her head, pills to keep her mood stabilised. Pills to make her feel positive, pills to make sure she didn't get too positive and go over the top. Pills, pills, pills, bottle after bottle after bottle.

'Gwenny – have I taken my tablets?'

She would look confused, her eyes swinging from them to me, anxiety in her voice.

What did I care? I was ten. What were all these drugs to me? Who takes all these drugs? Can one person really swallow everything on this cabinet? I'm your daughter, not your mother. You want to take these? You work it out! The protests banged around and around in my head.

'Mum! You ask me this all the time. How should I know?' I spat it out.

I've seen documentaries of other ten-year-old girls taking care of their mothers in this situation, ensuring they take their medications, on time, as prescribed. They understand the connection between medication and mood. I wasn't one of those daughters. I didn't understand, and I didn't care. My mother's drugs were not my responsibility.

Medication, electro-convulsive therapy and committal to a locked ward in a psychiatric institution were the sole treatments for my mother. Psychotherapy, cognitive behaviour therapy and other types of counselling were unheard of. I don't know what the drugs were, although I imagine lithium was a mainstay, a powerful drug with a fine line between a therapeutic and a toxic dose. The combination of anti-psychotics, anti-depressants, anti-anxiety medication and mood enhancers was, for my mother at least, like being hit with a sledgehammer. She became quiet, passive and robotic. She became dead to me, like a zombie, one of the living dead.

Mum struggled to function under the barrage, clinging to the routines she knew, finding sanctuary in their familiarity. She shopped every day, taking up her string bag in a mechanical movement, and leaving the house as if she was under a spell. I avoided going with her because I hated her robotic walk, and I was thankful that I was usually at school. She kept her head high and stared straight into the distance. At the kerbside she stopped to attention, before stepping deliberately onto the street. She did not take a step forward until both feet were lined up side by side, and when she reached the opposite footpath, she repeated the process.

She went to the same shops and bought the same thing each time: steak, chops and sausages from the butcher; peas, potatoes and beans from the fruiterer; and a tin of baked beans, a packet of ham and a steam pudding mix from the grocer.

These routines were Mum's refuge. 'I need your sheet, Gwenny,' was the Saturday signal to get out of bed. Time to drag myself out of its warmth, pull off the sheets and take the bottom sheet down to the laundry. When the bed was remade, the top sheet would go to the bottom and a freshly laundered sheet would go on top.

I would find Mum crouched in front of the brick kiln under the copper, her face flushed and anxious as she coaxed up a fire to bring the water to the boil. A muslin bag of blue powder hung from the tap that filled the copper. I stuffed my sheet in along with hers and Steve's and all our other white clothes and grabbed the long wooden stick that we used to stir the washing. A couple of hours later, we dragged the tangled mess out of the boiling water.

I didn't know that Mum had been taught to wash like this in the orphanage, doing other people's washing in squalid Dickensian conditions which belonged in another century. I just knew that I hated doing our washing in this way. I hated watching Mum drag boiling clothes out of the copper and drop them into a cement tub for rinsing. I hated watching how her hands became red and swollen as she wrung the sheets and clothes by hand and repeated the rinse in a second tub. I hated lugging out the load in the old cane basket with broken bits scraping at my knees, and I hated hauling on the cord of the wooden clothesline, struggling to pull the lines up to the right height and hold them fast with the cord wrapped around a cleat.

'Muuuum,' I whined, 'When can we get a washing machine? We could get the same as Kulpie. Nothing fancy.'

'No, Gwenny, no.' Alarm would spread across her face. 'Don't make me. You can't make me.' Her hands would come together, twisting and wrenching, a signal of inner anguish.

It was strange how often my mother took the part of the child, not so much in her conversations with me, which were so rare as to be of no consequence, but when she was around people of her own age. Her body would shrink into itself as if she was recoiling from a dressing-down, and her face would take on a pleading look as if she was begging you to go away and leave her alone. Or she might start to giggle in a girlish voice, for no reason in particular. She had a way of being in a room, yet not being there, blankly staring into the distance, and then bursting out into a deep, contemptuous laugh. When I saw the film *A Beautiful Mind*, the story of John Forbes Nash Jr's struggle with schizophrenia, I recognised the behaviours. There were other people in Mum's world, people I could not see, and not all of them were kind to her. As the years passed, they took up more space. Sometimes she would take both parts, her voice changing as she switched the conversation from one to the other, and sometimes she would listen in silence as the other person spoke, her head cocked to one side, her body twitching, her face changing expression, nostrils flaring and lips pursing as she took objection to what they were saying,

'Well! You would say that, wouldn't you!' she would fling back at them. It was her favourite retort to her invisible antagonist.

'There are those who are born to do housework, and those who are not. Those who are, should do it for those who are not.' That was Mum in her schizophrenic 'I am born to greatness' phase, and Aunty Myra humoured her. Until Uncle Bill became ill, she visited us every three months or so to do our housework, even though it was a long journey on two trains and one bus.

I looked forward to these visits, even though it must have been hard work for her. Simply washing the floors took half a day, with bucket after bucket of filthy water being tossed under the fruit trees, and another kettle of water put on to boil. At the end, Steve would pull out a dry woolly mop, place a cushion on top, and my four-year-old self on top of that. He would whiz and twirl around the room at top speed, using the pressure of my buttocks to shine the linoleum, while I wrapped my arms and legs around the handle and hung on determinedly, until finally I would be flung off and go spinning across the floor, crashing into the wall. Playing with my brother like that was the best fun ever. I wished Aunty Myra would come and do our housework more often.

Mum never did a lick of housework, and it was only after I went to summer camp when I was eleven, and came home to the realisation that we lived in a filthy house, that I took any interest in stepping up to the plate.

13

My mother's condition would be recognised as bipolar disorder today, or manic depression as it was called at the time. Underlying that were symptoms of schizophrenia. No doubt, modern doctors have yet another name for multiple psychotic disorders but, in my opinion, finding a precise label is irrelevant unless it leads to a treatment that restores the sufferer to stable health.

Whether anyone gave Mum a diagnosis back in the 1960s, I do not know. Steve and I weren't informed of the medical fraternity's conclusions for another thirty years – at the time they told us she had had a nervous breakdown, brought on by the stress of life. Until recently, mental illness was such a black slur, it was a taboo subject; Mum could tell no one for fear of being shunned by society and labelled a madwoman. It wasn't discussed, and whenever a mention of it was impossible to avoid, 'nerves' was the politest acceptable term to be used in conversation, and the issue was evaded.

It wasn't something I could talk about with schoolmates. I couldn't share my hurt and bewilderment with them, and confiding that my mother was in the 'loony bin' was unthinkable.

Did Mum suffer some unspeakable trauma in the orphanage, something that plagued her mind until it gave out? Or is abandonment and emotional neglect enough to cause madness? Growing up in an institution, devoid of a loving and supportive environment – can that affect a child's development so badly that it sows the seeds of insanity? Or was it repetitive emotional trauma that caused her psychosis? Or is it a genetic flaw? I will never know the answer to these speculations. The only fact I know is that Mum was not the first in our family to see inside a mental hospital.

While Mum was living at Burnside, on 3 October 1926, two months before her seventh birthday, her Aunty Lucy died in the mental hospital at Callan Park. The death certificate says she died of 'exhaustion of acute delirious mania; and exophthalmic goitre'. Thirty-one-year-old Lucy had gone so mad, she was both manic and delirious, and without drugs to control the insanity, her heart had given out under the strain.

I discovered Aunt Lucy's death certificate in the course of writing this book. When I absorbed the shock of this news, it was the second cause of death that caught my attention. Exophthalmic goitre is also called Grave's disease, an endocrine disorder that causes excess secretion of the thyroid hormone, leading to hyperactivity, a faster heart rate, higher blood pressure and increased nervousness. It may cause protrusion of the eyes, double vision and even loss of vision.

No one knew this information when Mum was shuttling back and forth to hospital. Perhaps my mother was never 'mad', but merely suffering from an overactive thyroid. This condition runs in our family, and Aunty Myra's scar was a testament to how severely she was affected.

If Mum's disease was a thyroid problem, then she could have told people of her physical illness and expected sympathy and support in return, instead of having to conceal she was suffering from mental illness. She hid that in the same place she kept all her secrets. It lived with all the other shadows in her head. Maybe *that* is why she spoke so little. She couldn't risk an idle slip of the tongue.

•

Steve and I learned to meld around Mum, to carry on with our lives. Her condition became a fact of life, just as our father dying was a fact of life. Her state of mind dominated our lives, but didn't stop us living ours. It swirled around me, affecting me, and yet I could separate Mum and my life as two different things. In a later moment of lucidity, Mum said I had been independent from the age of seven; and I guess she was just about right.

Mum's illness isolated her from life. She sat off to the side. She had no friends apart from Kulpie, although occasionally she would meet a new person and there would be some tentative social activity. She was never the centre of attention or the talkative person in a group. The only group occasions in which I can picture her are Cousin Esther's wedding or Kulpie's annual Christmas Day gathering. Mum would sit in a corner, like she was tidying herself out of people's way. If something was being shown or discussed, photographs for example, she might pick them up and examine them after everyone else had finished, but not until others had lost interest and cast them aside. Whatever she thought as she scrutinised each photograph, she kept to herself.

Sometimes, I might be visiting a neighbour or girlfriend's house, and Mum would just appear, come to fetch me away from bothering people, offering them money for having had me. I developed the feeling she was apologising to people for my presence, that I was somehow second-rate and not worthy. At first I felt hurt and confused, wondering what was so bad about me. Then I went through a defensive stage – why would she bother? My friends liked my company. As time went on it simply irritated me. Who was this strange woman, embarrassing me in front of others? I learned to detach and shrug it off. She was like a shadow that slid in and out of my life, and in time I accepted the distance and made no demands on her. We became like two moths battering around a flame, both needing light and warmth, stumbling into each other's orbit, but never getting close, lest we burn up.

•

A year or more after her initial breakdown, Mum was sent to Mt Wilga Rehabilitation Hospital at Hornsby. It was a grand house, built earlier in the century in the style of an English manor. The facility aimed to get people back into the workforce, and Mum attended as a day patient. I realise now it was an enormous effort for her to get up, dress, catch the bus and train connections and try to relearn her secretarial skills, but she put herself through that every weekday. She sat in a classroom taking shorthand dictation and practising 'the quick brown fox jumped over the lazy dog' on the manual typewriters. Whenever I went with her, I delighted in meeting the other patients, each with a different idiosyncrasy. I didn't see their abnormalities as a negative; I thought it was pretty cool that each one had something unique to show off. I basked in their friendliness and playfulness and lapped up their indulgent attention: the wheelchair man who stood me on the footrests as he whizzed me around the basketball court, turning wheelies until I was dizzy; or the lady dwarf, an adult I could talk with eye to eye. I was allowed to bash on typewriters in Mum's class, and joined the others in the dining hall for lunch.

Rehabilitation didn't last long. After one failed attempt at returning to the workforce, Mt Wilga and employment drifted into obscurity. A doctor provided a certificate that Mum would never work again, and she was put on to the Invalid Pension.

So we became a welfare family. If we were poor beforehand, now we were destitute. I hated it, and the older I grew and the more I understood our situation, the worse I felt. There was no money for anything but the most basic food and our meagre gas and electricity consumption. I loathed scrunching my feet into someone else's shoes which were already worn down at the heel, and dreaded going to school to hear some young girl shriek, 'You're wearing my old dress!'

There was such a stigma attached to being on welfare. It marked me out as different, and contemptible. In 1960s Australia, theoretically, anyone who wanted a job could get one, and people in our suburb took whatever jobs they could, without airs and graces, whether it meant they were a tea lady or an engineer. The land was booming, construction was everywhere, new houses and office skyscrapers were being built every day. There were more jobs available than there were people to fill them. The austerity of the war years was long since cast aside; no more ration books or minimalist clothing or making old things new again. Tram lines were dug up because who needed to use public transport anymore? Every other home had a brand-new car, and driveways were dotted with Holdens and Fords. Housewives rushed to furnish their homes in the latest materials, shiny vinyl couches and chrome-plated dining suites with laminated table tops. Even if you couldn't afford to buy things outright, well then, you could get it on the never-never, and the nice Walton's man would make it even easier for you by calling around to your door each week to collect your hire-purchase time payment.

If you needed welfare, it meant you didn't want to work. We weren't on the 'pension', something we had earned after years and years of toil and now our bodies were too fragile to contribute, and Mum wasn't in a wheelchair, too incapacitated to leave the house. She used to work to support us, and now she did not, and there was no obvious physical reason she didn't. An old-age pension was considered an entitlement, but welfare for younger people was a handout, and taking the dole signified that you were too lazy, or too drunk, to go out and earn money for yourself – a good-for-nothing bludger. There weren't clusters of people in the same situation. Welfare wasn't a generational thing handed down from parent to child. There was no sense the government 'owed' you, and people didn't manipulate their circumstances so they could qualify for the public purse. No one promoted the idea that you had paid tax into the government coffers and now it was your turn to have it back.

Accepting welfare was accepting charity – pure and simple. It was a gift from a socially minded system to support persons in dire need, and there was no pride in having fallen so low as to need support. I was the only child in my primary school who was being raised at the expense of the government. We had lost our independence, and now we were at the mercy of bureaucratic benevolence, one step away from the poorhouse. There was not much lower we could fall in our latent system of social class.

Even though many Australians became wealthy in the 1960s, and the ranks of the middle-class swelled, there were pockets of poverty all about. Old Guildford was one of them, and many of my schoolmates would remember doing it tough, while others seemed to have money to burn. Yet if they looked at it critically, they would realise they had a father who was working, and maybe their mother, too, and even if they were blue-collar workers on the basic wage, at the end of the week there was still enough spare cash for a present, or an extra treat in the shopping trolley, or something, anything, that went beyond basic survival.

There was never anything spare in our house, and some of those who thought themselves poor looked down their noses at us for being even poorer. I learned to mix only with those who showed empathy and tolerance, and fortunately for me, there were enough of those around. I'm social by nature and will talk to just about anyone, but at the core I like to have special friendships. That wasn't always easy at school, which seemed to me a minefield of spite and pettiness, with girls the worst. One moment the girls were ganging up on you and you were on the outer; the next moment they were in your corner and you were all ganging up on someone else. Swinging between being 'in' and 'out' was confusing and hurtful. The boys were easier to understand, but only interested in whether you could play sport. I didn't like girlie cliques and I couldn't kick a ball. I was bookish and chubby and had no talent for sport, and it was a godsend to find some special friendships to carry me through those turbulent years of infants and primary school.

Primary school children love to tease each other. Their ability to spot a weakness or difference in another person is like radar finding a target, and when they lock on, they attack mercilessly. There were so many things about me my classmates could seize on, and I never learned to shrug off their barbs. I felt every one. I recoiled from them, wanting to hide my head and block out my tormentors, as if by not being able to see them, they could not see me. In desperation, I tried to defend myself.

'If my father were here, he wouldn't let you speak to me like that.'

Howls of laughter greeted me. I couldn't understand why my outburst didn't have more impact, why it didn't touch some chord of sympathy and understanding. I was opening up my heart to my attackers, sharing with them that somewhere deep down I *did* miss not having a father, and all they could do was laugh at me? *None of them* had to live without a father. Could they not understand how lucky they were? Or what a struggle it was for me to get by each day at home with no one to provide for me, financially and emotionally, with only my brother to rely upon?

Their reaction had nothing to do with my baring my soul, though. They knew that in our world fathers didn't stomp into the playground to stand up for their children. You had to do that for yourself. In the absence of having a father of my own, I fantasised about how theirs might behave, and I had it very wrong.

14

Clump . . . clump . . . clump. I was used to that sound as the tyres of Cousin Bruce's car passed over the joins in the concrete on Parramatta Road.

Clump . . . clump . . . clump. I found it comfortingly familiar, a lulling repetition, a steady beat I associated with good things, happy times. The rhythm of the roadway and the rhythm of my visits to the Concord house went hand-in-hand.

It was late 1965 and coming up to the third anniversary of Mum's first breakdown. Earlier in the year, I lived with the Spearmans. This time I was with Nan and Jack and Cousin Bruce, as I regularly was. My cousins Esther and Pat were married, and Ron wasn't around.

When Uncle Jack was free, he enjoyed a hit at his tennis club. I dreamed he would take me along and we'd discover I had a natural gift for tennis, I would become a world-famous champion and he would be my coach. At other times I dreamed he and Cousin Brian would take me to the boxing ring and we would discover that I was a born boxer and I would become a famous female world champion and Brian, my trainer. Brian was the 1962 State Novice Golden Gloves welterweight champion, so he knew a thing or two about boxing. Uncle Jack was as proud of him as if he were his own son.

There were so many things I daydreamed about, with me in the starring role. Here I was, jumping into the flames of a raging fire to rescue a child, leaping into a raging torrent to drag out a drowning animal. In truth I was chubby, uncoordinated and lazy. I couldn't even swim. I wasn't an outdoor girl.

Cousin Bruce gave up slabs of his time to entertain me on my visits, patiently teaching me to play cards or board games. Aunty Nan probably daydreamed I would be more help around the house, or might show some interest in cooking or baking. That was as likely as me jumping into a raging fire.

I preferred it when Cousin Ron wasn't around. I found him to be unpredictable and frightening, so I was relieved he wasn't at home for my visit this time, but it did seem strange that he and Mum were in the same hospital simultaneously. They were due home now, and I was going home too, back to Guildford in Bruce's Ford Anglia.

A few days later a letter came from Aunty Nan. It sat on top of the fridge, out of my reach, while urgent whisperings went on between Steve and Mum.

I didn't know what was going on. My imagination went wild.

What was it all about? What had happened? Had I done something wrong on my visit? Was I in trouble? Was I being sent away?

I recalled the visit from a stranger a couple of years before. She had balanced on the edge of the wicker chair in our living room, delicately avoiding snagging her stockings on the torn and broken binding. Mum had turned to me. 'You don't want them to take you away do you, Gwenny?' I saw the look of alarm, I heard the unspoken words . . . 'They'll lock you in a horrible place. Stay here! Don't leave me!'

'No!' I'd said, on impulse, not knowing who this stranger was, what they were talking about. 'No! I don't want to be locked away.'

Was this happening now? Was the letter for me, about me? What had I done?

In the end, Mum showed it to me.

8th September 1965

Dear Joyce,
I am returning the two pounds you gave Bruce. I don't want anything for looking after Gwendoline.

Thank Gwendoline for the nice card. Did she make up the poem?

Trusting you are well.

Love Nan.

Ps – 9th September 1965:
Since writing the above I am sorry to inform you Ron passed away this morning. He took an overdose of sleeping pills. The funeral arrangements will be in the 'Herald'.

Ron was only twenty, and after a stint in hospital for depression or some other mental illness, he was discharged. On his first night at home he committed suicide by taking all his prescribed medication.

What state of mind was Aunty Nan in to be able to compose the original letter, write such a politely formal postscript, and then manage to post it the next day? Such was her strength of character, she maintained her decorum even in the face of this gut-wrenching tragedy.

Now, the biggest discussion was whether at ten years old I should or should not attend the funeral, and in the end, it was decided I should go. Apart from any other consideration Mum and Steve might have had, I insisted I wanted to be there.

I wasn't sure what to expect of my first funeral, but it was the burial that affected me most. Not because of the sadness or solemnity or finality or mourning. No. Quite the opposite. As the coffin was lowered, I was struck by the conversations taking place around the gravesite. Even as clods of earth were being tumbled into the void, people were clustering into private groups, exchanging pleasantries in hushed tones, and commenting on how long it had been since they had seen each other. I was astounded. I thought they would be wailing and beating their breasts, or at least standing in a respectful, silent huddle of black figures. I didn't expect it to be a social event like a family reunion; it was as chatty as Esther's bridal shower had been. Back at the house Aunty Nan passed around sandwiches and cake and cups of tea in her best china. Voices hushed when she came near and people pressed her hand in silent comfort. Grief, tears and anguish mixed with 'Hello' and 'How are you?' and 'Good to see you' and 'We must catch up again in better circumstances.' I still had a lot to learn about funerals.

•

At the end of the following year, in the lead-up to the six-week summer school holidays, the year I turned eleven, Cousin Bruce suggested including me in their family holiday. I was so excited. I was used to sleeping in one place or another, to be sent first to this house and then to that, to this family and then to that, but this was something else. I was going on holidays – just like my schoolmates did every year – and every day was going to be an adventure. Then, when the school year started again, I would have tall stories to tell, just like my schoolmates.

Uncle Jack rented a house at Blackheath in the Blue Mountains for two weeks. It was a rambling weatherboard place standing high at the end of a road overlooking the Megalong Valley. The house had no structure or order to the layout, and each room beckoned you to come and plop yourself down in its cosy confusion. Each window had a different view of the mountains and the valley with the mist rising in the morning. At the end of the street, a short walk brought us to the edge of sandstone cliffs, their sides cut sheer and glowing rich ochre in the sunlight, and the eucalyptus forest tumbling down to the valley far below. The dense brush covered any walking trails, but we knew they were there, meandering their way up and down the sheer cliffs and along the path of the river. Uncle Jack, approaching his sixtieth year, was fit and trim and delighted in leading us on bush-walks through the magical crags and valleys and waterfalls. Sometimes we went to Blackheath public pool, where Uncle Jack taught me to swim. I couldn't swim well, and I couldn't bring myself to dive into the water, but I learned just enough to keep myself afloat and swim a short distance, which was more than I had ever managed before.

Even though Aunty Nan was a few years younger than Uncle Jack, she wasn't fit and was not the outdoorsy type at all. She wasn't interested in hiking or swimming or playing tennis, not even in playing cards, but she joined us on most outings, even if we abandoned her to wait on a park bench here and there. Then when we returned home hot, exhausted and sunburnt, it was Aunty Nan who sorted the washing and got the dinner ready.

Aunty Nan cared for me and loved me in a predictable and reliable manner, but didn't share anything of a personal nature. That fell to Aunty Myra, because in the interval between Ron's death and the Blackheath holiday, puberty came knocking.

One night, Aunty Myra and I lay awake in her room, she in her bed, and me on the *chaise longue* at the foot. The lights had been out for a while, and we had been quiet all that time, but we could tell from each other's breathing we weren't asleep. Suddenly her voice reached out through the darkness.

'Gwenny?'

'Mmmm?'

'You know how you have a hole for doing wee?'

'Umm, yessssss.'

'And another for doing poos?'

'Hmmmm Hmmmm.'

'Well, there's another there too . . .'

'Huhh?'

'Yes, it's between those two.'

'I don't think so . . .'

'Yes, really. Why don't you just have a little feel and see if you can find it?'

'Huhh?'

'It's okay. Just have a little feel and see if you can find it.'

I rustled around underneath my pyjama pants.

'No. Nothing there.'

'Yes, there is. Why don't you have another little try?'

I felt some more under the covers. Rustle, rustle. Rustle. Wiggle. I couldn't find anything of interest. I gave up.

'No – nothing else there. I really don't think I have one.'

She sighed, and paused.

'Okay. Well let's not mind about that for a moment.'

Pause . . . Silence . . . Then again her voice in the darkness.

'Gwenny – I want you to imagine a fence.'

'Mmmm?'

'So this fence starts at your belly button and goes down to your knees.'

'Okay.'

'And it goes round either side of you.'

'Okay.'

'Now it doesn't matter what anyone ever tells you. This fence is too high to climb over, too wide to go around, and too low to crawl under. Do you think you can remember that?'

'Umm, yessssss.'

'Now . . . you're sure, Gwenny? Are you sure you can remember that?'

'Sure. Yes . . . ummmmm – why do I need to remember this?'

'You'll find out, Gwenny. Just wait a while. You'll know soon enough.'

Satisfied, we drifted off to sleep.

I remembered her advice for a long time. But perhaps not as long as she was hoping for.

•

I'm glad Aunty Myra introduced me to the idea my anatomy was not as I imagined, because there would have been nothing so terrifying for a young girl than to arrive at her 'time' without any knowledge of what was happening.

Mum was in no way prepared, and after the initial fuss was over, I asked her, 'What does this all mean?'

'Well, now you can have a baby.'

I asked her to explain more to me, but it was beyond her ability – maybe even beyond her own knowledge. When the drama repeated itself a mere three weeks later, I knew I needed advice. We had evening lectures on growing up at school, the boys had Father and Son, and we girls had Mother and Daughter. The classes were a chance for the parent to introduce the topic of puberty to their pre-teen children, but Mum hadn't come to my session. There was literature circulated as part of the program. I needed to get my hands on some of that.

I went to see the mother of my school friend Lilly. Not only was Mrs Hawkins a good, down-to-earth woman, she was also a nurse. Whatever I had to say wasn't going to shock her. She even made jokes about her breasts, calling them her two fried eggs.

'Would you have any of those girl books please?' I asked politely, standing shyly at the front door.

'Certainly, Gwenny! What would you like? *Lorna Doone*? *Black Beauty*? Something else?'

Panic inside.

I took a deep breath.

'Ummmm, not those sort of girl books . . . the ones when you're not a girl anymore.'

Understanding rushed across her face. 'Come on in. The girls aren't here, so let's have a good talk.'

She sat me at her dining table and brought out the books I needed, sitting beside me to help me understand some of the diagrams and answering questions as they popped into my head. When I explained I was only using rags for protection, she sat back and looked me in the face.

'Come with me.'

She led me to a drawer in one of the bedrooms. Displayed inside it was a range of sanitary items on a clean white sheet.

'I've kept these ready for when Eloise or Lilly will need them, but they're not quite there yet.' She showed me the manufactured pads and the belt, which was worn around the hips, and how to clip them together.

'Here you are, take some of these to get started. Show them to Steve, and ask him to bring you some home from the chemist. He still works there sometimes doesn't he?'

I'm not sure how much it pleased Steve to fetch packets of sanitary pads home in the little shopping basket clipped to the front of his bicycle, but it was a huge improvement for me. Modess pads had never before been wrapped in so many layers of brown paper.

The trouble with relying on books for an education is that sometimes there is a gap between the picture in the mind of the author, and the picture in the mind of the reader. Something gets lost in translation, for example, what is beige to one person is fawn to another.

I studied the books Mrs Hawkins lent me, and generally understood what happens during a woman's cycle, and about how babies came into being. I got the part about the sperm meeting the egg, and I got the part about them joining together blissfully and going to live in the womb for nine months.

It's where and how the sperm and the egg encountered each other that I wasn't sure about. Somehow I got the idea that when a man kissed a woman, the sperm ran down her throat, into her stomach and down to where it could get on with business.

When Uncle Jack arrived for his next visit I shot out the back door. There was no way I wanted our greeting kiss to result in me having his baby when I was just eleven years old.

15

My final year of primary school, 1967. This was the year we were the 'big kids' on the block. This was the year most of us turned twelve. This was the year we had Mr Silby as our teacher.

We called him the Marlboro Man. He was a dead ringer for the man on the TV ad. Some said he really was the mountaineer who climbed the peak to stare across the valley – sucking on a Marlboro cigarette, or the cowboy who rested the herd at the end of the day, staring into the campfire – sucking on a Marlboro cigarette. We girls swooned over his rugged, outdoor good looks, me included, even though I wasn't interested in boys yet.

Boys were beginning to annoy the hell out of me, and I learned a good swift smack in the head was an effective way of dealing with them.

No, I wasn't interested in boys then – but I *was* on the threshold of a weird time.

•

Mum and I were shopping. Neither of us enjoyed shopping, but I needed a new outfit. We had taken the easiest approach, choosing a drapery store in Granville that sold a mish-mash of items, from wool and knitting needles to clothing, and they offered personal service. Between us we chose a conventional grown-up suit, a two piece skirt and jacket, the kind of thing you wear to visit grandparents. It was ultra conservative and slightly old-fashioned, but I liked it. I felt smart and elegant in the fitted jacket and knife-pleated skirt. I looked like a woman . . . more than that, I looked like a *lady*. It was a treat to have something new and I had Steve to thank. Every week he saved money from his pay packet, two dollars for Mum and one for me, for the express purpose of keeping us clothed.

In the change room, the assistant turned to Mum.

'Perhaps I may also suggest a little brassiere for your daughter?'

'Oh . . . do you think?' Mum expressed surprise.

'Mmmmmmm,' confirmed the assistant.

'Oh . . . well . . . maybe . . . a training bra?' Mum was hesitant, taken aback.

'No, Madam. I think we can go straight in to an adult size 32B.'

And so it was my boobs were pushed in to a sensible cotton bra, size 12B, with hooks and eyes on an elastic strip at the back. When the elastic wore out, it was simply cut off and replaced. The original bra could last a lifetime.

There was instant containment. The veritable sheep dog bra – round them up, and point them in the right direction! I was astounded. My breasts had been jiggling around for more than a year, and yet no one – least of all me – had taken any notice, despite the fact that I lived in t-shirts and sloppy joes when not in school uniform. I was mortified . . . not about being fitted for a bra, but from the knowledge that it should have happened earlier. The assistant sensed my embarrassment, and murmured soothing words as she adjusted my straps, our eyes meeting in the mirror. 'There now,' she gave me a reassuring pat. 'I am sure you will find that much more comfortable.'

Mum was a brilliant knitter, and had made me a cute, short-sleeved twin-set in pretty green which suited my eyes. The effect of the bra on the sweater was startling.

When it came to school photo day, we could wear our choice of clothes. I wore the suit, the newest thing I owned, and under the jacket I wore the sweater of the twin-set and under the sweater, *I wore the new bra*. I strode into class feeling proud and dressy.

Of course the weather turned hot, and as I left the classroom for mid-morning break, I discarded the jacket.

Fifteen juvenile male heads swung in my direction. Sniggers, stares, nudges . . . some stared directly at me, and some didn't know where to look.

Suddenly I was embarrassed – not proud! I hunched my shoulders and put my jacket back on.

I've been hunching my shoulders forward ever since, even though I long ago lost any suggestion of a good bust line.

•

Around that time I had other things beside boys and bras to worry about. I was to sit an exam for the Commonwealth Junior Secondary Bursary, a government fund that helped with the cost of education. It was a way of keeping bright children from poor backgrounds in school. Even in the public school system, textbooks and uniforms were expensive. Gaining a bursary would take a load off Mum's mind.

The application forms arrived. The bursary was means-tested. The family's annual taxable income had to be less than $3600 or you weren't allowed to sit the exam.

Mum and I looked over the forms together.

Father's Taxable Income . . . that was easy, no father, no income. Strike out the whole column.

Mother's Taxable Income . . . well, Mum had an income. We lived on her Invalid Pension. It was worth around $20 a fortnight, a princely $500 per year and not taxable. We wrote NIL in that column.

I qualified to sit the exam.

I don't know what the authorities thought of the answers on the form, or how it compared with the other applicants. Maybe there were thousands of us living on air.

The exams were held towards the end of the school year, close to the time we sat our regular school tests, except every subject was examined on the same day. Six or seven papers one after the other.

There were two of us sitting the bursary at our school. We were put into the administration building, and quarantined from contact with the outside world for the whole day. Even in our lunch break we were monitored.

There were three strangers already in the room. 'We are the invigilators,' the eldest announced, 'We will roam the room quietly as you work. We will let you know when it is time for a break. If you need the toilet at any other time, raise your hand, and one of us will accompany you. We will announce the allotted time as we hand out each new paper. When we call "time-up" you must stop immediately. We will remove that paper and hand you the next. Do not look at it or commence until we give you the signal. And under no circumstances should you look at your classmate, or try to talk to each other.'

As we sweated through one paper after another I was all too aware I was competing with every other poor child of my age in the country. A pass was not good enough. I had to gain a place in the top 2000, the number of bursaries on offer. This had to be my best effort; there were no second chances.

It was an intense situation for a twelve-year-old.

I was successful. The total value of the bursary over the four years would be around $500 – roughly equal to a year of our household's income.

It was no great surprise, nor any great achievement, that I pipped my classmates Doreen, Suzanne and Lilly, and took first place in the school examinations. I was honed from my experience with the bursary. All the same, Mr Silby praised me on my report card. 'Gwen has worked assiduously all year and deserves her success.'

Assiduously. It's a nice word. It has a certain ring. I like those kinds of words. I even liked *loquacious*. I seemed to get that on my report cards a lot, although never from Mr Silby. Thanks to Mum's insistence on using a dictionary, I even knew the meaning of both those words.

•

Speech Night 1967 was a large event hosted by Granville South High School. I knew I was to receive the prize for coming first in class. I also had a part in the class play, and a role assisting backstage, so I had no need of a seat in the audience. I expected to go with the Hawkins family, until Steve and Mum surprised me by saying they would be going as well. I was thrilled she had made the effort, although I wasn't over the moon with excitement. I knew her interest would be transient. It was a rare moment of enthusiasm that would wane as quickly as it flared.

Mrs Hawkins had made me a dress for the evening, in preparation for when I would appear on the stage. It was a cotton polyester material in a swirling paisley pattern – very now for the hippies of the 1960s. Miniskirts were 'in', but I was a young girl attending a school function, so my shift dress most definitely finished at my knees. She had also sewn me a conventional red velvet dress with a nipped-in waist and white lace collar. It was hanging in her shower recess so that steam from their bathing would lift the velvet up. I loved them both. It was the last chance Mrs Hawkins would have to help me with my clothes as the family was transferring to Melbourne at the end of the year, taking away my good friend Lilly. I felt devastated to be losing them. It was a repeat of the Joanne separation. Best friend and mother figure, both lost in one blow.

The evening opened as usual with 'God Save the Queen' and progressed as these things do, with performances from each class, and presentation of academic and sporting prizes.

We'd reached the end of the regular awards, and I was standing in the wings nattering with other prizewinners, when we realised someone was still speaking into the microphone. He was saying something about the Returned Services League (RSL), something about a special award for the Dux of a different school each year, and that this year it was the turn of Old Guildford Public School. None of us was paying any real attention. We were hearing, but not listening.

'Gwen, go, go.' A teacher was pushing me back to the stage. 'Go! Can't you hear them calling your name?'

I stumbled onto the stage. An elderly man in a suit was beaming at me, one hand outstretched in a handshake, the other snaking around my shoulders to point me at the microphone. I was stunned. It dawned on me what was happening. A familiar calm washed over me. I'd experienced this sensation many times before when faced with a confronting situation. It was as if something washed through my body, repressing the urge to panic and leaving me composed and steady. I took a deep breath and, smoothing my dress down, I gathered my wits and stepped up to the microphone to make my first public speech.

You know those times in your life when you replay a scene, an argument, a bantering session, and you wish you had thought of something different to say? This will stick forever in my mind as one of those moments.

The first words tumbled out well enough, but I was soon in trouble.

'I would like to thank the RSL for awarding me this . . . er . . . this . . .' I was stuck. I either had to come up with another word for what I was getting, or risk repeating myself. I had to think quickly. I racked my brain – it was a blank. The silence was in danger of becoming embarrassing. There was nothing for it but to press on.

'For awarding me this . . . er . . . this award . . .'

To this day I cannot remember what the award was; all I can remember is repeating myself and how I could have continued with 'thank the RSL for bestowing me this award,' or some other polished outpouring of gratitude proving just why I deserved it that year.

A week or so later I answered a knock at our front door. There stood the man from the presentation night, together with another man I didn't recognise.

'Hello lass,' he beamed at me confidently, 'we meet again.'

'Can I help you?' I asked politely.

'Well, it's the RSL that can help you! We've taken up a collection and would like you to accept this Christmas gift from all our members.'

He waved at a cardboard carton behind them. Clearly it had needed the two of them to carry it down the path to our veranda. It seemed almost large enough to hold a body.

'Is your mum home? We'd like to present it to her.'

'She's sleeping,' I said absently. I was fixated on the box. 'What's in it?'

'What's not in it would be a better question. Here, have a look for yourself.'

He was pulling the flaps open.

'Ham, turkey, heaps of canned food. Toys, books . . .'

I peered into the box. It was as he said, packed with food and giftwrapped items. I poked around, lifting things out and turning them over in my hands. There was so much! I'd never seen anything like it. I felt a thrill of excitement. We had never had Christmas in our house. Maybe this year would be our first.

Mum materialised at my side. 'What's this?' Her tone was suspicious.

'Good morning, Mrs George. I was just telling your daughter how the RSL has taken up a collection to brighten up your Christmas.'

'We don't need anything.' Mum looked at the box in disgust.

'Well, this is something we do every year for a needy family in the area. We'd love you to accept it with our best wishes.'

'And who said we're needy? What sort of people do you think we are?' Mum spat out the words. I could feel she was digging in for a fight.

The man tried to reason. 'Oh, Mrs George, there's not a family in the district who wouldn't appreciate something extra at this time of the year. We didn't single you out. This is something that goes along with presentation for Dux.'

'You would *say* that – *wouldn't* you?' She was glaring at him now, her voice taking on a vicious note.

The RSL man tried hard to win her over. He tried repeating we hadn't been singled out for special attention, that no one had been prying into our situation, no one was talking about us behind our backs. He explained again this was something the RSL did every year and presented to the family of the school Dux regardless of their circumstances. Mum was having none of it. I had rarely seen her so angry.

'Well you can just take it back where it came from. We don't accept charity in *this* house!'

It was her final word on the subject. She despatched him off our doorstep.

I felt frustrated and embittered towards Mum as I watched the men struggle back to the car with the carton. Inwardly, I fumed that it wasn't her right to make this decision. After all, hadn't it been me who had done the hard work in the exams? I felt sorry for myself at the loss of all those treats. What surprises were inside? *She* wasn't going to give me anything! Why couldn't she have at least let me keep one or two things? Just for *once*, we had the chance to have a Christmas celebration because I had *earned* it, and I *deserved* it – and here she was, depriving us all.

What did she think was happening when people clothed me, took me into their homes, fed me, took me on outings, paid my way, advised me, encouraged me? Wasn't *that* charity?

Maybe she was unaware what was happening under her nose. Maybe there was a distinction because people dealt with me directly, rather than asking for her approval; and help always came from outside our home. Perhaps someone standing on her front doorstep was crossing another of her invisible lines. A strange man offering food and gifts did not fit her delusions of grandeur. He should have come to the tradesman's entrance. If we had one, that is.

I was a long way off learning the pride and inner dignity that comes from taking the high moral ground. Mum was merely trying to do her bit so our family could hold its head high. It was one of the contradictions of her illness. Refusing *this* offer of help – while accepting others – made sense to her. The distinction was important to her. It bolstered some sense of self-worth and pride.

We didn't die of starvation that Christmas. In fact, we spent the day at Kulpie's just as we often did, eating our once-a-year treat of cold roast chicken and other delicacies spread from one end of her table to the other in a neverending smorgasbord of delight.

So maybe in this, my mother taught me a lesson – grovelling for handouts is demeaning and unnecessary. But now, as an adult, I see it differently. If someone is offering assistance when you're in need, accept his or her help graciously, and look forward to the time when it can be you offering another person the leg-up.

16

Most little girls dream about being a princess. When I was quite young, I fantasised I *truly was* the Queen of England's daughter. I imagined it had been impossible for the Queen to care for me herself, so she had left me on a random doorstep in faraway Australia, to grow up in obscurity. It made sense of why I felt I was the odd one out, never belonging where life had dropped me. In time, this belief faded away and was replaced by acceptance of my identity and place in the world.

Any childhood I had was rapidly falling away from me now. I was thirteen years old and in high school. We all thought of ourselves as growing up, but I was growing mature and self-sufficient faster than the other girls were. I had to, because it was up to me to look out for myself. I didn't go to Aunty Myra every holiday now, nor did I spend many weekends at Aunty Nan's. I was still close to Kulpie, but had no need to go to her for after-school care.

I basked in the triumph that had been my thirteenth birthday, my official entrance into the teenage world, when I had invited a select group of school friends home and prepared all the food myself. Nothing too challenging, but nevertheless the like of which had never graced our table up till then – parsley-flavoured mashed potato wrapped in ham or devon slices, oranges pierced with toothpick sticks of cheddar cheese and red and green cocktail onions, home-made sausage rolls, savoury stuffed hardboiled eggs. I'd arranged for one of the girls to bring her portable record player, and the dozen of us danced around in the living room pretending at being grown-ups, while Mum sheltered discreetly in her room.

Now the universe conspired to send me three messages and, when all three fused, everything I knew of myself changed. The messages weren't delivered all at once, in a rush, like an 'Oh My God' lightbulb moment. They drifted in on waves of consciousness and presented themselves for inspection, to be turned over and over in my mind, questioned, considered and mulled over. They revealed themselves, one after the other, deliberately and in sequence, over a period of six months or so.

It all began a few months after I started high school. The first message came in Mrs Morgan's biology class. Mrs Morgan intimidated me. She scoffed at my answers in quizzes, holding them up as examples of stupidity to be mocked by the rest of the class. She never named me, but she knew I recognised my own work, and it was the silent, knowing mocking that hurt me most. I sat through each lesson longing for it to be over. So I surprised myself when one day I realised I was actually listening to her tirade on genetics.

Families pass physical characteristics from one person to another? *Really?* Eye colour, hair colour, body shape, these were not random acts of God? It was a revelation, a moment of enlightenment. I knew I was the odd one out, but I didn't know it shouldn't be so. I was the short, chubby, hazel-eyed, dark-haired, olive-skinned offspring of an Anglo-Saxon, tallish, slim, blue-eyed, fair-haired, light-skinned gene pool.

'Find another ancestor.' Mrs Morgan's response to my muddled question was abrupt.

I cast further afield. The black and white photo of my father did not provide much insight. I held it up to the mirror and compared our reflections. Two strangers blinked back at me in the glass.

I looked to Uncle Jack's family. The children had the piercing brown eyes of Aunty Nan and the dimpled chin of Uncle Jack. All had fair, Anglo-Saxon skin.

My difference was even more noticeable in Aunty Myra's family. They were so lean they were wiry, with blonde hair and round blue eyes. Only Cousin Phillip had dark hair, but his eyes were the roundest and bluest of the lot.

What a conundrum.

Mrs Morgan pushed on with the theory of survival of the fittest. 'In the animal kingdom, the young buck pushes out the dominant male as he ages. It's only those in the prime of life who procreate. This ensures the species will survive.'

'It's the same in humans. There's an optimum age to bear children. After a certain point, nature takes over and removes our fertility.'

Really?

I did a count back. I knew for sure Mum was thirty-five when she gave birth to me. That was beyond question. Dad was a different matter. I knew he was *much* older than Mum – but how much older? I had to dig around to get that information.

A few weeks later as I was leaving class, I paused to speak to Mrs Morgan.

'Can a man father a child when he is sixty-five?' I asked.

'Sure.' She was hurrying to her next class and showed no interest in why I might be asking the question. 'Sure. It's possible. But not likely.'

I didn't know what else to ask, so I left it at that. She hadn't said it was impossible, but a seed of doubt had been planted in my imaginative mind.

The second message was delivered through a book. I devoured books as I did food. I ate whatever was in front of me and I was always ready to eat more. It was the same with reading. I finished a book every few days, so I didn't read on any one theme, just whatever was at hand that seemed of interest. Quite by chance I read a book about a young girl who always felt out of place. It wasn't until she was grown up that she discovered her mum and dad were actually her aunt and uncle, and the woman she thought was her aunt was her mother. I followed her rollercoaster journey of discovery, her hope and disillusionment, anger and reconciliation. I considered this story over and over. The message in this book was that if someone has a powerful reason to keep a secret, such as having a baby and not being married, then they will hold things very close to their chest over years and years. They lie and cheat, but they do it because they think they're being kind. It's meant to be for the best.

The third message came from the gods. Shortly after I read the book, a school friend's mother decided to have a séance. It was by chance; someone had bought a ouija board, and as far as her daughter and I knew, it was merely a different kind of fun game to play. We squeezed into their breakfast nook, Doreen, her sister Wendy and me cramming along one bench, and Mrs Coddington sat with some other adults on the opposite bench. The board lay on the table in front of us, the letters of the alphabet spelled across it and the words 'yes' and 'no' at each end. An upturned drinking glass was in the centre of the board. We all placed our hands on it.

'Concentrate,' one of the adults told us. 'Then spell out your question and see where the glass moves.'

We played for a while, asking questions and giggling as the glass moved around the board, spelling out an answer letter by letter. It came to my turn.

The question popped into my mind. My fingers came to life. I spelled it out laboriously, letter by letter.

'Will I ever see my father again?'

The glass moved steadily across the board and came to rest on 'yes'. Confusion raced through my mind. What to ask next? I spelled out a statement, not a question.

'My father is dead.'

The glass shifted, moving slowly, inexorably towards 'no'.

I looked up at Mrs Coddington.

'It's not me!' she said, meeting my eyes full in the face. I could tell by her expression she was as taken aback as I was.

I looked around the table. Doreen and Wendy weren't giggling; they peered at me curiously, waiting to see what I would do. The other adults didn't know me, so they just looked perplexed, wondering what was going on.

The cynics will have many rational explanations for this event and what flowed from it. All I know is, that's the last time I ever tinkered with a ouija board.

•

Apart from begrudging that life was unfair to deprive me of a father when almost everyone else I knew had one, it had been years since I'd thought of my father as a real person. Now he was at the top of my mind, as if walking with me and demanding I pay him attention. I thought about all the times I had seen Mum and Aunty Myra having whispered conversations, how the room went silent when I walked in, how no one ever talked to me about my father, and how he never brought me any presents. How I actually couldn't remember any moment that I had ever shared with him.

I dug deeply into the shadows of my memory, trying to remember any event involving my father. I sensed a memory, but its shape sat just beyond the reach of my consciousness. I let my mind drift, digging ever deeper, sifting through the filing cabinet of my brain. It was as if I opened one drawer after another, examining the accumulation of knowledge stored there, until I came at last to the earliest of my memories, mere snapshots of a moment in time.

Here I am a toddler, wearing the corduroy overalls Aunty Myra made me. I am grasping the shovel from the fuel stove in both hands. I am playing in the gravel on the side of the road. The road has no gutter; it slopes away to merge with the grass of the footpath. Muddy pools lie here and there. Is there someone with me? I mentally scan to the edges of the picture. No. I am alone.

Here I sit on the knee of an unseen man; a colouring book is balanced in my lap, open at a fresh page. I am holding a brush dipped in water. I am ready to splash it over the drawing. He covers my pint-sized hand with his, steadying my grip, and guides me as we stroke the wet brush inside the drawing's shape. Instantly, coloured pictures spring to life from the white page. I can feel the sense of wonder wash through my little body and I look up to his face in amazement. How did that colour happen? Where did it come from? Is it magic? I strain to see his face. I try hard – but it is not there.

Here I have scrambled up onto a bed to reach the window, my fat knees balanced unsteadily on the narrow sill. I can see myself from behind as I press up close to the glass. My mouth is open in a shout; I am calling out to someone as I thump at the windowpane with chubby palms. I seem agitated. I can see the back of this person walking away up the hill, heading for the main road. Who is it? I strain to make out the figure. Is it a man? Whoever it is does not look back. Perhaps he cannot hear me.

•

Beside the fuel stove in the corner of our living room was a cupboard. All manner of things ended up in that cupboard. Mum was a hoarder who kept every piece of string and brown paper that found its way into the house; she smoothed the paper and folded it neatly and wrapped the string into balls, which got bigger and bigger as she added to them. She kept them in my old brown kindergarten case and put the case in the corner cupboard. Whenever I put it away I noticed a tattered book with a green cover. Its contents were of no interest – I couldn't understand most of the words.

Now I burrowed around in the cupboard and hauled out the old book, its cover torn and hanging off. I flicked through the contents. It was a textbook for Italian speakers to learn English.

A story came into my mind. A story from way back, about riding in a train through a long, dark tunnel. In a place where the mountains were so high people cut through them so they could get to the other side. The mountains were very high and the tunnel was very dark and the train rolled along inside for a long time before coming out on the other side of the mountain.

I could remember the story but not the voice or the face of the one who told it. I could remember how I felt when I heard it, and how badly I wanted to be there, to be enclosed in the dark tunnel walls, to hear the whoosh of the air as the train sped through, to burst into the dazzle of daylight and to see it glinting on that white stuff called snow.

It was Uncle Carlo who told me that story. Uncle Carlo. A ghostly memory with no face and no place. A shapeless form of a man who once used to visit us. A man who would help a young girl paint pictures on white paper. A man who would tell stories in a twisted accent.

'One day I take you on that train.'

'When?' I had demanded.

'When you are older.'

'When will that be?'

The last time I saw Uncle Carlo, I was too young to have any concept of time.

Now the pieces fell into place. Uncle Carlo was the elusive figure in my faded memory. There *were* no memories of my father, at least, not the one with the weird name of George George, the remote and absent man who had died six years before. The man I thought of as my Dear Dead Dad, and whom I acknowledged and mourned lackadaisically. The one whose photo stood proudly beside my bed. The war hero with the chopped-off fingers.

Mum was in the kitchen the day I confronted her. I sat down on the step that divided it from the living room and spoke to her back. I didn't feel tentative, nervous or angry. Not at all. I felt grittily determined. I wanted the truth, and was not prepared to accept evasion. To achieve that, I *had* to stay calm.

'Who *was* my father . . . George . . . or . . . Uncle Carlo?'

Mum spun around as if struck, eyes wide.

'I was going to tell you when you were thirty.'

In that moment of self-justification I understood the truth. The World War I flying ace, the man whose photo had sat beside my bed for so many days and nights, had nothing to do with me. No wonder he never brought me a present. I was not his child. *My* father was Uncle Carlo . . . but . . . *who* was he?

I suppose Mum had clung to the thought of waiting for my thirtieth birthday because she imagined I would be mature enough to hear and understand her story, or because it was so far in the distant future that it comforted her not to have to deal with the reality of the situation. Now here she was facing a mixed-up, hormonal thirteen-year-old, who was demanding an answer, demanding a heart-to-heart conversation. I wasn't going to be fobbed off.

We kept our guard. Mum stayed rooted to the spot where she had turned, one hand resting against the kitchen table. I stayed motionless on the step. If I moved towards her, or showed any emotion, the barrier would come down and she would scurry to her bedroom, and once there she would close the door on me and life, and anything that threatened her fragile stability. She stared at me like a frightened animal caught in a predator's gaze.

Then she started to speak, in a slow, measured tone. The words didn't tumble out one over the other in a rush of confession, nor were they evasive or halting. Quietly and calmly she told me her story, as if she had practised what she should say when this day finally came. I have no illusions it was the whole tale, but that portion of what she shared, I believed to be the truth.

'We worked at Waltons together. That's how we met. Working at the department store. He came from Italy. He'd migrated here a couple of years before . . .

'He loved you. We were going to be a family. He visited here sometimes . . .

'My mother didn't like him. She didn't like the idea of an Italian in the family. It didn't work out. He didn't stay. He went back to Italy when you were four . . .

'No, Gwenny, I never heard from him again. I don't know where he is now . . .

'No, Gwenny, no photo.'

'But Mum . . . weren't you married to George?'

'Married? No, Gwenny. I was never married to George. I've never been married.'

'But there's a photo! Your wedding photo!'

'What photo, Gwenny? What are you talking about?'

I dashed to the living room and dug around in the cupboard, coming back triumphantly with a yellowed envelope of black and white professional photos.

'This, here!' Now I was standing beside her. I pointed at the shot of her, a thirtyish young woman in a silky formal dress, leaning against George. His arm was snaked around her slim waist. She was wearing the linked belt of silver metal butterflies that showed off her trim figure; I had always longed for it. She looked radiant, her cheeks a rosy bloom and her small mouth curled in a smile. Streamers trailed over their clothes and piled around their feet.

'See, it's your wedding celebration.'

Mum allowed herself a laugh, a hiccup that caught in the back of her throat. 'Gwenny, that's a New Year's Eve party. Look, here's a photo of Steve at the same party.'

Steve's six-year-old self looked at the camera shyly, his arms full of the same streamers which had fooled me into thinking it was a wedding party. He was dressed in a smart suit. The party must have been formal, but it was no wedding. I had looked at both photos so many times, how had it escaped me they were taken on the same night?

'Then why did you tell me George was *my* father? Why did you lie?' I wasn't so much indignant as perplexed.

'No one told you that, Gwenny. You just assumed he was. I didn't realise until he died and you kept his photo. I thought it better just to leave it at that.'

Silence fell. Mum looked long and hard at me. She must have been satisfied with what she saw, because suddenly she broke the silence.

'Gwenny, there's something else. Everyone thinks I'm a widow. Lots of women became widows after the war – even if their husbands came home. They think my husband died and left me with two young children.'

There was a pause as I let this sink in. Mum was opening herself to me now, all the little details she had kept to herself over the years. I tried to make sense of what she was telling me. She had two children. They had two different fathers. She had never married. Mum had never married? But in the Australia of the forties and fifties, every mother had to marry. Now here was Mum saying she hadn't. That meant she had broken a taboo. That was not acceptable. So she had invented a story to cover up. Mum was good at creating a fantasy world. She lived in it more than she lived in reality.

Thoughts flooded in on a sudden flush of empathy that took me by surprise. It was a moment of rare insight – like a tableau of events unfolding in front of me. How must it have been: to leave your mother and family, to come to this barren suburb alone and ill equipped, to fend for yourself, to fabricate a life, to watch every word that slipped from the tongue, to be careful to act in thought and deed as if you were someone, some being, other than who you really were – not just to the outside world, but even to your own children. No wonder her mind cracked under the strain of it. My poor mum. What a tragedy.

Instinctively I wrapped my arms around her, and after a moment I felt her arms around me. It was a shock. Physical affection wasn't one of Mum's characteristics. We held each other like that for moments, perhaps a minute; our bodies blended together, each feeling the warmth of the other. It was the one and only time we hugged. For that one moment, I felt close to her.

As we broke away, she implored me. 'Gwenny – you *have* to keep this secret! It's important for us. It's important what people think of us. Not just me. It's for your sake, too.'

It was just as well that a few months earlier I had read the book that had given me a clue to mixed-up parentage and what happens when you learn of a change in your identity. It went a little way to preparing me for the subsequent confusion of feelings, but it didn't stop me from falling into introspection and cynical disillusionment. I spat out the emotion in poetry.

They try to pretend
That life is fun,
A joy with no end
And a shining sun.
As a child it is pure,
Filled with carefree days.
Our innocence is a lure
But only a phase.
So soon we grow older,
The blind gain sight.
A little less bolder
We see our plight –
The sun is less golden
Now life has grown solemn,
Dogged with worries and cares.
My dreams are nightmares.
Days are a sequence
Of troubles with frequence.
Joy is an ecstasy,
A child's fantasy.

The knowledge was a heavy burden. As I mulled over the story, connecting strands of lost memory with my feelings of isolation, the full significance of my situation dawned on me.

I wasn't just fatherless; I wasn't just dirt poor; I wasn't just the only kid growing up on welfare. I was illegitimate – a bastard! Somehow I was instantly worthless, instantly unacceptable to society.

For once, it wasn't my imagination running away with me. Illegitimacy was no small matter, it was a serious social stigma. To call someone a bastard was no term of endearment and, as far as the law was concerned, you had no rights. Even birth and marriage certificates declared you were *illegitimate.* A good man would think twice about marrying a bastard. He wouldn't want his children to carry that slur.

In the 1960s, Australian society had a veneer of respectability. Behind closed doors, there may have been violence, alcohol, gambling, neglect and other dysfunction, but everyone looked and acted like the perfect nuclear family. Mum, dad – a *married* mum and dad – two or three kids, the fibro house on the quarter-acre block, one car and one television.

Everyone – it seemed to me – *except for us*. Now I really knew why.

I tried hard to keep the secret. I *did* try, at least for a few weeks, maybe even a few months. The trouble was I was not my mother, and I did not want to be. If keeping a secret, even one as vital as this, meant you had to make yourself so sick that you kept going back to hospital and had to take oodles of drugs and live like a zombie half the time, then what was the point of life?

On the other hand, if you were accepted in society and made close friendships, as I had with Joanne, Lilly and others, and everybody praised you and gave you prizes when you did well in school, as long as they didn't know you were a bastard . . . but they would all turn away from you if they did . . . then what was the point of that? I would have to spend my life hoping they would never find out. Wouldn't it be better to know beforehand which people would turn against you? Before you got used to having a good friend and good school reports and all the other affirmations of belonging to society? In Lord Tennyson's words, *'Tis better to have loved and lost than never to have loved at all,* but that wasn't my view of the world. Better to have prepared yourself for the worst so you weren't too hurt or surprised when it happened. That had always worked for me. That's why I was always the first to make fun of my faults: being fat, or too hairy, or too talkative. That way, nobody could criticise me more than I did myself, and it took the wind out of the sails of anyone who was intent on slinging arrows in my direction.

The newfound knowledge plagued me. The secret would not go back into its box. I couldn't imagine how I could walk around with it held inside me for the next fifty years.

Finally, with a mixture of fear and bravado, I shared my story with Vicki. She and I had been friends for years, ever since she started at my primary school when her family was transferred to Guildford by the Defence Department. She was the eldest of five children, and I was often at her house, listening to music, going on picnics in the family Citroën, going to church with her mother, or to Legacy meetings with her father. I was sure I could trust Vicki. She was the most grown-up young person I knew.

I pulled her into my bedroom and slid the door closed. Right under Mum's nose, I whispered out the story, making sure I emphasised the illegitimate point. I held my breath for her response.

'Well,' she said brightly. 'That explains why you're so dark. And you're growing up so fast. Have you looked in the mirror lately? You're getting hollows under your cheekbones. You've lost any baby look. It's very pretty.'

'But Vicki. Don't you understand? I'm a *bastard*!'

'So?'

'Can you still be friends with me?'

'Of course, silly! What a pity there isn't a photo of your dad. It would be fun to see if you look like him.'

What a wave of relief swept through me. Vicki was interested, supportive, understanding, and at the end of that day, she was still my friend.

The trouble with secrets, though, is once you've told even one other person, by definition, that information is no longer a secret. So it was with me. Since I had shared it once, I shared it more often. I didn't exactly shout it from the rooftops, but I didn't exactly shy away from telling people. It's *how* I did it that causes me to cringe today. More than one person received the benefit of this experience:

'How do you do,' I offered my hand to the staid-looking matron.

'How nice to meet you, dear, and welcome to our church.' I scanned her in one look, a pill-box hat on close-curled permed hair, cats-eye glasses, a conservative two-piece suit, gloves, handbag and sturdy flat shoes. The sort of woman who might welcome you one moment and cut you dead the next, if you failed to meet her standards. No point in mucking around, better make sure of where I stood.

'I'm a bastard, best thought you should know that straight up.'

•

There was no one in the family I could turn to. The family was safeguarding Mum's secret, too, and had done a good job of that for thirteen years. I could hardly approach any one of them now and say I knew Uncle Carlo was my father. I couldn't pry for information, or ask someone to tell me more about him, to fill in Mum's sketchy outline. People didn't talk about such private matters, even people as chatty as Aunty Myra. They might not even know who Uncle Carlo really was. Maybe they had never even met him. I would be exposing Mum's shame to the family, and she had been so particular about the need for secrecy. It was one thing to tell outsiders, when I knew it would never get back to Mum, but to hold her up to scrutiny within the family circle would not do at all.

Nor could I ask Steve if he felt as badly about illegitimacy as I did. Did he feel worthless too? Did he feel he wasn't as good as the next person? How would I start such a conversation? I couldn't think how to do it.

Steve had done his best to be a caring big brother, even though I rarely recognised it was at the expense of his own comfort. He had taken me to the circus and the cinema, had let me join outings with his mates, taken me on drives when he got his first car. One of our favourite pastimes was to hang out at the back of Sydney's Mascot airport, leaning up against the wire perimeter fence as we watched planes take off and land. At times like those I felt close to Steve, when we were spending time together and having fun. I cherished how Steve had taught me to be observant in all things, whether it was the features of jet airliners or the way the grass grew on the side of the road.

On the other hand, there had never been many conversations in our house, even lighthearted ones. There was no chatter around the dining room table or around the radio at night. We didn't have a way of sharing our innermost thoughts, or our hopes and dreams. Poverty didn't bond us together; nor did we look to each other for emotional comfort, or stand together in the face of adversity – apart from banding together to protect Mum – and hardship didn't make us better siblings. It was nothing like they show on American movies, with everyone reaching harmony in the mandatory happy conclusion. We discussed practical things such as chores, school, work, appointments, the occasional joint outing, those sorts of things. We were already growing apart as our independence increased – so how was I to start now with something as important as this?

Steve and I understood it was our responsibility to shelter Mum from the traumas of life. We held joint accountability to ensure she didn't go back to hospital again. Steve already felt I had caused too many of her breakdowns, at least that's what I thought. He believed maintaining emotional distance was the right way to behave, but I was so much more outgoing than he was. He couldn't understand my extroversion and chattiness. Mum needed calm and quiet.

I wasn't going to upset the apple cart now by sharing that I knew Mum had sex outside marriage. It's hardly the thing to say to a boy about his mother. I didn't think he knew, and I couldn't picture him taking it well if I told him. He would probably think I had made it up as a way to hurt Mum.

As for any responsibility to myself, I was too immature to understand I was owed some care and consideration, too. I put the whole episode into a Pandora's Box of insecurities which I kept to myself, and let it fester there. Picking away at my self-esteem. Picking and chipping away in the background. No one in the family asked if there was anything troubling me. Mum never revisited our conversation. She behaved as if it had never taken place.

17

I was still in the middle of this trauma, still only thirteen, when the Nixon family moved from the Northern Territory and into our street, buying a tumbledown house across the road from Kulpie's. They had a foster daughter, Rachel, and she had a story to rival mine.

Under Australian government policies of assimilation and integration at the time, welfare authorities had removed Rachel from her Aboriginal mother when she was just a toddler, even though her mother loved and cared for her.

'But what happened?' I asked her.

'Well, I can remember sitting in the police station.'

'Was your mum there?'

'No, they'd already taken me away from her. I can't remember much about that, just screaming and crying. Then I remember sitting up on the sink in the police station. I remember watching my legs dangling down.'

'Then what?'

'Then Mum Nixon came flying in the door, shouting out for me. She was yelling at them not to take me to the mission home.'

Rachel continued her story. 'Mum Nixon told me about it when I was older. How she heard the police had taken me off my mother and were all set to put me in a home. She was Mum's good friend. She came racing straight to the station and fought for them to hand me over. She was able to convince them that she and Dad Nixon could look after me. It probably helped that he was a white man. She said another ten minutes and it would have been too late. But I wasn't allowed to see my own mum again. That was about ten years ago. I've lived with the Nixons ever since.'

I took to Rachel immediately. She was a year older than me and was only an inch or two over five feet, but she had a lean body, a straight back and an inner pride that made her seem much taller. I noticed her voice, which was melodic and well modulated; and I noticed her beauty. Her eyes were dark and doe shaped, fringed by dense, glossy eyelashes, and thick eyebrows winged over them. She had a pout, and her lips were permanently rose tinted. How I wished I could look and sound more like her. I tried to shape my eyebrows like hers, but all I managed to do was pluck them away. I tried to get my ample bosom to look pert and trim like hers, ironing a criss-cross crease into my cotton bras, but it was never successful, my round melons filled every fold of the fabric. I slapped at my thin lips to make them redder, but they never looked luscious like hers. Her poise and beauty would never rub off on me, but that didn't stop us bonding like sisters.

We used to sit in the gutter outside her house. The local council had laid kerb and guttering in our street, finally bringing Old Guildford into the modern era. I was happy to see the end of the dust and gravel; the kerbing created cleanliness and order. I liked the fresh white cement and how the storm drains carried away the rubbish that built up in them. I thought it brought us a notch closer to the stateliness of Concord, where Aunty Nan and Uncle Jack lived.

Then the council sent all the ratepayers a bill for the work. It tipped Mum over the edge into an anxiety attack; we couldn't afford to pay for a single frontage property, let alone that our bill was double since we owned a corner block.

It was a tense time. Steve and I were on tenterhooks waiting to see whether Mum would cope with this crisis or whether she was off to hospital again. Eventually she rallied, but it was a tough few weeks until the council relaxed its demand.

Rachel and I put the gutter to good use as a place to escape and share our thoughts.

'My parents are so strict!' Rachel lamented. She was upset they wouldn't let her go dancing with her cousins.

'My mother doesn't care where I am!' I howled in response.

Neither of us could decide who was worse off.

•

The Nixons were an unusual couple. He was a slightly built Anglo-Saxon who was on an eternal quest to improve the dilapadated house he had built on the cheap, using Rachel as his builder's labourer. Mrs Nixon, a long-limbed Aboriginal woman, was at least a decade older and already past her eightieth birthday. She had at least ten adult children of her own, plus all their descendants and cousins – dozens of family members scattered around Sydney and other parts of Australia. Her health was failing and she was crippled with arthritis, but there was nothing wrong with her mind – she had no trouble expressing her demands.

Under her insistent direction, Rachel was expected to run the house – shopping, cooking, washing, cleaning, even nursing. It was a wonder she had time to attend school and study as well, yet she was a keen student, with an eye to excelling in biology and working in a laboratory.

Rachel kept house not only for her foster parents, but also for the many relatives who dropped in and stayed a day or a month or more.

'Gwen!' she called to me on one of my frequent visits. 'Look what I've done to Bernie's shirt.'

She showed me his shirt, the bright-yellow one he was so proud of wearing because it showed off his glossy dark skin to perfection. She'd splashed bleach on it in a laundry accident. White streaks now ran down the front and back.

We stared at the damage. Trouble was looming. Rachel's 'brother' Bernie – one of Mrs Nixon's sons – would not take it well.

'Dye,' we nodded in agreement.

Dashing to the chemist shop, we quickly returned with a packet of yellow dye. There had only been one shade in stock and it was practically iridescent, but we were desperate. In a few hours Bernie would be expecting to find his shirt freshly washed and hanging, ready for him to wear that night.

We followed the instructions to the letter, the two of us hunched over the cement laundry tub at the back of the house. We rushed to get the shirt dry and ironed.

'What do you think?'

'Looks like a sunflower,' I said doubtfully.

'Well, we'll just have to hang it up and see if he notices.'

Bernie noticed. He put it on and admired himself this way and that in the bathroom mirror. The shirt was a yellow sunbeam against which his skin gleamed like burnished copper. He turned, and his wide smile and perfect white teeth dazzled me. It was like a light switched on in a dark room.

'What did you wash this with?'

'Omo,' Rachel muttered.

'Gee, it's come up a treat! It's really brilliant!'

'Yes, well. Haven't you seen the ads? They reckon Omo's the best of the lot,' said Rachel.

Bernie rode off on his motorbike.

'Don't ever breathe a word of this to anyone.' Rachel's eyes danced at mine.

Bernie was a few years older than we were, in his late teens or early twenties, with a regular job which meant he could contribute to the household, and most importantly, it meant he could own a motorbike – a shiny, powerful, thrilling beast.

I *loved* to ride pillion! Perched on the back seat, miniskirt tucked under my thighs, hands resting on Bernie's hips, wind pushing the hair off my face; it felt as if the three of us were one entity: me, man and machine. We were united in momentum, leaning in to the corners, watching the tarmac whoosh up towards us, adjusting our hips as we straightened up. Feeling the power beneath us as we gunned down a straight road, every fibre of my being tingling with the exhilaration of the ride.

Whenever he stayed at home, Bernie took over the sleep-out at the front. The three of us were in there one rainy night, lounging on the bed and singing along to his strumming of the guitar. As we competed with the sound of the rain on the tin roof, I was captivated in the magic of the moment. I felt entranced: the three of us there together, the weeping of the guitar, our voices soaring above the thundering noise of the rain.

Suddenly, there was Mum, standing on the front step, looking through the open door, an umbrella held over her head. I sat up straight, startled. What on earth was she doing here? She never came to visit the Nixons.

'Mum?' I stood up. A feeling of dread swept through me. Had something bad happened?

Mum said nothing. She glared at me and jerked the umbrella over her shoulder – meaning I was to follow her as she turned for home. My mind was in a whirl. I couldn't think what the problem might be, or why she had decided to come for me. If something had happened to Steve wouldn't she say straight out? Had I broken something? Did she think I had stolen something? What on earth was the matter? As we trudged through the rain, I tried to ask what was happening, but she wouldn't say a word, and I knew not to ask anything more. Her face said plenty, though . . . shooting me glares every time I dared look her way.

By the time we got home I felt as guilty as sin, despite the fact that whatever I had done was still a mystery. Everything at the house was normal, and Mum went to bed without a word. I was bamboozled and racked my brains for an answer. The best I could come up with was it had something to do with Bernie. It seemed to be just the fact I was sitting on the bed with him that had her so riled.

How could she have known? I wondered. She didn't have eyes in the back of her head, did she? Hah! For all I knew, she really did have a hotline to God. Maybe he told her. But why? Where was the harm in it?

Back at school, I went over the story with my friends.

'You were sitting on the bed with a man? Weren't you scared you'd get pregnant?' said one.

'Don't be silly,' I said. 'You have to do more than that to get pregnant.'

'Yeah,' said someone. 'My sister told me all about it. *And* she told me about the pill, too.'

'The pill?'

'Yep. She's just been to the doctor. You take a pill every day for six months and it stops you from getting pregnant. She said it stops the sperm from getting to the egg.'

I thought about this for a while.

'But when you stop taking the pill, won't the sperm just be waiting in the woman's belly? Won't you just get pregnant then?'

The others thought it over. None of us could understand how the pill could be a solution to pregnancy. Contraception wasn't a topic covered in the mother–daughter pamphlets. Everyone knew good girls didn't have sex before marriage. The pill was only meant for married women.

18

Rachel and I needed money, and she knew how we might get it. We approached Joe, the owner of the fruit shop at the bottom of the ramp to Guildford railway station.

'May we work for you in the school holidays? We're *such* hard workers. You're here on your own. We can be of real help to you.' Rachel was at her most polite, her doe eyes entreating him to say yes.

Joe wiped his hands on his leather apron and sized us up. He wasn't much taller than we were.

'You gooda girls?'

'Yes,' we nodded earnestly.

'You gooda wid cuzdomer? Can you cound change righda?'

'Yes, yes.' We were bouncing with eagerness.

'How old you?'

'Fourteen!'

'Thirteen!'

'Oh. Verry younga.'

'But we work hard . . . and *cheap. Please* give us a job.'

Joe hesitated for a moment, and then made a quick decision.

'Labour departmen' man coma aska da question – you say you my nieces. Okay?'

We looked at Joe: short, nuggety, dark, curly hair, eyes like coal, olive skin covered in spiky black hairs. We looked at each other. It was hard to imagine we three were related.

'OK!' we chorused.

Half an hour before the end of my first day on the job – which had gone without a hitch – I turned to serve the next customer. It was Steve. I did a double-take.

'Oh . . . hi. What are you doing here?'

'Ummm. I just thought I'd drop by and see if everything is okay.'

He looked concerned and he sounded serious. He was talking quietly, and staying out of earshot of Joe.

'Oh? It's fine.' I was confused. What was there to worry about?

'Well, I just thought. Your first job and all.'

I had blundered straight into employment with all the confidence of youth. What should I worry about? Joe was a nice man, a family man, an *old* man in my view. It was straightforward, simple work. Greet the customer. Ask what they wanted. Help them select the fruit. Don't let them squeeze it too hard. Weigh it, bag it, tot up the bill on a piece of newspaper, take their money, and count the change into their hand. Put the parcels in their string bag. Smile. Thank them. Maybe tell them, 'See you soon,' or 'Have a nice dinner,' or 'There you are – that'll keep you going on the train trip.' Yet, something had brought out Steve's protective instincts, and that was unusual. He hadn't enjoyed his first taste of the workforce, so maybe he imagined it would be just as hard for me.

Steve waited around until Joe was closing and I was taking off my apron.

'You want to have a go at driving the car?'

'What?'

'Come on. We'll go up to the car park behind the hotel.'

Steve had bought a brand-new Toyota Corolla using money he had inherited from his father, George. He sat me in the driver's seat, showed me how to coordinate the clutch and accelerator and how to change gear. Like all new drivers, my first few attempts were a series of kangaroo jumps, but it wasn't too long before I was going around and around the car park in a figure of eight. Steve seemed relaxed enough in the passenger seat.

'You're cutting the corners too fine. Don't go so close to that cement barrier.' That was the closest to a rebuke he could muster.

My big brother and me, hanging out together and having fun.

•

Rachel and I settled into a pattern of working on alternate days, or working together on busy days. It wasn't long before Joe learned just how much he could trust us. He started to leave us with the keys to open the metal roller doors and set up the fruit and vegetable stands on the mornings he went to the markets for fresh produce. We all got on well, just as if we were real members of his family. He always treated us with respect and consideration, and I never imagined it would be otherwise. Rachel says he gave us each a set of Mikimoto pearls when we stopped working for him a year later. I don't remember that, and I don't own any pearls, but Rachel remembers it because she sold hers later when she was desperately short of money.

I might not remember the pearls but I will never forget that first pay packet: a whole six dollars for a week's work, ten per cent of what Steve earned, and *he* was an *adult*, doing demanding office work and being ordered about by bosses, *and* paying tax as well. I felt as though I was rolling in clover.

Mum took one-third of my pay as board, but it still left me with the fortune of four dollars a week, and I squirrelled it away to fulfil my dreams, starting with decorating my bedroom. Until the previous year I had never had my own room, just a corner of the front living room, with a little screen around my bed so I could undress in privacy.

It was like the screens glamorous movie stars peeked over when men came to call on them in their dressing rooms, except there were no rich admirers in my world. It was Steve's mates coming in and out all the time, and I was getting older, and curvier. Kulpie's builder son-in-law volunteered to build a wall, and we ended up with a hallway and a bedroom for me. It was a plain affair, small and irregularly shaped, but I could see in my mind what I wanted it to become, and now I had the means to make it happen.

Steve helped me get started. I chose lilac, and we painted the room together. The shade didn't come out evenly on each wall, but I didn't care. At least it wasn't like the rest of the house, where the paint was so faded everything looked a nondescript shade of off-white, with old dried paint peeling off in drifts like snowflakes as people walked past.

Little by little my room took shape. Steve turned his hand to carpentry and I discovered how to use a sewing machine. Joe paid me regularly and I saved diligently and spent wisely: a chenille bedspread, a shaggy floor rug, wall decorations, and glass-blown vases. I cherished each piece, but was particularly proud of my purple paper lampshade, which covered the bare ceiling light. Even though it diminished the light in the room, I welcomed the softening of stark outlines and admired the shadow patterns it played on the ceiling. Everything was accumulated painstakingly – work, pay, save, spend – and piece by piece my bedroom blossomed into an oasis as if a gardener was tending delicate blooms. When I stepped into my room I saw a Moroccan-style Bedouin tent, exotic in purple and blue, rich with fabric and texture and cluttered with eclectic nick-nacks. Brass incense holders filled with aromatic sticks flourished on the wooden mantelpiece above the fireplace, and saturated the air with exotic scents. Sometimes, I was tempted to dance around the room naked.

My thirteenth year signalled other changes too, although I was too self-absorbed to realise at first. I had overlooked that Mum had not been hospitalised for some time. I had developed a level of conscious indifference where she was concerned. Had I been paying attention,

I would have noticed that when I crested the hill on my walk home from school, she might be standing at the front gate, or sitting in the sun on the veranda, knitting industriously.

'Haven't you noticed, Lynn?' Kulpie said, 'It's been a long while now since she last had a breakdown. She seems to have sparked up because you are growing up now. She comes and visits sometimes and talks about you. Shows me what you are reading.'

It grated when Kulpie told me that. This habit Mum had developed of reading my books was a constant source of annoyance. I'd turn on her in frustration. 'Mum! Can't you just wait until I've finished? I'll only be a day or two! You can read it then. Why are you always losing my place?'

Kulpie was right, of course. There *were* subtle changes in Mum's behaviour. Now when I slipped out of the house in the morning, avoiding her room, she sometimes came running up the street after me, arms akimbo. 'Gwenny! You forgot to kiss me!'

No, didn't forget, *Mum*, I'd think, as I squirmed under a squelchy kiss on the cheek.

I didn't want my mother involving herself in my life. I had managed fine this far without her. There was no way I would confide in her about anything, and I couldn't unburden to her if I had troubles on my mind, for fear of transferring those troubles to her mind.

Sewerage was connected in our suburb. Mum formed a temporary friendship with the plumber, inviting him in for tea and biscuits, but when the job was completed, the friendship ended. Although it was only August, Steve left out the customary Christmas gift of money and beer for the last visit of the sano man, together with a note: *Now we have sewerage, this is the end. Christmas came early for you, my friend.* I loved Steve's sense of humour which was always on display around his mates. With no annoying parents to curtail their high-jinks, our house was their 'go-to' place, and there were times they practically lived there.

Mum came around to the idea of a washing machine. In the store the salesman turned to Steve, enquiring, 'And who is it for, the mother, or the little wife?' Steve squirmed. He didn't need this reminder I was growing up so quickly.

The hopes of a recovery led to Mum being referred to a sheltered workshop. As part of her occupational therapy, she made serving trays with basket weaved edges. They taught her how to paint bright pictures on the bases. The smell of enamel paint still lingers in my nostrils. It didn't mean that she became engaged with life, though. My fourteenth birthday came and went. Two weeks later, Steve stood in my bedroom doorway. 'Did Mum buy you a present?' he asked.

I shook my head and gave him a resigned look. 'Hmph,' he shrugged and walked away.

Two weeks later he was back with a giant-sized bar of chocolate. 'Happy Birthday,' he said. It was a small gesture, but I took comfort from it. Now in his early twenties, Steve was immersed in his own life. He'd given up his first job because he felt under-valued and taken advantage of, and when he discovered that the new recruit earned more than he did, he moved on to Garden Island dockyard. He was busy: working, commuting, carousing, and training in the CMF. Making time for his kid sister was not his top priority, nor did I want it to be. I was too busy getting up to high-jinks of my own.

Armed with a taste for money, I started hounding other people for jobs. It was a simple exercise. I rode the bus to Parramatta or Villawood and targeted a street of small shops, walking up and down asking the shopkeepers for after-school and Saturday work. They all said 'no' on the first few attempts, but I just kept coming back once or twice a week, and eventually someone would cave in. I worked steadily through high school, in a cake and doughnut shop, another fruit market and a hardware store. I worked the six-week summer holiday at Luna Park, earning as much money as Steve if I worked extended shifts, and the best part of that job was we were given free tickets to the rides. I took these back to school at the end of the holiday and sold them off for half the regular price of the ride. I even earned money working from home when Steve's bachelor mates started bringing their ironing to me. I was never going to be a millionaire, but I was no longer destitute. It felt liberating to have money of my own. I had money to spend on a social life.

My social life had started innocently enough, based around family time with various friends and neighbours, watching television movies, singing, dancing, picnics, swimming in the Georges River with Steve and his mates. Going to church with Vicki's mother, I sat there waiting for the hand of God to reach out and ask me to walk with Him, but He was always too busy to send me the lightning bolt that would tell me I was called to his side. Whenever summer rolled around, I gave up waiting and went to the beach instead.

It wasn't long, though, before I was playing out of my depth. I was fourteen and hanging around with an older crowd, girls who had left school and were working. They all had jobs at Formfit or Hestia, famous for 'Holding Every Size Tit in Australia' they told me, and they enjoyed a drink or two before going on to the teetotal Rivoli dance hall. The pub across the road from the Rivoli offered a ladies' lounge, with décor that was slightly more upmarket than the front bar. There was carpet on the floor, and tables and chairs, rather than just the long bar with a trough for spillage and spitting. In this pub, as in any other pub in Australia, women were barred from the front Saloon Bar.

The arrangement was I would wait at the door of the Rivoli while the rest of the girls nipped across the road and had a couple of drinks before the dance. Advocaat and cherry brandy was a popular choice.

That worked to begin with, until the time I was desperate for the toilet and it was too early for the hall to open. The pub had a big burly bouncer, whose job was to keep out underage drinkers and other unwelcome would-be patrons. I decided I would let him know my girlfriends were inside, and could I use the facilities for just a moment please? He looked surprised I was even asking him and indicated for me to go right on in.

So I did. Then, since he clearly wasn't expecting me to come straight out again, excited but nervous, I went up to where my girlfriends were. Surprised at first, they shouted me a drink. It was blue and tasted of lemonade. Now it was my turn to be surprised. Is that it? I thought. So what's all the fuss about alcohol? Best of all it had this cute paper umbrella on a wooden stick. Over the next few weeks, I gathered a collection of paper umbrellas which I hid in a drawer at home. Then one weekend I cut my fringe and that night the bouncer threw me out before I got a foot in the door. The short fringe had taken years off my appearance.

I'd met these girls through Rachel, but she was still tied to home. She was in a steady relationship, and on occasions Mrs Nixon allowed her out with her boyfriend, Dave, but she drew the line at letting her come out with us. We were roaming all over Sydney, to the beach, to the bowling alley and to pubs and clubs as far afield as Coogee. For me, it was as much about the bands, the music and dancing as it was about the drinking – but by the time I was fifteen there was plenty of that, too.

Occasionally a suspicious bouncer would approach our group and single me out. 'What's your name?'

'Bernadette Devlin.' I'd throw it back at the bouncer with my chin tilted in the air. None of them ever got the joke, never realising this radical, left-wing Irish firebrand was my current idol. She had captured my attention with her youth and her stand for Irish parliament in the unrest of Northern Ireland. Protestants called her Fidel Castro in a miniskirt.

'What's your date of birth?'

'Twenty-third of April, 1952.'

'You got that off pretty pat.'

'Well, when you've had eighteen of them, you get to remember when it is.'

'I see. You don't look eighteen.'

'Can I help it if my hormones are deficient?' I'd reply, glancing down at my breasts thrusting above my singlet top.

Cheeky bitch. Some bouncers let me stay – others threw me out.

It was a juggling act, but I seemed to be on top of it all. I had plenty of energy, and there was a time for everything: schoolwork – including spots on the debating team and the dramatic society – after school and Saturday mornings for work, and the rest of the weekend for play. My grades slipped a little, but I was still topping many subjects. I worked hard, and I played even harder.

One night I was home late again, but before Steve got home from the pub. He was out most nights, so I couldn't imagine walking in the door to find him already there and waiting with a look of thunder on his face. I used to let myself in the front door and quickly slip into bed, pretending to have been asleep for hours. Lately, Steve had taken to opening my bedroom door and standing silently in the doorway, while I lay still in the dark, breathing in and out deeply and evenly, playing possum.

'Where have you been?' His question that night was a shock. Normally he just walked away after a few minutes. I ignored him. 'I know you're not asleep. I'll ask you again. Where have you been?'

'At the bowling alley.'

'That's a lie.'

'No.'

'Yes! I just followed you home! I saw you sitting up in the bus with those blokes. Who were they? Where were you?'

So, it *was* Steve's car I'd noticed a few lengths back. Going slowly so as not to have to stop every time the bus stopped to let someone off. Had he been following me ever since I left the pub?

'I was with my girlfriends. It was a brother and his mates.'

'You're lying. And those girls are trash! You shouldn't be hanging around with them.'

'Don't speak about my friends like that!'

'Friends! They're gutter girls.'

Steve was riled now. He'd stepped into the room and was looming over my bed.

'What have you been up to?'

'Nothing! Leave me alone. What I do is not your business.'

'The hell it isn't!'

'What would you care!'

'Oh . . . you little . . .' Steve exploded. He wrenched the covers off me, and slapped me hard, once, twice, three times around the buttocks. This was the first of many fights that ended with me in tears.

•

I was fourteen, going on twenty-four, a child physically mature beyond my years, but I was insecure and desperate to fit in somewhere, desperate to be loved. My moods were all over the place. I was prone to dramatic outbursts, or at other times I wallowed in dark thoughts. It was hard to know just what each day would bring and how I would react to it. Most of the time I didn't know who I was. Some days I was carefree and careless, and other days I was in deep despair. On the eve of my fifteenth birthday I wrote a poem that expressed my inner turmoil.

Echoes of screams –
Walls closing in,
Smother.
Horror, endless terror –
Pain.
Faces, tortured,
Mouths open, eyes bulge –
Lifeless.
I want to scream
On and on.

Running,
Never ending,
Don't stop –
You'll die.
Scared inside –
Where am I going?
Don't know.
Can't think.
Lost.

It was around this time when I 'met' Barry. I was leafing through the afternoon paper, catching up on the gossip in the Dear Del column. Next to reading my horoscope, this was my favourite part of the paper.

'Dear Del, I lied to my boyfriend to make him love me, but now I am scared he will find out.'

'Dear Del, I have strong feelings about a man, but he is not a strong character . . .'

'Dear Del, My best friend stole my boyfriend, but now she has dumped him. Should I take him back?'

'Dear Del, I am a nineteen-year-old instrument fitter in the Air Force, and I would like a penfriend.'

That sounds like me, I thought. I tore the ad from the paper and rushed off to introduce myself, and a few weeks later, in October 1970, I received the first of dozens of letters.

'Hi there! Thank you for writing,' it began. 'Well, after I wrote to Del, I received letters from about fourteen girls. I didn't know just who to write to, but after much reading and re-reading I chose you. So here I am.'

I reached out to Barry as if he were a life 'boy' and me the drowning person. I poured out my anxieties and daily dramas to him, letter after letter. Barry was at Fairbairn RAAF base in Canberra when we started writing, although at one stage he was transferred to Wagga Wagga for part of his training as an instrument fitter, before being transferred back to Canberra. He had a girlfriend, two parents and three siblings, so he had plenty of letters to write, but he was still lonely.

'I am 5'10" tall, brown eyes and fair hair,' his first letter explained. 'I love sport of any kind, but I concentrate more on basketball, hockey and cricket.'

I took him at his word, because we had never met face to face, and although we talked about it in our letters, we never exchanged a photograph. Having film developed was expensive, and I didn't own a camera. I'm not sure he did, either.

Barry was never far from the end of my pen. Our letters flew back and forward at an average of one each a week, sometimes more often, sometimes with a short break. We wrote of our families, his work and the mechanics of aeroplanes, and my schoolwork (when a male student had beaten me in maths, 'Hooray for the "Male Sex",' Barry wrote, 'you were lucky the boys *even let* you come second!'). We wrote about our hobbies, what movies and music we liked, and we wrote about our picks for the Melbourne Cup – he won that year on Baghdad Note. 'I reckon she's a sure winner,' he wrote when telling me he had ten dollars each way, as well as drawing her in the sweep.

He bought himself a cassette recorder with the winnings, so he could play his eclectic collection of music tapes ranging from Al Martino to the Beatles, the Animals and the Easybeats to Percy Faith and Roy Orbison.

We competed with each other to write witty, lighthearted pieces, pages and pages of nonsense that would have made Spike Milligan proud. Without looks, dress and body language to get in the way, we gave free range to expressing and describing ourselves through thought. Occasionally, our minds met despite our outer reserve, our mutual self-analysis revealing self-doubts and insecurities, weaknesses we weren't prepared to expose to anyone else. After a while, a chemistry built up between us. I began to feel I knew him better than if he had been there in person. One extra-long letter he wrote a year after our first trailed off with, 'I'm trying to sign off, but I don't want to, because I've found a missing link – you – through the medium of this letter – someone I can talk to, seriously, without being laughed at.'

I felt exactly the same, and there were many times in the future months when the only person I felt I could truly confide in was Barry. Even so, some things that were ahead of me were just too awful to share with anyone, even such a trusted friend.

19

Despite Steve's efforts to be a caring big brother, by the time I was fifteen, he was twenty-four and tensions were mounting. My curvy body was trying to grow up to be Sophia Loren's, and I was sassy and full of false bravado to go with it. Steve was a young man who knew what young men wanted, but he was shy when it came to women. He admired them from a distance, and was polite and respectful to his mates' girlfriends. Although he had a girlfriend now too, he didn't have much personal experience, and was alarmed about the experiences he thought I was having. When we argued, which seemed more and more often, he thought I was melodramatic, and I thought he had a short fuse.

'He's just your brother. It's not as if he's your father or anything. Why do you let him hit you?' one of my friends said when she saw the marks on the back of my thighs.

'Well . . . It's *like* he's my father,' I justified. 'Besides, how can I stop him? He thinks I deserve it.'

It wasn't that Steve woke up in the morning determined to fight with me. It's just I was no longer the baby sister who wanted to hang out with her big brother; and he didn't want a kid sister tagging along in any case. Life and hormones came between us. I was meeting boys everywhere – at school, at dances, at friends' houses, and Steve imagined I was leading them on. He didn't seem to realise not every boy was as serious as he was and most of the time they were playing a game, paying attention one week, dropping you the next. I loved to dance and to live life, and carry on as if I were on the stage – quite the opposite to his reserved and careful approach to life.

Steve saw danger around every corner. He was frustrated at my outgoing style and blind to my moments of introversion, so in desperation, when he didn't know what else to do, he slapped me. It might start out as a cross-examination of what I had been doing or where I had been, but it would inevitably escalate. Perhaps it was a sense of helplessness and frustration that sent him into such a rage.

Mum knew Steve hit me, but she did nothing about it. She hid in her bedroom and avoided the conflict, her usual way of escaping anything she couldn't deal with. She never asked me if I was hurt, or how I felt. For all I knew, she had told Steve to do it. Steve wouldn't dream of hitting me in the face – it was only on the back and legs – so nothing much ever showed apart from on sports days, and teachers never seemed to notice.

No doubt Steve hoped the punishment would change my behaviour, but the outcome was the direct opposite. I was rebellious, and I became even more so. If I was going to get a hiding, I decided I may as well make sure I deserved it.

I tried to stop him finding out my business. I always knew when he was nearing home because of the bend at the bottom of Crawford Street where he had to change down a gear to get up the hill. I heard the Corolla change gear the moment it entered that bend. It was a sound I listened for with fear and trepidation, and I would jump straight into bed and pretend to be asleep. Sometimes, he would stop at my bedroom door, then, perhaps doubting his suspicions, would think better of it and go to bed himself. Other times, he would barge straight in and start with the accusations.

I did plenty that warranted reprimanding, but even if Steve had tried gentle guidance instead of a belting, I would have objected to what he had to say. I thought I had all the answers.

•

I had been working weekends at another local fruit market – a barn-like building in Villawood that was always packed with customers, some buying their fruit and vegetables by the case. They were heavy, busy, nine-hour days which paid the massive sum of one dollar an hour. It was a fortune, and I was on a mission to save a pot of money. It had been plain sailing for six weeks, but when trade turned slack and I was caught playing noughts and crosses with another girl, both of us were sacked on the spot.

'Take'a da' money and go now. I pay you work – no play.' That is what the matriarch of the Italian family business had snarled as she pushed a brown envelope across the desk at me. I slunk out of the office feeling miserable. It was the first time I had been sacked. It wasn't a good feeling.

At home in my room, I pulled a tin from its hiding place, counted the money inside and added the contents of the brown envelope. I had one hundred dollars. I regretted losing my weekend job and all that extra income. I had meant to work right up to Christmas, because my friend Jeanette's parents had invited me to join them on their holiday to Adelaide. Her brother Dave and Rachel Nixon were going steady, and Dave didn't want to go with the family because he was old enough to look after himself. I'd been asked to go in his place as company for Jeanette. They might have asked Rachel, but there was no way the Nixons would let her go. Jeanette's parents would pay for petrol and caravan hire, but I was to share in the food costs and cover my own expenses, including meals on the way. More money would have been nice, but I assured myself a hundred dollars was enough.

Steve was concerned when he heard of the plan. 'Are you sure you'll be all right with these people?'

'Why not?' I was wary. I didn't want to miss out on this trip. I had never been out of the state before. Never been on a road trip which took you halfway across the country, never been on a road trip, full stop! I'd never stayed in a motel or caravan; never had breakfast served in my room; never had a holiday with a girlfriend. I was already planning some of the places we could go.

'Well. What if something happens? An argument, say?'

'I've money. Plenty! Look!' I showed Steve my tin of savings. It seemed to reassure him.

'Okay. If something goes wrong, don't stay there. There's a train from Adelaide. Get straight on that. You've got enough there for the fare.'

What could go wrong? I thought to myself. It's a *holiday*. We're going for *fun*, not to fight. God, Steve, sometimes you can be *such a square*.

•

Rachel had a fiery temper. If she was worked up over something, she'd let you have the full brunt of her emotions and thoughts, no holds barred. She hit you with a broadside, smothering any protest. She didn't need to swear because she could cut you dead perfectly well using the Queen's English. Then it was over. The next time you saw her it was all forgotten, unless you were one of the few people she'd decided to write out of her life forever. As for me, she once described me as a snail. She said I sheltered in my shell until I thought it was safe to come out. If anyone touched my feelers when I popped my head out for a look around, then I pulled back inside and didn't come out again until I felt safe.

It was an apt description at the time. I felt things too keenly and my feelings were too easily hurt. It was an accident of astrology. I was born under the sign of the crab, and like the crab, I had to grow a hard shell to protect my soft inner core. Sass and false bravado were ways of covering up. The day Rachel thumped on the back door, though, I didn't have my 'feelers out'. I was unaware and unprotected.

The thudding on the back door was set to knock it off its hinges.

'What on earth . . . ?'

I ran to open it and took a step back when I saw Rachel. She was fired up – her tiny body was almost shooting off sparks.

'Wha . . .'

'Why did you say that about Dave and me!'

'What do you me—'

'Don't play smart with me. You know what you said. His mother . . .'

'Mother?'

'. . . His mother told me everything! How could you talk about me behind my back! What kind of . . .'

'Rach . . . ?'

'*Friend* are *you*. *You're* just jealous – well that's *your* problem!'

Her body was rigid, drawn up as tall as her five feet, two inches would allow, standing proud and defiant on our back step.

'I don't . . .'

'We're done. Don't . . .'

'Know what . . .'

'Ever speak . . .'

'You're talk—'

'To me again!'

'—ing about . . . Rachel?' But she had already spun on her heels and was storming down the eight back steps, through the courtyard and into the street.

I slumped against the back door, my mouth agape, my throat constricted and my heart twisted into a little ball. My stomach churned and my legs began to quiver. Tears pricked at my eyes as I watched her march down the street with her head high, and her back straight, without even one backward look.

I fell into a chair.

What just happened? I asked myself.

We had returned from Adelaide the day before and I'd been looking forward to sharing it all with her – the drive, the motel, the pool, the movies, the huge stack we had eaten at Pancake Kitchen, life in a caravan and how we couldn't go to bed until we finished playing cards because the table was the base of the bed Jeanette and I shared.

Then I remembered. One night as we sat around the table, the conversation had turned to Rachel and Dave. It was clear his mother wasn't in favour of the relationship. She didn't come right out and say she didn't want an Aboriginal daughter-in-law, but she was from whiter-than-white Irish heritage, fair-skinned with blonde hair and freckles. Gossipy and opinionated and used to ruling the roost, she had implied that perhaps her son could make a better choice of girlfriend. I hadn't agreed but I hadn't defended Rachel, either. I didn't want to find myself on the train back to Sydney. Yes, there had been ten minutes or so of conversation about Dave and Rachel. Had I been quiet, or had I said something out of turn? Whatever the truth, it seemed clear Jeanette's mother had happily put words into my mouth, which would have been typical of that woman. She took pleasure in being malicious, imagining it was in her hands to decide what was right and what was wrong, and that it was her responsibility to set the standards others should follow. Now my treasured friendship with Rachel lay in tatters.

Later in the year I heard Rachel and Dave were expecting a baby and were planning to get married. That should have been my trigger to contact her and make peace. I didn't.

Don't go where you're not welcome. That was my motto, and my motto had held true for me. It didn't occur to me Rachel might need me back in her life at that time. I was too focused on having the door slammed in my face if I tried. So I was of zero support to Rachel then. I left it to her to come to me and mend the bridge.

20

As 1970 dragged into 1971, the year I would turn sixteen, my life became increasingly confused. Barry was my lifeline, his words comforting and guiding me through my ridiculous and desperate search for love and acceptance. I wrote letter after letter telling him of my latest lost love, and he treated each one seriously, replying with constant reassurance.

'There are lots more fish in the sea – I wouldn't even bother to chase that one up to hit him!' was Barry's advice when one boyfriend dumped me. The next one didn't make the grade, either: 'With regards to your situation with John, you've done the right thing and if you never see him again you'd be better off. I'd drop him if I were in your position.'

It was around April or May of 1971 that I met Colin. I was digging in the front garden, swinging a rusty mattock high over my head, thumping it into the weed-choked, rock-hard soil. I was determined to transform this barren patch into a sea of purple and gold, my favourite colours, colours of passion and happiness. Imagining the yellow daffodils and purple violas I would grow in a profusion of bright colour and happy faces, I ignored the fact that nothing I planted ever grew. The soil was infertile, and I knew nothing of growing seasons. I thought if I stuck something in the ground and watered it, it would grow to look like the picture on the packet. Silly me. The only things that ever grew in our yard were straggly bush roses and kikuyu grass.

A car stopped.

'Hey girl, whatcha doin?' It was my boyfriend, John.

'What does it look like?' I gave him a surly look. I was still seething over our last argument. He dropped his eyes.

'Yeah. Well. I'm only here 'cos my sister wanted to see you.' He jerked his head at her. Sue, sitting in the back seat, flicked me a wave.

'They just let her home,' he added.

I dropped the mattock and walked over, wiping my hands down my jeans. Sue wound down the window.

'Hi Sue. How you doing?'

'Not bad. Feel a bit strange, but. Trying to catch up again with everyone.'

'Was it awful?' She had been sent to Parramatta Girls' Home for a stint. For her own good. That's what the authorities said.

'Pretty bad . . . yeah . . .' her voice trailed away.

John and another guy swivelled around in the front seat, watching us talk.

'Oh and yeah . . .' John cut in, 'this is me mate Colin. Lives down the road.'

I nodded at Colin, noting straight brown hair flicking over his forehead, brown eyes, lopsided cheeky grin. Tatty jumper with holes at the elbows.

'We been work'n on me car,' Colin said. I nodded. I didn't look any better in my old jeans and flannelette shirt rolled up at the sleeves. Hair screwed back in an untidy ponytail. No makeup. I was dressed for garden work, not for going out on the town.

'It's a Ford Zephyr, Mark Two.'

'Right,' I nodded. As if *that* meant anything to me.

They drove off after ten minutes of half-hearted conversation, and I turned back to my gardening. I didn't give Colin another thought.

A few days later, I was shocked to find Mum at our front gate when I got home from school.

'There you are!' She rushed towards me. 'I thought you'd never get home.' Lunging at me, she dragged me down our front path, almost pulling me off my feet. I could feel her body trembling as she herded me into my room.

A cascade of blooms enclosed in clear cellophane splayed across my bed. I had never seen anything so magnificent. I fingered the pink satin ribbon holding the thick wad of stems together, trying to calm the surge of adrenalin.

Could these really be for me? Don't get too excited, there must be a mistake. Any moment now the deliveryman will come back. He's got the wrong house.

I could feel Mum up close beside me, bouncing on the spot with excitement. 'Gwenny, they came an hour ago. Aren't they beautiful? Who sent them? Oh! Gwenny! Your first flowers! Such a display! Delivered to the door. I had the man bring them in here to your room. So big! I couldn't carry them.' The words tumbled out in a jumble. She was bursting with the thrill of it, as if they were for her. Her face was flushed and her eyes sparkled like a schoolgirl's.

'The card, Gwenny. Open the card!'

My heart was thumping. My cheeks felt hot. No one had ever sent me flowers before, not even a posy, and here I was staring at a gift so extravagant it must have cost a week's wages.

Mum pointed out the florist's card. I opened the envelope, my fingers trembling.

'They're from Colin,' my voice squeaked. Colin? Colin was sending *me* flowers? What was he up to? He had to know John and I had been seeing each other.

A week later another bouquet arrived, just as splendid as the first, this time with a note asking me out.

Dear Gwen, (wrote Barry)

No! I will not be cynical and say Colin is softening you up. At least I hope he isn't. I think you deserve a break. However, not being nasty, but I said John would put the ol' hard word on you, much to your disappointment. I was right – he did & he may have got 'knocked back' but all the same – he did. Best of luck with Colin.

Sweet man, Barry.

I may have shared some doubts with Barry, but I dumped John immediately and it didn't take much for Colin to win me over. A couple of bouquets, some consideration, kindness, shared jokes and a hundred compliments and I was hooked within a few weeks. We seemed to have so much in common. We were close in age, he was eighteen and me almost sixteen when we met. Colin was a 'change-of-life' baby, arriving fifteen years after his parents thought their family was complete; although he had two brothers and a sister, his experience with the age gap in parents and siblings was similar to mine. We both felt isolated and misunderstood, and we both nursed resentments about how our families treated us. He liked to laugh, and he liked to talk me up, and he had any number of grand schemes and rosy ideas that swept me along. He didn't act all tough and macho when it was just the two of us. He was tender and open about his feeling for me, telling me all the things he loved about me, how different I was to all the others girls he knew. It made me feel special. We both had a lot of love to give, and no one to give it to. We both needed a lot of love and reassurance, and now we had found each other.

It was a whirlwind courtship. We were together every day. Even though it caused arguments with both our families, we couldn't seem to stay apart. We thought it was their fault others couldn't understand our great need to be together. Feelings and events that should have taken months to grow and develop happened within weeks.

'Slow it down, Lynn,' Kulpie looked at me sternly across her dining table. 'You're both too young. Do you want to end up like Rachel? Sixteen and pregnant?'

'No.' I felt uncomfortable under her glare. I wanted to agree with her, and at the same time I felt a fierce loyalty to Colin. I couldn't explain to Kulpie that I didn't know how to slow it down. It seemed out of my control to pull back. Besides, Colin and I weren't 'doing it'. Heavy petting, sure, but he respected me too much to demand sex. I felt I was safe.

Colin had left school at fifteen hoping to be a jockey, but when that came to nothing he took whatever came his way, mainly truck driving. He was puffed up with pride that he was earning a few dollars every week, and sometimes sneered at his friend Roy who stayed on at school to go to university.

'It'll be years before you're in the dosh, mate,' he threw at him.

He was deaf to Roy's patient explanation that over time he would earn much more than Colin could dream of. Colin saw no value in education, and it was a miracle he managed to finish third year. It was totally opposite to my ambition to get a university scholarship.

'He's not your intellectual equal,' Aunty Myra was anxious, 'it will make you unhappy in time Gwenny. Mark my words. He will hold you back.'

I shrugged off her advice.

You don't understand, I said to myself, he *loves* that I'm smart. That's what makes me different to all the other girls he's taken out. That's what makes me so special.

No one in my family liked Colin, and after the night of my sixteenth birthday party there was no hope of changing their opinion. The party for my thirteenth had been such a triumph; I imagined this would be too, only more grown up, and with more people, so I decided to hold it in the backyard. I was so excited, arranging the music, food and alcohol – even though my school friends' parents would have been outraged if they knew about that. I hadn't arranged any supervision; Mum was in bed and Steve was out for the night.

The party was gate-crashed by a hundred people, all bringing more booze. It turned into a riot, the neighbours called the police; somehow Steve got wind of it and turned up, trying to restore order. In the melee that followed, Colin broke Steve's jaw.

I'd been too drunk to remember everything the next day, but I readily accepted Colin's explanation. 'If he hadn't barged in, he and his mates, throwing their weight around, it would never have come to this,' Colin said to me. 'It wasn't my fault. It was just an unlucky punch, an accident. I didn't mean to do it.' Steve was not there to refute this claim.

'Of course, of course, I know, you were just protecting me,' I agreed.

•

A couple of months after my party I was unpacking stock at the back of the hardware store. I liked working there. I liked the oily smell of the hardware, the down-to-earth customers and the hands-on things I was learning, such as cutting keys and mixing paint. I'd even worked out a quick and easy way to check stock deliveries. This was a time when hardware items were supplied in bulk and not pre-packaged, and I was in tradesmen's class 101. The boss was kind to me and liked the way I worked, and the other staff were good natured, even if they made fun of me at times. I was good at mixing paint, but they confused me the first time they told me there was an order for striped paint. It took me a few minutes to wake up to that joke. Another day, stock had arrived in a large carton marked 'Modess', and when I saw it, they said they had left it for me to unpack because it held 'ladies' things.'

'But we don't sell that,' I protested.

'We do now,' was the quick reply.

I opened the carton doubtfully, only to discover it held the usual jumble of tools and hardware. They all laughed.

'Gotcha! You should have seen your face,' roared the ringleader.

I laughed too, with relief. I wasn't looking forward to finding a place to display sanitary ware; I'd much prefer to deal with the tradie who wanted a bastard file, although the first time that happened I called the boss because I thought the customer was swearing at me, but it turned out it was a special size of grain on the file.

Now it was the boss calling me.

'Gwen! Your boyfriend's here.'

'You're early.' I started forward. 'I don't fin—'

I stopped when I saw the look on his face. His best friend Roy was with him, and he looked serious.

'What's happened?'

'It's Mum,' Colin's face crumpled and his body slumped towards me. 'Can you come now?' his voice cracked.

'What is it? Colin? Roy?'

I lipread as Roy mouthed silently over Colin's head.

'She died.'

I felt shock bolt through me. He was only eighteen. Too young to imagine his mum could die. I held him to me and let him cry, right there in front of my boss and the burly blue-singleted customers. He was as soft as a rag doll in my arms.

•

His mother had welcomed me from the start.

'I'm happy if my boy is happy,' she said as we shared the washing up, 'and you're a nice girl.'

Colin's mother was trim and petite but she had a heart condition and often felt off-colour. Ever since leaving school a couple of years earlier, sometimes Colin stayed home from his latest unskilled job to help around the house, much to his father's rage, because he thought Colin was just slacking off. In truth he probably was, exaggerating his role in washing and housework, but I didn't see it that way – I believed him wholeheartedly, and resented his father's accusations. People often misjudged Colin and no matter what he did, his mother defended him to the rest of the family. Colin's father in a rage was an awesome sight, but she would hold her ground, stressing Colin's good points, and taking the blame for him missing work or losing another job. Colin felt she was the only one in the family who loved and understood him, and who saw him for the sentimental, kindhearted person he believed himself to be.

They had the occasional argument, and the night before had been one of those times. He had stormed off to work without kissing her goodbye. She had dressed in her regulation white dress, shoes and hat, and taken herself off to bowls. She was the champion of the local women's bowling club and loved the sport passionately. She often won for the team, and had again today, but just as she rolled the winning bowl, her heart seized and she fell forward. It was instant death.

Colin was shattered. He was hurting inside and in need of comfort, and it was me he turned to. We were both getting in deep now.

We shouldn't actually have been a couple. Our relationship should have gone the way of all others before it: full of eagerness, chemistry and unfulfilled anticipation for a few months, then crashing and burning when enthusiasm waned and differences came to light.

Colin and I were very different people. He was a knockabout Aussie bloke who liked to get out into the country and shoot kangaroos and rabbits for sport. He liked to gamble on horse and greyhound races. He tinkered on his car most weekends, getting dirty and smelling of grease, sometimes for days. He didn't dance or read books or write letters: he did none of the things I had been doing for the last few years. He wasn't a sparkling conversationalist or a debater like I was, but he did have the gift of the gab, and could turn on the charm at the drop of a hat. He had a store of jokes and funny sayings.

'Accelerator's further to right!' he'd lean out and yell at a slow driver in front. I thought his jokes were funny, and he *was* funny. He made me laugh – most of the time.

Even Barry grew concerned, writing me a long, long letter full of good counsel and gentle warnings of what he was reading between the lines. Yet, the more others objected to our relationship, the more I stuck by Colin. If I had been honest with myself, I knew we were starting to argue over petty things. It seemed every time I tried to suggest we see a little less of each other, the conversation twisted into accusations.

'So! You saying you don't love me?'

'No. I do . . . it's just . . .'

'Just what?'

'Well, I don't know. Something . . . you know . . . maybe we should . . .'

'Honey. I love you,' he would be wheedling now, 'you know that. I'd do anything for you. Don't listen to other people. They're just jealous. You do love me – don't you?'

'Yes,' I'd reply weakly, pushing away any doubts.

My world was starting to focus on him to the exclusion of anyone who wasn't his friend or family. I wasn't hanging out with my girlfriends; I wasn't going to the dance or the bowling alley. Even my letters to Barry had trickled down to twice monthly, and were in danger of stopping completely. I was still at school, studying, working and seeing Colin. He was the centre of my world. We didn't go to any social events. We went for long drives in the Zephyr, watched horror movies on TV, played Everly Brothers records, and listened to the greyhound races on the radio. Or did crosswords – because they were my passion and Colin said he wanted to increase his word power. Occasionally we went to a movie at the drive-in. We played cards with his mates. We visited his family. All very domestic, routine, home-style activities. As far as we were concerned, planet earth had a population of two, and the rest of the naysayers could go to hell. The closer I felt to Colin, the tighter the net pulled around me and the more difficult it became to talk to anyone about the niggling doubts that crept into my mind from time to time.

On one of our aimless drives, we found ourselves at Newcastle's Nobbys Beach late at night. Colin's arms encircled me as I stared out to sea, the moon glittering on puffy whitecaps, the sea and the sky and the surf immense and unending, the sound and the motion lulling and rhythmic.

'Marry me,' Colin whispered into my hair.

'Mmmmm . . . some day . . .' I murmured, wrapped in the mysticism of the moment. I didn't think he was serious, and I wasn't actually paying attention. My thoughts were far away. I was listening to the old man of the sea calling to the moon above. In my mind, I pictured him carrying the ghosts of ancient mariners on his back, holding up their souls in the frill of the ruffled water. Then, just as the moon goddess reached out to save them, I saw him dash them, body and soul and all, onto the rocks below us. I felt desolate and uplifted in the same moment. It was as if I had shrunk to a being smaller than an atom, while all around me the sky and the stars and the sea grew larger and larger, until I was nothing but a speck in the great void that is our universe, and yet I felt calm and complete.

21

I was aware of my miniskirt riding up as I rammed my left foot on the floor. I could feel the fabric brushing against my bare upper thigh as, with my right foot suspended in mid-air, I strained across the pool table. I had my line of sight now, the fingers of my left hand spread in an arc, the pool cue neatly pivoted between my thumb and forefinger. If I moved to hitch the skirt down all would be lost, and if I leaned any further forward my left foot would also lift off the floor. I knew Colin's brother, Dale, would scream 'foul' the second he thought I might take my shot while lying on the table. It was a technical point. I'd played enough pool to know the rules, even if I suspected they were just rules blokes made up to suit themselves. I was enjoying this moment too much to ruin it, swelling with pride to know Dale was open-mouthed in amazement that I had caught up to him, and now he was watching me like a hawk, unable to believe I might actually win the game.

Let him *sweat*, I thought. Stalling a moment longer than I needed, out of the corner of my eye I could see he was fidgeting. Everything I had heard about Dale told me he wasn't used to losing, and it was going to be me who showed him how.

Ahhhh, sweet Lady Justice, she was with me tonight. I knew the angle exactly, and pictured the trajectory straight into the corner pocket. I took a deep breath and steadied myself one last time.

'Hit it smoothly,' I muttered under my breath, 'keep it steady, look what you're shooting for. Don't blink.'

My cue ball smacked the black exactly on the sweet spot; everyone heard the echo. I knew it was perfect the moment I connected. The ball dropped cleanly into the corner pocket, no hesitating at the edges or jamming over the hole. I drank in the sound of the ball on wood as it rolled down the chute, just like the sound of a ten-pin bowling ball running down a gutter. There was a gentle chink as it joined the seven spots I had already sunk.

'Yesssss. Winner!' I shouted triumphantly, dancing a jig and swinging my cue over my head.

'Go girl!' Colin shouted, through the almost closed grin that hid his broken tooth. 'Whaddya think of that, bro'? She's okay, hey?'

'Hustler,' Dale pretended to glare, 'your girlfriend's a hustler.' It seemed like friendly banter, and Colin was laughing. Dale towered over me.

'No! Scout's honour! It's what happens when I drink – my eyes just seem to focus better. All the balls line up.' I was wide-eyed and innocent and we were all laughing now.

'True, bro', I've seen it before.' Colin backed me up as he looked at me with pride and affection.

'Well. I guess it's time you had another scotch and dry then.' Dale headed for the bar. I felt a momentary twinge; I'd already had two, maybe three drinks. I knew if Steve found out where I was and what I was doing he would slap me for sure, but then he seemed to slap me for anything these days – so like the old saying went, 'better to be hung for a sheep as a lamb'.

'Hey, honey, after this drink we're going back to Dale's place. He wants to show you where he lives – I told him okay.'

'Well . . . okay . . . sure. So long as you get me home on time. Okay?' I wanted to be safely tucked in bed before I heard the gear change of Steve's Corolla at the bottom of the street. I didn't want to have to explain what I'd been doing.

I didn't feel drunk at all, even though I knew what it felt like to be drunk on scotch. But that time I'd finished off with a tequila – so I guess that was what did it. Scotch was probably okay. Yeah, that would be okay. One more. A quick look at Dale's place. A cup of coffee. Should be home by ten-thirty . . . eleven. Tops. Should be fine. And I'd made Colin happy. Just look at his face glow.

When we'd arrived at the pub an hour or so earlier, the locals had given us curious looks, but as soon as they heard Colin was Dale's brother, they made us welcome. I had made a special effort with how I looked that night; I wanted to let Dale know it wasn't just he who was important in Colin's life. I felt like the bee's knees in my zip-fronted lilac miniskirt, cream lace top and perky cardigan. My dark hair was brushed out and curling around my shoulders and my face fully made up with eye shadow and mascara. I thought I saw admiring looks from the others I met. Nobody guessed I was just sixteen and I sure as hell hadn't let on or I would have been thrown straight out of the bar. Now I was on a high, cracking jokes to anyone who would listen. It was strange that I was feeling so relaxed after having been so reluctant to meet Dale.

Colin said everyone had Dale wrong, no one understood him. Maybe, as Colin had always insisted, he wasn't such a bad bloke after all.

'You know, honey, how people are always down on me, too, and you know they've got both of us wrong. What did we do to deserve it? You know how much it cuts me up. Besides, it's not his fault if he doesn't always think straight – remember Mum told you how he nearly drowned in a swimming pool? Not enough oxygen.'

Colin looked up to Dale in a way that he didn't with his other brother, Edwin, even though Edwin was the oldest of the four siblings. Edwin had another life: married with a couple of children, he had a steady, responsible job, head of sales at a furniture store. He'd done time but he'd learned his lesson and was never going down that road again, and he didn't want to see Colin make the same mistake. Edwin seemed almost boring to Colin now – at least conventional, with none of the glamour he saw in Dale.

Dale was a different matter. Dale was the black sheep of the family, the one of whom everyone despaired but loved nevertheless, even if they kept their distance while making excuses for his behaviour. He was big, well over six feet tall, and solid with it; he didn't mind throwing his weight around when it suited him, swaggering and flashing money to burn. People fetched at his command and Colin lived in the reflected glory of being his baby brother, the Aussie terrier to his brother's Doberman. Colin would have followed his older brother around constantly, idolising and emulating him and panting for people to show him just an ounce of the same respect – but of what good was a five-foot-five, sixty-kilo, ten-years-younger brother who still lived at home, to Dale's life of petty crime? All Colin could hope for were the scraps of attention Dale tossed his way from time to time, such as tonight, when the two of us had driven into the city to meet him at his local pub.

I hadn't wanted to go. I had only met Dale briefly and I didn't like him, or what I'd heard about him, and I certainly didn't want to hang out with him. I'd refused many times in the past, and left Colin to visit without me, but I was hoping he would eventually tire of hanging out with Dale on his own, and see him for what I thought he was – a bully and a petty criminal. I was sure I could influence Colin to turn away from him. It was just a matter of time and patience. Instead it was Colin who won. He had insisted, pleaded, it was time for the two most important people in his life to get together.

'Spend some time with him, please. You'll see what a great guy he is. And he *really* wants to know you.' Colin cajoled and sulked until I relented, naïvely philosophising: I know I am Colin's saviour. I'll show him crime doesn't pay in the end. But I can't just object without spending some time with Dale. That will only make Colin have to choose between us. So I'll just go this one time and that will convince Colin he's not worth his admiration. Colin loves me; he'll see it my way . . .' One justification after another swept round and round in my head, and even though I felt bad about it, I stepped into the car that night, all dressed up as the sacrificial lamb.

Caught between good sense and the desire to rescue Colin from himself, I stepped fair and square into the fox's lair.

•

I rocked gently from side to side as I tugged at the hem of my yellow checked school uniform. The vinyl seat felt sticky against the back of my thighs. I wished now I didn't wear it so short. All girls were allowed a length halfway between the knee and the groin, and Mrs Morgan lined us up periodically to shove a wooden ruler up our inside leg to check we weren't violating the rule. It was the teachers' way of saying that while minis were the current fashion, *they* were still the ones in charge. Now I wished it were winter. At least then, I would be wearing my grey box-pleated tunic and I would have been thankful for all of that extra fabric. I could have folded it around me, bunched it around my legs so they couldn't see so much skin. I felt exposed, sitting a foot away from the desk of the middle-aged detective. Sunlight streamed through the open slats of the dust-speckled venetian blind, flashing across his papers and catching me in its spotlight. I pressed my legs hard together, but that only stretched the light cotton tighter across my thighs. Was it my imagination, or was he staring up my dress?

Another detective sat against the edge of the desk, half on and half off, one leg tucked behind the knee of the other, his arms folded across his chest. A third leaned against the wall just inside the office door, long and lanky in a white business shirt and thin black tie, hair clipped so short it was almost a crew cut. I could feel his eyes watching me in profile, and it made me uncomfortable that I couldn't see his expression without twisting around in his direction. I felt so very alone and terribly anxious. I was in such conflict. I was terrified Steve or Mum would get involved, and I was desperate to stand by Colin. Meanwhile, these detectives were making me feel like a criminal.

The oldest one was talking at me. 'So – this is your story – right? You went drinking with your boyfriend and his brother. You played some pool and then went back to the brother's place. Everything was fine and friendly. The three of you were hanging out in the brother's bedroom. The guys were drinking beer – not you. Your boyfriend needed to relieve himself and his brother took him out to the backyard to show him where the toilet was. The brother came back alone, and he locked the door behind him, but you didn't notice that. You were talking and then you got scared, then he attacked you. You wrestled with him but he threw you on the bed and spread your legs and did the deed. Sometime later, your boyfriend came back but he couldn't get in the bedroom because the door was locked. So he ran back outside and started belting at the window. It was all too late by then, and then the brother let him back in, and the two of you left. That's when your boyfriend told you his brother had knocked him out when they went outside. You and your boyfriend hung out together in the car for another couple of hours and then he took you home. That pretty well sum it up?'

Did it? It didn't sound like that when I had told them. Haltingly – holding back the tears. Trying to explain how I had come to be in a pub in the first place, admitting I had been drinking under-age. Acknowledging it was a stupid thing to do. Yes. Under-age drinking is a criminal act. Yes. I knew that before I did it. Trying to explain why I had been there – why I wanted to support Colin – how I believed I had the power to persuade him his brother wasn't worth his admiration. They weren't much interested in that. 'How much did you drink? Were you drunk? Did you come on to him?' That's what they were interested in.

'Why were you in his bedroom?'

'Can't remember. That's just where we went.'

'What was wrong with the loungeroom?'

'Don't know. Don't remember. Don't remember seeing one.'

'Did you ask to go to the bedroom?'

'What? No! That's just where we went. As soon as we arrived. Dale took us there.'

'So! How come your boyfriend needed to go to the dunny? Who suggested it? Him – or his brother?'

'What? How can I remember? He had some beer. He doesn't drink much. He needed to go. Is that so unusual?'

'Okay. So his brother shows him the way. And then he knocks him out. Cold. You didn't hear anything?'

'No.'

'No struggle? No grunting? He didn't yell out?'

'No – nothing.'

'Just like that, hey? Where were you?'

'In the bedroom. Like I told you.'

'So the brother comes back – what then?'

'Well, I was sitting on the end of the bed. There were two beds. Singles. I was sitting on the end of one.'

'And?'

'I dunno. We shared a joke. Laughed. Waited for Colin to come back.'

'Mmmm?'

'He got weird. He said Colin wasn't coming back. I didn't understand. But I got nervous. I started to stand up. That's when he pushed me back.'

The quizzing went on. They fell over each other in their questions. What? How? What was said? What happened next? What did you do?

I felt exhausted. Guilty. Confused. I didn't want to be telling this story – the one that had been playing over and over in my mind. They had made me tell it twice already. I had promised myself I wouldn't tell anyone. Now here I was, spilling it out to three strangers, three strangers who were looking at me as if I was dirt.

From my right I heard a match strike. The matchstick arced through the air and landed near a wastebasket at the end of the desk. The lanky detective was lighting up. He pushed his body away from the wall. 'Well, young miss. Let's go over it one more time. Just before we type it up.'

Across the desk I met the eye of the senior detective. 'Again? Do you think I'm lying?' It was a weak act of defiance.

I heard the drawn-out intake as the lean one took a long drag on his cigarette. The cigarette paper burned with a loud crinkle. He blew out with a sigh through pursed lips and the pungent aroma of smoke drifted past my nostrils. He spat onto his bottom lip from the tip of his tongue, then felt there with his fingertips for a stray tobacco strand. I heard his fingertips rasp together as he crushed away the faint trace of it.

'Well . . .' He strolled around to face me square-on. 'Someone's lying, so let's go back over why you didn't come forward until now.'

I could have given a hundred reasons. Because Dale was a big, bad crim and I was scared he'd have me killed. Because when Mum heard about this she'd have another nervous breakdown and they'd put her back in hospital. Because then Steve would be so angry I was scared what he'd do. Because my boyfriend is so ashamed he didn't protect me that he begged me to keep it quiet. Because I'm so ashamed I didn't fight back that I *want* to keep it quiet. Because how can I bring this grief into a family who is still in mourning for their mother. Because everyone knows there's no point complaining to the police, because half the time it's them doing the raping. Because everyone knows there's no point going to court because the defence will tear you to shreds. Because they'll make me live through every moment of the rape again. Because as soon as the jury hears I was drinking they'll decide I was just asking for it anyway. Because everyone thinks girls who get raped are asking for it.

I didn't say any of these things. I just mumbled, 'I was scared.'

'So you're not scared now?'

'Yes. I am. I am still scared. *I* didn't come to the police. Mr McKerrow called for you. You know that.'

Mr McKerrow. Kindly, genial, trusting Mr McKerrow. Mr McKerrow, who had been Steve's English teacher at his high school. Who was principal now at mine. The same man who ambled around the playground, smiling beneficently at students as he passed. The same man who always stopped when he saw me, knowing he should know me specifically but never remembering the connection. Never remembering my name. 'Hello, lassie,' he would say, his small eyes twinkling in his chubby, ruddy face, his large, round, red nose with the knobby end crinkling up, his smile reaching from one cheek to another. It was to him I had been sent hours earlier, after a teacher had exploded in frustration.

'Gwendoline! You haven't been paying attention. Again! Where has your head been these last few days? Do you think I'm here just for you to waste my time? Well? Well? Well don't bother answering me then. You can answer to the principal.'

Kindly, genial Mr McKerrow had wheedled the story out of me, shed a tear with me and assured me it would be all right. Kindly, genial Mr McKerrow had insisted I make a complaint to the police, convincing me it was my duty, if not to save my own honour, then at least to save that of the girls who might be victims in the future. He convinced me I was the one who could see it through, who had that special strength of character.

It had been all handshakes and courteousness and doffing caps to him when the three detectives arrived in his office, but as soon as they had me in the police car on the way to the station the atmosphere had changed. On the phone they had promised to come in an unmarked vehicle, but they hadn't kept their word. Now everyone would know I had been taken away in a police car. I wondered how many would guess why. I could be sure there were plenty of rumours flying around at school as I sat here spotlighted in the sun, being grilled by three suspicious men. They were suspicious of me, and me of them. Police in our area didn't have a good reputation; they were well known for pulling young girls over for vagrancy if the girls were out walking without any pocket money on them. They'd offer to waive the charge if the girl would agree to 'get in the back' for ten minutes. It had never happened to me – but I'd heard enough to know what went on if you were tricked into it.

If I hoped for tea and sympathy from the examining doctor then I was in for a shock. As he snapped on a pair of rubber gloves he jerked his head towards a trolley. 'Clothes off, get on that. Lie back, legs apart. Use the sheet.'

It was quick. Whether it was a policewoman who stood just inside the door or one of the detectives, I can't remember. I just remember the police doctor: white coat pulled over his street clothes, small build, old face, bushy eyebrows – a man nearing retirement age. He barked out findings over his shoulder.

'Penetration confirmed.'

'Virgin?' came the response from the doorway.

'Can't say. No childbirths. Recent sex. Some residue . . . can't say whose.'

'Signs of violence?'

'Bit of tearing . . . could be a rowdy session with the boyfriend.'

'What! How can you say that!' I found my voice. 'Everything, everywhere . . . hurts!'

'Yeah?'

Couldn't he *see*? I'm the *victim* here! Wasn't it obvious?

'Look at my arms. Look where he grabbed me . . . look where he held me down.' Why was he making me prove myself? Tears and rage were boiling up.

'Mmmm . . . yeah . . . bit red, scratched . . . coupla bruises. You mighta brushed against something.'

I couldn't believe what was happening. I was mortified – and defiant.

'My ribs. My body. I can't even walk straight. Look where he forced my legs. Look where he ground into me with his knee.'

'Yeah. There're bruises there all right. But they could be self-inflicted.'

'Self-inflicted? There?'

'Well, you mighta' put your boyfriend up to it. Look. You wouldn't be the first girl to go all the way and then point the finger at someone after. We see it all the time. This incident happened a few days ago. Anything I'm looking at should be yellow by now. This is fresh. You can get dressed now. We're done.'

Did he think I was a piece of trash? There was no point trying to explain I had never had sex with my boyfriend. I wanted to curl into a ball and howl my eyes out. My throat constricted with the effort to hold the tears but I wouldn't let them fall. I wasn't going to give him the satisfaction of seeing me reduced to begging for his compassion.

I walked out of there as gingerly and subdued as I had walked in. I stayed that way for a few more days, barely able to breathe in and out without pain, hardly able to squat to sit on the toilet until the internal pain started to ease and the bruises came to the surface, welling up from some deep place. It was another week before they had all turned yellow, looking sickly against my light-olive tan. It wouldn't have made any difference to the doctor. He needed me brought in on the night, half-torn clothes hanging off me, covered in debris and stab wounds. Stabbed in places I couldn't have self-inflicted. Preferably with the knife still in me and an intact set of fingerprints on it. Preferably the fingerprints of a repeat offender. And it would have had to be clear I had been a virgin a few hours earlier. Even better if it could be proved I would never be able to bear children. And definitely no such complicating factor as a boyfriend – particularly not one related to the offender! Then a girl might have a chance of being taken seriously in court – assuming, of course, she was still alive to tell the tale.

Over the next weeks I discovered this callous treatment was the detectives' version of tough love. They were preparing me for what to expect if I went to trial. They did carry out an investigation, and when they interviewed Colin and got an account that was even more garbled than mine, they were clearly doubtful about him being knocked unconscious. Colin insisted he had been struck from behind with the torch Dale used to show him the way to the toilet. The detectives didn't buy it, and it was even starting to ring hollow in my ears. Yet I couldn't bring myself to believe I had been set up. Not by my boyfriend, not by Colin. It didn't fit with our relationship. He had cried harder than me afterwards, holding my stiffly shocked body in his arms and spurting out between sobs, 'I'm sorry, I'm sorry,' crying over and over, 'I should never have insisted . . . I didn't know, I never guessed . . . how could I know that's why he wanted you there. It's my fault, he's too strong. I was knocked out cold. You gotta believe me . . .' on and on, hugging me and consoling me and kissing me so fiercely it was as if he thought he could kiss all the hurt away.

There came the day, a month or so later, when the detectives sat me down and counselled me. 'Gwen, we think it's best you drop it.'

They were speaking as gently as they could, which caught me off-guard. I wasn't used to their consideration.

'Look, you've gotta see it's coming across as if you're lying. *We* think it's to protect your boyfriend, but who knows how the jury will see it? You're just not a reliable witness. Neither of you are.'

I sat there taking in the significance of what they were saying. The senior detective's voice cut the silence. 'Drop it, love. You gave it a good run, but it's time to give it up now.'

One part of me was angry that I had gone through so much just for it to end like this. A bigger part of me was relieved that it was finally over.

•

I have always believed the universe has a way of righting the balance in the world in the same way that water finds its own level. I have always had the innate trust that what goes around, comes around. It's my version of karma, the idea that a random act of kindness brings rewards on the giver, and that bad deeds eventually catch you up.

Maybe I didn't always believe this. Maybe it was a belief born just as 1971 was drawing to a close, about three months after the rape, the night Dale was shot dead at point-blank range with a .45 pistol – in the head – in his own home. So close, the gunpowder residue was on his face. 'Between the eyes,' some newspapers reported, writing it up as a gangland killing. At the trial the killers pleaded it was an accident, even though they had barged into the house.

'We were sick of him standing over us, making threats against us. So we went round to give him a good hiding,' said one defendant.

'When we went into his house I asked him where "someone else" was, and when he said that person wasn't there, I said "cop this" and let go right into his face,' said another.

It wasn't reported that 'someone else' was a woman. The wife of one of the killers, killers who themselves were well-known criminals, not the kind of guys you want to get off-side in a hurry. Certainly not the kind of guys whose wife you want to have a fling with. Dale may have got one over me, but he brought the wrong woman home the night he was killed.

'I shot him all right. Someone had to. He's been going around too long iron-barring people,' said one of the defendants. The jury strongly recommended mercy. The judge didn't see it their way, even though the detective sergeant on the case described Dale as a well-known member of Sydney's underbelly: 'thief, bludger and standover man, vicious and quick-tempered'.

Too bloody right, I thought, pity the two guys who did it got life. Should have got a bloody medal.

But Colin didn't see it that way. He took it hard, first his mother, and now the brother he idolised. As we clung together in his grief I could feel the walls of emotion closing in on me. I truly believed I was all he had left. The idea that it was me who had the higher need of comforting never occurred to me.

22

The rape happened in September 1971, a few months after my sixteenth birthday. As the police investigation proceeded in the background, my fears were for myself. I had no way of knowing Dale had only a few months to live, and I wouldn't have cared even if I had. Instead, I waited anxiously for signs of an impending period. Every time I went to the toilet, I stared at my panties, willing for a sign of blood. Thank goodness for my short cycle. I didn't have long to wait. My relief was immense.

I shared my story with as few people as possible: the principal, the detectives, a doctor I consulted for follow-up attention and Colin's father. Colin and I believed we had no choice but to tell him, as he would hear about the police investigation anyway. He was angry – anger born of despair and frustration. He was angry with Colin, raging about his weakness, even though his brother was so much bigger, and challenging him over and over about the details of his part in that night, until even in my own mind I was beginning to question if Colin had told me the truth. Then his father turned his anger on me.

'And you!' he shouted, 'couldn't you save yourself? Why didn't you just reach out for a bottle and smash it over his head?' I cried and shook, and confessed something I had been too ashamed to tell anyone else – that for all my bravado, I was so terrorised that I went limp, unable to move or breathe, so terrorised that I couldn't scream or fight. I didn't understand how I could be so paralysed with fear.

'I was so scared. He might have killed me . . . so . . . so I just . . . detached. I can't explain . . . a part of me just wasn't there . . . I didn't fight . . .'

Colin's father looked at me blankly. His belligerence had subsided, and he dropped into the nearest armchair. He stared hard at us, first Colin and then me. He opened his mouth, then closed it again. He looked defeated, all the bluff and bluster burnt out. Then he dropped his head into his hands.

'Thank God my wife isn't here to know this day,' he moaned hoarsely.

I saw his shoulders heave and his body shake with silent sobbing. I hesitated for a moment, then I sat on the arm of the chair and slipped my arm around his shoulders. We sat there together, both with tears oozing from eyes squeezed shut. We both had our losses to bear. He was right. Thank goodness Colin's mother had been spared this pain. There is, after all, some salvation in death. Colin flapped hesitantly in the background and stayed out of it. This was between his dad and me.

I was desperate to keep my mouth shut. There was so much shame and stigma around rape: even the most innocent victim couldn't hope for understanding and consolation. There was no such thing as a rape crisis centre or counselling. The onus rested with the girl to prove her virtue. What could I prove? Only that I had dressed up, put on makeup and gone out drinking. Begging for it. That's what they would say in court. I could picture the jury nodding. Without doubt, Your Honour. She was asking for it. What was the man to do?

I had been a 'woman' for five years. I had a period every twenty-one days. My hormones were raging. It was true that a man could get me going, and there were times I despaired of how long I could resist their advances. It was only by reminding them and me that I was 'jail-bait' – a minor, under the age of consent – that we halted our passionate encounters. So, could it be true? In some unconscious way, had my sixteenth birthday signalled my time had come? How would I answer, when the defence lawyer challenged me on whether I had thrust myself at Dale? Had I subconsciously wanted this? Did I send out come-on signals without even knowing? I was filled with shame at the thought of it.

And what of Colin? What really was his role? Was it credible that one blow to the head with a torch could knock a man out? He was so contrite. How could I possibly accuse him of collusion? He loved me. How could I even *consider* this possibility?

There was no one I could turn to, least of all Steve or my mother. God no! She would be back in hospital before I had even finished my story. I had survived Dale's attack and so I kept my mouth shut and acted as if nothing had happened.

•

At the start of October 1971, amid all this trauma, my penpal Barry was transferred back to Canberra. It was only four or five hours' drive away. I longed to meet him, and Colin encouraged the idea. Maybe he saw in Barry an ally who would chase away my fears and doubts, or maybe he just wanted an excuse to get me away for a weekend. It was a daring, reckless plan on my part, because I knew Steve would never agree to me spending the weekend with Colin, even if I insisted we would have separate motel rooms. In the end, I lied to my family, and so did Colin. I pretended I was going away with a girlfriend for the October long weekend, leaving Colin right out of the picture.

Colin and I took a room together, and we shared the bed platonically, although, if he ever found out, I would have had a hard time to convince Steve that we weren't having sex. For me the comfort was in the intimacy of our bodies so close together. When I woke in the morning I felt the warmth of his arms and his kisses washing away the strain and the hurt of the last weeks. I felt so completely in love, as if we were two persons merged into one. I felt such peace, and with the excitement of meeting Barry after two years of intense letter writing, it was as if my world was complete.

When I first saw Barry I was disappointed. He was just as he had described, five feet ten inches tall, fair-haired and brown-eyed, but he wasn't good looking, nor had he ever claimed to be. Not good looking in a movie-star way. His face was a bit too long, his nose a bit too broad, his eyebrows met together in the centre above close-set eyes. His top lip was hidden by a thick moustache. His hair was thick and crinkly, and with its airforce cut, the bulk of it was sitting in a clump on top of his head. His chin was strong though, and his bottom lip full.

I chided myself in the same second as I felt the disappointment. For two years I had been writing to Barry as if he were someone I had known all my life, when in truth he was a stranger to me, a shadowy figure who was barely a man himself. Old enough to fight in Vietnam, yet not old enough to vote. I had poured out my heart and soul to this man, holding some things back, but not many.

Underlying every lighthearted witticism or deep thought lay the need to be reassured that someone cared what I did or thought, and I knew from the way he wrote back that Barry cared for my wellbeing, just as I cared for his.

How could it be important whether or not he was good looking?

I was on an emotional high for the next two days. Whenever Barry was off-duty the three of us went out together, and we were relaxed in each other's company. Barry had a serious girlfriend and I was Colin's girlfriend, so there was no crossing that line. Colin and I had come as a couple to pay a visit to an old friend. I was sharing a bed with my boyfriend, and Barry knew. He might not have thought it a great idea, but he didn't say anything.

All the same, Barry looked hard at me when it came time to leave. It was the moment for a kiss, but it was fleeting. He showed too much respect to risk offending Colin or me. We never met again, and there would never be another chance. Barry was killed in 1978 in a peacetime training exercise.

Time came to return home to face the music. The weekend was so perfect that I hoped I would get away with my lie. I was still on a high when the Zephyr blew a tyre on the drive home. I was so late getting back there was no way to avoid being found out. Steve was not impressed – not one little bit. In *my* mind however, after all I had been through in the previous month, it was worth every second of the risk, even though I didn't enjoy the argument that followed. I never enjoyed that.

Colin and I had only been back a week or two when we had an argument which should have ended our relationship. I cannot remember what it was about, but I remember what happened. We were in the living room at my house with a friend of Colin's. Mum was in her bedroom and Steve was out for the day.

Colin and I started to argue about something. Maybe we raised our voices; maybe we had been arguing for a while; or maybe it was sudden, it doesn't matter. What does matter is, Colin hit me. He struck me on the head so hard it felt as though my brains bashed against my skull, and I fell onto the couch. Colin's friend intervened, and they went off together, leaving me huddled and crying. Mum stayed in her room. If she was aware of what happened, she stayed out of it.

That should have been *The End*. I should have shut Colin out of my life and never had another thing to do with him. But love born of insecurity is a twisted passion. It wasn't long before I was making excuses for his behaviour. I probably blamed myself. Soon we were seeing each other as often as before.

This time, though, when we 'made up' we went 'too far'. When a girl is no longer a virgin, there is no honour left to defend. I wanted to feel loved, and if having sex was the way to feel that, well, so be it. I was spoiled goods anyway. So why not take comfort in passion? We'd been teetering on the edge of intimacy for months. It felt as if this was the right time.

A night or two later, we sat in the Zephyr outside a chemist shop a few suburbs away, far from any prying eyes that might recognise us. We were having a stand-off over who would go in and buy condoms.

'I think you'll have to do it. It'll be better coming from you. You're the girl and all. They won't ask so many questions.'

'They'll think I'm a slut!' My stomach curled into a painful knot.

'No they won't. They'll understand.' Colin – full of his false bravado and empty promises. What would he know?

'Yeah, sure. What schoolgirl waltzes in to a chemist shop and asks to buy frenchies?'

By the time Colin agreed he should do the buying, the chemist was closed.

'I guess we'll just have to be more careful,' he said, 'it'll be alright, hon, promise, you know I'll never hurt you. You know how much I love you.'

•

I wrote so much to Barry, but some things I held back. I didn't confide in him about the rape, or the police investigation, or Colin hitting me, or what happened when we made up. I did write about the insecurity and uncertainty that followed. He knew something was wrong and he was forced into the role of counsellor, desperately trying to offer advice about our relationship without knowing what was causing my despair, although he had enough experience and intuition to guess sex had a role in it.

He offered one definition of love after another: pages of heartfelt feeling. If he had cradled me in his arms and stroked me gently, he couldn't have tried harder to comfort me. And who else would have thought to quote Goethe?

This is the true measure of love,
When we believe that we alone can love, that no one
Could ever have loved so before us,
And that no one will ever love
In the same way after us.

Colin tried to comfort me, too, tried to show how much he loved me, showering me with flowers and a card he addressed: 'To not just the best girlfriend a boy could have, but the best *friend* a person could have,' and inside: 'I know I have treated you pretty bad at times honey . . . hope you'll forgive me.'

I forgave him all right, not knowing he was only just getting started on the bad treatment.

The card was written on 25 October 1971, the same date as my last period. We needn't have caused ourselves so much anxiety over the condoms. After Dale, my body had granted me one reprieve. I should have known there were no second chances in my world. Even if one of us had summoned up the courage to enter that chemist shop, it would only have been a matter of closing the stable door after the horse had bolted. Too little, too late.

23

I didn't know what to do. Now I could understand just how cruel I had been to Rachel. When I heard she was pregnant, I should have realised she would be scared and confused, in need of a friend. We were best friends. Friends fight sometimes. I should have gone to her, reached out, explained myself, asked her to forgive me and forgiven her in return. She would have welcomed the comfort. I hadn't, I was so young, too young to know all of this. I could hardly turn to her now for advice.

I kept my suspicions to myself and considered my options. In reality there were only three: abortion, adoption or marriage. Being an unmarried mother was not an option in 1971 – not if you planned to stay in your home town. It was rare to find the family who would rally around a girl in this situation, who could withstand the neighbourhood gossip. They would have to be very progressive and very strong, or be able to pass the baby off as belonging to another relation. I had no idea how Mum had managed it twice – but it was obvious it had not been good for anyone, not for *her* health, nor for *our* emotional security. I knew she wouldn't support me on the basis of shared experience. She seemed to have completely blocked out that there had ever been a man or two in her life.

I briefly considered abortion and rejected the thought. Abortion was illegal and usually performed by backyard operators, and sometimes resulted in death. The only way to obtain a legal abortion in a hospital was by having medical evidence that to proceed with the pregnancy would cause permanent physical or mental harm to the mother. I thought this meant I had to be ill in the same way as my mother. I didn't consider myself a candidate.

I thought about adoption. When I was a child, there had been many times I wished I had been adopted. I thought I was living in this family by mistake. I could see the attraction in adoption providing a loving, secure family, something I had yearned for. But this was *my* baby and I had *so much* love to give. I wanted to be the one to do the nurturing. *I* wanted to raise my baby.

So that left marriage. I didn't want to marry Colin. It was too soon and it didn't fit with where I thought my life was going. I couldn't put my finger on what was wrong, but I had an underlying uncertainty about our relationship. The more Colin pushed for commitment, the more uncertain I became, and yet the more my family objected to our relationship, the more loyalty I felt towards him. I felt pushed and pulled, and I didn't know where I belonged. I should have run for the hills when he hit me, but he seemed so remorseful afterwards and wrote me such heartfelt words of apology that I had forgiven him and thought I understood how it had happened. I didn't see the relationship was emotionally co-dependent. I had never heard such mumbo-jumbo. We didn't talk that way. I was ready to love anyone who said they loved me, and it was Colin who was saying those magical words.

Finally I came up with a plan. I would move to Perth and say I was visiting Joanne van den Avoort for the Christmas holidays. I would get a job there and pass myself off as a widow. It had worked for Mum, so surely I could pull it off too. I just wouldn't return home at the end of the holiday. No one on the east coast need ever find out about the baby, and no one on the west coast need ever find out who I really was.

I needed money for this plan, and I knew where it was. The $500 from my junior bursary had been quietly accumulating interest in a bank account. Attending a government school wasn't so expensive after all. One way or another money had been found to pay for my uniforms, textbooks and exercise books. The only flaw was that Steve was the trustee of the bank account; I couldn't access the funds myself. I couldn't tell Steve the reason I needed the money; I would have to come up with a story to get his signature.

I never went through with the plan. I assumed Colin wasn't clever enough to sense the change in my mood but he guessed almost immediately that I was pregnant. He was so happy! It was all blue skies from his point of view. He had taken the proposal on Nobbys Beach as a serious matter, even though all he had done was whisper into my hair as I stared out to sea.

'Mmmmm . . . some day . . .' I had murmured back. Now fate ended any excuse for procrastination on my part.

We kept our mouths shut and I didn't go to a doctor to get a proper pregnancy test. I did go to my head teacher and warned her I wouldn't be returning to school the next year. She was shocked and dismayed. I had just sat and passed some serious exams, and won both the Senior Secondary Bursary and the Commonwealth Scholarship. She knew I would have to decide which one to accept, but everyone expected I would continue at school for another two years and then win another scholarship for university.

'You can't break off your studies now,' she said.

I looked at my feet and mumbled about a home situation. After long discussion with my other teachers, she told me they had come to the conclusion I would make my way in the world, whichever path I chose. I couldn't tell her my path was already determined. I kept my counsel. Since the exams were finished, I snuck away from school and tried to keep a low profile. Not for me any exuberant celebrations, excited meetings to compare examination results, or plans for a future after school – I simply disappeared. From time to time when I was out in public and I spied a former school friend or his or her parents, I scurried out of sight quickly, hiding in a doorway or behind a fence. No doubt the schoolyard gossip grapevine came to know the truth when I did not return for Year 11, but it was never from my lips. Ten years of school and study connections – cut off in a snap, just like pruning away a diseased branch from a flourishing bush.

24

Colin took on a contract for an ice-cream van. It was a mug's game, paying the rent on the van, buying the ice-cream ingredients and running the power all night to stop the mixture going off. The only person who was ever going to make any money from it was the franchise owner, but it took us a while to realise that. The first time we managed to make $100, I was so excited I bragged about it to Barry. I worked with Colin whenever I had the chance. He drove the van and I managed the serving hatch, juggling out-of-control children as they jostled and shoved for a soft-serve. I tried to keep the area spotless, but the smell of sour spilt ice-cream rose up even from the cleaning rags. Every time we reached a service station I rushed into the toilets and threw up. At night I would drift off with the sound of 'Greensleeves' dinging in my ears.

Alas my love, you do me wrong to cast me off discourteously . . .

Kulpie was over the moon for me when I got a job as an office junior at an advertising agency in the city. She kept telling me what an experience it was for a young girl just out of school to dress up for work, take the train to the city, part of the throng of workers emerging from the underground into the hum of the business district. In her mind, I would be office manager in no time. She didn't know I was pregnant, that I was going nowhere in the business world, and I didn't spoil her dream, not yet.

My duties were whatever the other staff wanted them to be. One moment I would be ironing shirts for an advertising shoot, the next I would be running errands. The only regular duties were to buy the manager a rose for his button hole and to make morning and afternoon tea for everyone.

The manager was sensitive about the rose. I was only allowed to buy it from the stand at the Hilton Hotel. It had to be a small, unopened bud. It must never be pink. Pink would imply he was homosexual. I wondered why he bothered to worry so much about the colour of the rose, given his preference for seersucker suits in small checks and girly colours. Maybe I just didn't understand the difference between flamboyant and gay.

The morning tea run was hazardous: they all had their particular orders and weren't happy if I got them mixed up. It's scary when you're faced with the most senior woman in the office stamping her dainty foot, dropping her bottom lip and fuming at you for buying the wrong colour icing on a doughnut. It makes the schoolyard appear mature by comparison.

I lasted three weeks. It was my first experience with advertising personalities. I just couldn't get my mind into their creative head space. They seemed self focused and petulant to me and they didn't think much of me, either. I left without a reference. I felt bad about disappointing Kulpie, but I knew I had a much bigger disappointment to share with her. It was a secret nibbling away in the back of my conscience, but I couldn't bring myself to tell her. I hadn't told anyone, especially not Mum or Steve.

Until his death about ten years before, when Steve was fifteen, his father had given him all kinds of expensive toys. Most of them were sitting in a tin trunk under the house. Now I was at a loose end at home, the weather outside was rainy and overcast and Mum was asleep in her room. I decided to drag out the trunk and get out his toys. I didn't consider asking his permission. After all, Steve was a grown man who hadn't looked at them in years, so what was the harm? I took over our living room floor, spending the whole day spreading out train track, building gates and signals with his Meccano set, houses and train stations with his Bayko set, arranging his Dinky cars here and there, and setting the Hornby engine and carriages on its way. Then Steve came home.

He went ballistic. B-A-L-L-I-S-T-I-C. We had the mother of all fights. The months of tension and anxiety he had felt about me, wondering where I was and what I was up to, all his frustrations at my lifestyle, his contempt of my choice of friends and boyfriends, the overwhelming responsibility of his years as my father figure – everything exploded from him in a furious burst of terrifying rage. We screamed at each other in an outpouring of hatred and desperation. We hurled abuse at each other from one end of the house to the other, with no thought for Mum or where she was, what she was hearing or whether she was frightened. Our tempers waxed and waned. Each time we neared burnout, another grudge flamed into life, until suddenly Colin appeared, throwing himself into the melee as if we were two dogs to be torn apart. This only added to Steve's fury. When it came to a short fuse, it was a competition between Steve and Colin as to who would lose control first. I made a dash for the front door, heading for the safety of Colin's car, but Steve caught me just as I reached the garden path. In the chaos he lunged for me again, knocking me into the garden, and as Colin pushed in to shield me he screamed at Steve, 'Ya arsehole! Stop hittin' her!' He was yelling obscenities at Steve, disjointed explosions of fury, and I could hear the panic in his voice; it was all he could do to stop from blabbing out I was pregnant.

Shaken, I went to see Colin's father. I pleaded with him to let me live there, assuring him I would keep the house, do the shopping, cooking, washing, everything – if only I could have food and shelter. At least until I got work and could set up on my own. Thank God he agreed. It didn't mean Colin and I were setting up house together. He kept his bedroom and I slept on the living-room couch. That was the deal. We still hadn't told his father I was pregnant, and even this crisis did not worm it out of me.

As I stormed out of my mother's home for what I thought was the final time, I shouted defiantly 'From now on, every mistake I make will be all my own!'

And that is about the most truthful thing I have ever said. So many, many mistakes lay ahead, and I hold responsibility for every one of them.

25

Not long after I moved to Colin's house, a group of his mates came over for a Saturday night poker game. I had only played for an hour. I left the table with such bad stomach cramps, I could hardly bear to sit up.

I took a couple of painkillers, made a hot water bottle, and hugged it to my stomach as I stretched out on the lounge, soundless, willing the pain to leave my body. I dared to hope it was my period, even though I had already missed two. No one had actually confirmed I was pregnant, so could it be possible the dramas of the previous weeks had caused them to be late? I was in agony, but it would be worth the pain if that meant it was about to start. I hoped it would be soon. I was so desperate for that to be true that I wouldn't consider any other option, even though months before a doctor had diagnosed appendix problems.

The guys played on beside me, circled around the table, coins piled in uneven rows in front of them, and an untidy heap of copper and nickel growing in the centre. The steady chink of coin hitting coin muffled as they played on. Now I was out of the game, dollar notes were being added to the pot and the stakes were getting higher.

'I'll see your two and raise you five.' It was greeted with a roar. Colin's friend Bob was getting serious – he'd played plenty of poker when he'd been on the inside and now he had nothing else on which to spend his pay packet.

I lay there as the hot water bottle went cold and pain seared my body. My insides felt as if they were tangled together. It was a blessing when I drifted into a light doze, my breath coming in shallow gasps and my belly muscles clenching against the pain.

The game broke up around midnight and Colin ambled over to the lounge. 'Up you get, girl. Everyone's going home.' I heard him through a daze. He shook me awake and tried to pull me to my feet, but I couldn't move from the waist down. I was paralysed.

A rush of excited voices and feet scurried around me. I felt the four of them haul me from the couch; they manhandled me the length of the hallway and across the veranda. It was a blur of arms and legs and curses and 'what the hell's happened', as they slid me into the back seat of the Zephyr. Brett jumped into the driver's seat and Colin into the back. He cradled my head.

'Hurry, mate!' His voice sounded panicked.

Parramatta Hospital in the early hours of Sunday morning was quiet. I was dragged onto a stretcher and within minutes I was in an examination room. I struggled to distinguish who were nurses and who were doctors and who was somebody else. Perhaps the doctors were the ones huddled around my stomach, poking and pressing and muttering, and the nurse was the one holding a basin to my face as I threw up with each feel of my gut. Everything else in the room seemed white: the enamel basin pressed to my lips, the towel that wiped my mouth, the walls, the curtains and the fluorescent light blinding my eyes. Colin and Brett had disappeared.

The doctors massaged my stomach and prodded deeply with their fingertips. They pulled up clumps of skin and watched what happened when they let it go. They played ball with my belly fat, rolling it back and forward, pushing further with the flat of their hand on each roll, as if they were trying to reach back to my spine. I gagged and vomited and begged them to stop.

Suddenly they did so as if on signal. I turned my head and saw two more doctors silhouetted in the doorway. The nurse and doctors left the room in a hurry and pulled the door closed behind. Outside, I could hear the murmur of voices, which swelled for a moment as the nurse returned to me, then were muffled again as she closed the door behind her. The voices stopped. The door opened again and one of the examining doctors stepped up to my bedside. It was the first time he had looked me in the face. He was only young: his face was clear and unlined and there was no sign of a five o'clock shadow.

'Could you be pregnant?' he demanded.

My gut clenched again. The shame that ran through my body felt like a cold shaft running from head to toe. His face loomed over mine, the fluorescent light casting a halo around his head. He leaned closer to me and repeated the question.

'Could you be pregnant?'

I closed my eyes so I wouldn't have to look in his. 'Yes.' The word was carried on a rush of air. I had been holding my breath.

'Okay.' He turned on his heel. I felt the nurse move a few steps away from me. Away from my shame.

Silence. I knew the nurse was still there but it was as if she was rooted to the spot. I pressed my eyes closed and let the tears flow silently, drifting across my cheek and soaking into my hair, which lay in a tangled mass.

There was a shift in light and sound as the door opened again. The young doctor was back, this time with an older one in tow. The young one looked down at me, sympathetically. He didn't seem to realise I wasn't married. He talked to me gently as though he thought I had planned to have a baby.

'We think you're having an ectopic pregnancy.'

I didn't want to meet his eye, but I didn't know what he was talking about, either. I focused on a spot over his shoulder and raised an eyebrow in question.

'It means the baby is growing in the wrong place. It should be in the womb, but instead the egg has stuck in the fallopian tube and the embryo is growing there. It's not good news, I'm afraid.'

Silence again. It was a lot to take in. The nurse shifted stance. The doctors waited for a response.

My throat was dry and burning. It tasted of bile. My first words had no sound. I tried again.

'Maybe it's appendicitis?' It was a whispered question.

'Appendicitis? Why would you think that?'

'Been having . . . stomach cramps . . . months. Doctor says appendix . . . maybe . . .' Was I grasping at straws?

The older doctor stepped forward and began to quiz me on dates and symptoms and what I had done about it so far. Who had examined me? The GP. Where? In his surgery. Had I been referred to a specialist? No. Had I been to a hospital? No. Was I sure it was appendicitis? Well that's what the GP told me. Then why hadn't he treated it? I don't know. Maybe he didn't think it was serious.

The doctors exchanged a glance.

'Well, it *is* serious now,' the older one said gruffly as the two men left the room.

Time passed. The nurse and I said nothing to each other. Hospital sounds reached me from a distance, a phone call now and then, an ambulance siren, angry words from some drunk with a broken leg, trolleys wheeling along corridors. No sign of Colin or Mum. I was entombed in a white cave, abandoned to endure the pain in my body and heart in mute suffering.

The young doctor reappeared. 'Okay,' he was matter-of-fact as he dragged up a chair, 'we're pretty sure you have an ectopic pregnancy, but we can't rule out appendicitis, either. We'd like to do an x-ray, but are reluctant to if you're pregnant. So we're going to admit you for observation to see your symptoms first-hand, and run some blood tests over the next few days. Your husband is sorting out the paperwork now, and you'll be sent to the observation ward for tonight. He can visit you in the morning.'

'Husband?' The word sent a shockwave through me. The doctor didn't seem to notice my expression.

'Oh – and they'll give you something for the pain up on the ward.' It was an afterthought thrown over his shoulder as he left the room.

The observation ward looked dim as my trolley was wheeled to a spare spot. It was a long, dormitory-style room, eight beds lined up neatly to the left and the right and a generous walkway down the middle. The curtains around each bed were stacked against the wall so the nurses had a clear view of each patient from their station at one end of the room.

Two nurses bustled around me. The first busied herself sticking a cannula into my wrist while the second started tying my ankles and thighs to the metal side rails of the bed. When the first nurse had finished, she tied my wrists to the bed.

'What's happening?' I asked in alarm.

'You're to stay very still,' she said soothingly, 'we don't want you to roll over or thrash around. If it is your appendix, we need it to calm down. We don't want it to burst – now do we?'

I didn't need reminding to stay still. Every time I shifted even slightly, the pain seared through me as if I had been sliced with a knife. The cannula had twisted in the strapping and the needle was uncomfortable. The feeling in my legs was returning. Something the doctors had pressed on seemed to have sparked them back to life, and now they were tingling. The pin-cushion jabs of sensation were excruciating. I felt thoroughly miserable.

I didn't have a choice in the matter though. By the time the nurses finished, all I could do was turn my head to the left and right and lift it forward just as far as my neck would stretch.

Lying there in the gloom, it seemed as if I was in two places at once. On the one hand I was exhausted and drowsy and desperate to close my eyes and drift into sleep and discover the whole damned nightmare had disappeared by morning. On the other hand, every sense in my body seemed more alert than ever before. The smell of hospital antiseptic assailed me; the taste of bile was acrid in my mouth; the indentations in the acoustic ceiling were individual pin-pricks I could count. In my mind, I could reach out and touch the patient in the bed beside me, and all around me were their sounds. I could tune in from one bed to the next, assessing one from the other, visualising what lay behind the sound.

A picture popped into my mind, of a white rabbit lit by the light of an angel. The rabbit was straining on its haunches, its front legs tucked under its chin. Its ears lifted so straight and high it seemed they would tear away from its body. Its eyes were bulging and fixed on the angel. Every muscle seemed tensed and alert, but paralysed as if the rabbit couldn't move. Then I realised the light wasn't that of an angel. No, it was more like the headlights of a truck. A truck that was about to mow down that rabbit.

The realisation struck me. This is what fear feels like, and this is how I feel right now. I am that rabbit, that truck is going to destroy me and I don't have the power to run.

When I'm nervous I talk a lot. Words and stories tumble out of me in a furious rush. I lose the control to put thought before speech. Now, lying there in the half dark, tied to a metal bed, surrounded by strange smells and sounds and the movements of men and women I couldn't see, my first time in hospital – I started to babble. Under my breath at first, then loudly enough that my voice drifted down the dormitory.

A young nurse heard me. 'You okay?' She touched my bindings, 'You need a pan?'

'A pan?'

'You know, for the toilet. Let me know when you need to go and I'll help you onto a pan so you don't get up.'

Wee in my bed? I thought. Not bloody likely.

Sister came along. 'Everything okay, Nurse?' Sister's voice contained authority, with a hint she thought the nurse was time-wasting.

'Yes, Sister,' was her meek reply.

'Well then, move along and see to the other patients. They're bringing up that broken leg shortly.'

The nurse slunk away.

Sister stared down at me. 'How old are you?'

'Sixteen.' My reply was as meek as the nurse's.

'First time in hospital?' There was a hint of sympathy.

'Yes.'

There was a pause before she asked. 'Would you like me to stay a while?'

'That would be nice.'

There was a scrape of a chair being pulled up. Her face disappeared as she sat beside me. I turned my head in her direction. All I could see was the round face of a watch pinned upside-down to her sister's bar on the breast of her uniform.

The silence was uncomfortable.

'Sister . . . I know some jokes.'

'Really? Well let's hear them. We could do with a laugh around here.'

Mummy, Mummy – Why is Daddy running?
Shut up and reload.

Mummy, Mummy – I hate my brother's guts!
Push them aside and eat your vegetables.

Sister wasn't laughing. I pushed on with Mum's favourite. The one the men at the sheltered workshop had taught her. She didn't know what it meant of course.

What's the difference between egg and beetroot?
You can beat an egg but you can't beat a root.

I was on a roll now. The words were taking on a life of their own; I wasn't waiting to sense if Sister was amused. My mouth and my commonsense were in two different places.

Bruce and Sheila meet at a party.
They get on really well and by the end of the night
Sheila is back at Bruce's place and they get it off.
When Sheila leaves the next morning Bruce promises
to call her but he never does.
Three months later Sheila phones him out of the blue.
'Bruce, Bruce – it's me, Sheila!'
'Sheila . . . Sheila . . .' Bruce struggles to remember her.
'You know, Bruce! – Sheila! You, me, at that party –
and then we went back to your place . . .'
'Oh yeah. Sheila! Yeah – hey – great root! Yeah, Sheila! So how ya' doing
– what's happening?'
'Well Bruce, it's like this. I'm pregnant to you and if you
don't marry me I'm gunna throw myself off the Harbour Bridge.'
There's a pause from Bruce, and then he says –
'Good on ya, Sheila! I knew you were a good sport!'

There was another scrape as Sister pushed her chair back. Her face appeared above me. 'Well,' her tone was haughty, 'there's clearly nothing too much the matter with *you*.'

I lay there listening to her retreating footsteps, feeling hot and ashamed. Why had I done that? Apart from offending her, I had embarrassed *myself*. I wished a hole would open up and drop me in it. I *am* a nice girl, I tried to remind myself. That was just a silly thing I did because I'm scared. I'm smart, I'm thoughtful, lots of people care about me.

Not anymore, my other voice cut in, not as soon as they find out you're pregnant. You know those pains had nothing to do with a period coming. It's all over for you, girl. You're on your own now.

That night on the ward went on forever. The longed-for sleep never came. Two beds down from me an Italian woman felt the same need to talk to herself as I had.

Hail Mary, full of grace.
The Lord is with thee.
Blessed art thou among women,
and blessed is the fruit of thy womb, Jesus.
Holy Mary, Mother of God,
pray for us sinners,
now and at the hour of our death.
Amen.

I had never heard the prayer before. Words jumped at me. *Fruit of thy womb, pray for us sinners . . .*

She's on to me, I thought, she doesn't even know my bloody name and she already knows my shame. God! I wish it were my hour of death. Let me die . . . tonight . . . *please.*

All night long she repeated the plea, switching from English to Italian and back again. By morning I was fluent in the first line, *Ave Maria piena di grazia.*

Colin came to see me shortly after lunch on the first day. I had been transferred to the surgical ward. He beamed his lopsided grin at me, trying to close his mouth over his chipped tooth. 'I've got it under control.'

What a busy dream weaver he had been while I lay bound and helpless. He had scampered from the doctors to the admission office with his fanciful tale, telling them I was his wife and we were ecstatic we might be having our first child. One part of me loved him for trying so hard to protect my reputation and understood his lies were to shield me from criticism and scorn. Another part of me damned him for presenting me with yet another dilemma: how to look and act like a married woman.

'Don't worry,' he whispered as he tugged my friendship ring from my right hand and slipped it on to the third finger of my left hand. 'You know I'll always stand by you – *and,*' he said importantly, puffing himself up with pride, 'I told them you have health insurance with the Druids, just like me. So you'll get better care here. They've put you in the Intermediate section – that'll make sure they look after you special-like.' There was that lopsided grin again, and his eyes twinkling at mine. He was so sure of himself it made me want to believe him.

Colin knew that when I left school Mum's pension no longer covered my medical care. I had meant to take out private health insurance just as soon as I got a job, but my first job had come and gone so quickly I hardly had time to think of it. Colin was a member of the friendly society, the Druids, and he was convinced he could persuade them, on the strength of his wishing to marry me, to include me in his cover. He was years ahead of his time: entitlements for de facto partners was a figment of his imagination, as the Druids would make abundantly clear to us. In the meantime, though, I was to be treated a cut above the 'run of the mill' public hospital patient. Not that I was in any condition to recognise the difference – if indeed there was one beyond the bill upon discharge.

Mum arrived on the third day in that shadowy way of hers, appearing silently and without warning – no greeting, no kiss or hug. I was sitting up in bed by now, but resting delicately so as not to disturb whatever was happening on my insides.

She was wearing her little-girl look, her face long and eyes wide and limpid. Her eyes entreated me, screaming out her appeal as clearly as if she had spoken. 'Please don't hurt me. I didn't do anything wrong. Please, just make it be right, make everything be right.'

When she opened her mouth, her message burst out as if she had schooled herself on what to say all the way on her bus journey to the hospital.

'Aunty Myra says you must be pregnant, but you're not, are you Gwenny.' It was more of a defiant statement than a question. Her eyes bored into mine, imploring me to reassure her. The words hung between us. I licked my lips and took a deep breath.

'Yes, Mum. It looks like I am.' There, I had said it.

I knew it wouldn't be easy for Mum, but I didn't anticipate her reaction. She crumpled into herself, withering in front of me as I cut the thin thread of hope that Aunty Myra might be off the mark, even though she was rarely wrong where matters of commonsense were concerned. Aunty Myra – who had been the big sister looking after Mum's interests all these years – had certainly hit *that* nail right on the head.

There was nothing further to be said. I had destroyed any hope Mum held for a brighter future. Any secret ambitions she held on my behalf were shattered in that simple statement. She didn't – couldn't – reach out to me. She turned and left the ward as silently as she had come, and that was the last I saw of my mother for the rest of my hospital stay.

•

Wednesday night. My fourth night in hospital. I lay in bed, listening to the sounds of a hospital ward settling down for the night. The last of the supper crumbs had long since been cleaned away. Three meals and three snacks a day. That's what they fed you in this hospital. Not me, though. They fed me nothing except glucose through a drip.

'It's for your own good,' nurses reminded me, 'you could go to theatre at any moment.'

Even though they were reluctant at first, the doctors decided to go ahead with an x-ray. The results were inconclusive, and they didn't want to send me for another in case I truly was pregnant. Ultrasounds were unheard of. So the doctors had adopted a cautious 'wait and watch' approach.

The glucose solution dripping into my arm kept my body hydrated, but did nothing for the hunger pangs. I lay there feeling acidic bile roiling in my stomach. It was acrid and gurgled up my throat in a bitter backflush. My ward mates could hear my stomach rumbling and growling in the bedtime quiet.

When the sister-in-charge came on her rounds, I begged for food. I hadn't eaten since Saturday. Surgery seemed a distant non-event, something never likely to happen.

'Well,' her tone was doubtful, 'perhaps just some gruel off the soup. I'll see what the kitchen can manage.'

Time passed, then a young nurse arrived with a bowl of chunky, meaty broth. Moist lamb, melting in my mouth in sinewy tendrils, mixing all around with carrots and celery, a joyous mush of flavours and substance. I chewed quickly, knowing there had to be a mistake, desperate to finish before Sister came along and grabbed the food from me. I chewed and gobbled, shoving each new spoonful into my mouth before the first was properly swallowed. Then, scared I'd be found out, I hid the empty bowl in my bedside cabinet.

Later, Sister arrived with a bowl of thin liquid.

'Thank you, Sister,' I said demurely, slipping my guilty gaze away from her face.

Then I drank that right down too. Three hours later I was in emergency surgery. It was more than my inflamed appendix could cope with.

'You were lucky!' a voice told me in the recovery room. 'It burst just as we got you open. If you'd been any later getting into theatre we'd have had a job cleaning you up.'

Another doctor beamed at my bedside the next morning. 'And how are *we* this morning?'

I scanned his face – why had he stressed *we*?

'Yes,' he nodded, 'we had a good look and feel. You're definitely pregnant but everything is fine. It's all where it should be. It was quite touch and go there for a while. You might have lost the baby, but it's all fine now.

Every part of my body went cold. My stomach lurched into my

throat. I felt as if I was tumbling down a long tunnel. His voice became faint.

'Anyway,' he continued, 'we had a good look around while we were in there. You'll find the scar a little larger than usual. We removed an ovarian cyst, nothing to worry about. You just rest up now and look after the little one.'

He was so pleased with himself, as he should have been. He'd been called out in the middle of the night to deal with this emergency. He was a young doctor, a redhead with freckles. Now they were lit up all over his face. He and his colleagues had done a marvellous job. It was fantastic news for the married woman they thought I was.

I smiled wanly as I thanked him then as soon as he left I threw up. I kept throwing up for the rest of the hospital stay. I didn't eat again, one bowl of broth so soon before the anaesthetic had seen to that.

•

A week into my hospital stay, I was keenly aware of my financial situation and under stress to keep up the pretence of being married, so I agitated to be discharged. I coerced the doctors into it, two days after the operation and still with the stitches in. On discharge, they gave me a referral to have the pregnancy officially confirmed.

A couple of days later I sat in the outpatient doctor's clinic. He was happy to confirm the news. He congratulated me warmly. As I stood to leave his office, I felt the familiar roaring in the ears and the head confusion that precedes a faint. I slumped to the floor.

I had entered hospital weighing sixty kilograms and left a week later at fifty. I had a hospital bill the size of a year's wages, and a ten-centimetre raw wound in my side. I was a couple of months' pregnant: those who knew I was carrying a baby thought I was married, and those who knew I was single had no idea I was pregnant. My boyfriend spent more time out of work than in it, never saved a cent and had no ambitions. He always had the best of intentions but couldn't be trusted to carry them out. My mum and brother were barely speaking to me, and my 'father-in-law-to-be' would likely raise the roof when he heard the story.

I could hear Aunty Myra's voice in my ear: 'Well, this is a right old mess you've gotten into, old chum. A right old mess, indeed.'

26

It was only a week after leaving hospital that I applied for a job as a junior clerk, and the next thing I knew I was back in the workforce. I was still living at Colin's, and at the end of my first day, I travelled home with my head in the clouds and thoughts on dinner and table talk, but my ecstatic mood was dashed when I found a note from Steve in the letterbox. Written on a sheet torn off a writing pad, his anger showed through the sloping slashes and curt words.

Tried twice to see you. M in Parramatta psych hospital. We need to talk.

My heart sank. I dreaded having to speak to him. My anxiety was so physical that I threw up, right there, leaning against the fence, his note clutched to my stomach. It was many weeks since I had left home, and so far I had managed to avoid any contact with Steve even though he was still living there with Mum. He had no phone, so it would mean asking Colin to drive me to see him. I had no intention of doing that. Any discussion would have to wait until tomorrow when I could call Steve at work.

It was awkward. I had only been at work one day and I hated asking my boss to let me make a personal call. When I called him,

I was glad his workmates were near. He was furious with me, but at least he didn't shout at me when others were listening. He kept his voice low and controlled, but I heard the anger.

'I had to take her to Parramatta yesterday morning. She was in a bad way. Confused and erratic. Kept asking for you. I called in on the way to the hospital – where were you? I needed you in the car.'

I tried to explain. He talked over me.

'After I left her at the hospital I called back again. Still no one home. So I left the note.' He spoke resentfully, angry with me for not being available at his beck and call. I felt resentful, too: it wasn't as if I had planned any of this, or that I had been out playing around. I was at *work* for Chrissake! Even if I was out having a good time, what business was it of his? Why should he make me feel so guilty? It was the same as when I was a child – he was blaming me for Mum having another nervous breakdown.

Well, it was my fault *really* – I knew that. I just didn't need Steve's criticism. I felt guilty enough already.

'Anyway,' he continued, 'they've moved her to Rydalmere. She's sedated but still agitated. She's angry at *me* now. Says I threw you and her out.'

Whenever the lunatic demon invaded Mum's mind she was liable to rant on all manner of things, a mish-mash of fact and imaginings, spat out with such force and venom that she seemed more like an animal than a human. I could imagine her turning her fury on to Steve, her mind twisting him into the role of an evil torturer, rather than the hard-done-by loyal son he imagined himself to be. All three of us were victims of the voices that lived in Mum's head.

Mum was in hospital for two weeks, and all Steve and I managed to do was argue about whether I was visiting her enough. I resisted his demands that I make her my priority. I had so much on my own plate: a new job to learn, a house to run, social commitments. No doubt somewhere in my subconscious I felt bitter that she had never shown me great support, so why should I set aside my life for hers?

She had only come to see *me* once in hospital, hadn't she? So what did she expect in return? Steve saw only that she was worried about me, and was asking for me, and perhaps pinning her hopes of recovery on my appearance. Every time I said I couldn't visit at the time Steve wanted me to, was another reason for him to explode.

He was also pressuring me to return home. I refused, anxious about being alone in the house with him. 'You thrashed me. Don't you remember? You've got such a bad temper – how can I be there with you?'

Steve took offence. He clearly didn't have the same memory of the events as I had within my growing store of hurt and humiliation. Eventually, half-heartedly, I agreed to return home when Mum was discharged. There was no realistic alternative. Mum needed looking after.

By now, Steve knew I was pregnant, perhaps as part of Mum's ravings. He managed to contain his temper, but not his disdain. 'Like mother, like daughter,' he spat at me. Even though Mum wasn't there to hear it, if he had his time over, I don't suppose he would say that. It was too hurtful to Mum, as well as me. At least though, he didn't hit me. He never did that again.

'Perhaps it's for the best,' Colin's dad consoled me, 'I hadn't liked to mention before, but . . . well . . . the neighbours have been talking. A young girl like you living alone with two men. Tongues were bound to wag.'

Tongues would be wagging soon enough. It was time to let him into our secret. He and I had become friends while I was living there, but this wasn't something he was likely to accept, and I braced for the explosion.

I was surprised. All he did was look at me sadly, and turn to Colin.

'I knew I should have cut it off when you were born.'

Colin flinched, but he knew he had been let off lightly. All he had to do to make it right was to marry me.

•

A year earlier, when I was fifteen, I hankered to find my father. Mum humoured me, not by reminiscing about a great love affair and a special man in her life, nothing like that. She gave me a box containing letters he had written to her over the first few years of my life. Everything I knew of my father I learned through those letters. Mum couldn't bring herself to add any stories to my limited knowledge, nor did she have any photographs to share. I sorted the letters carefully, arranging each in sequence and putting any stray sheets into their correct place in time and meaning. I pored over them, searching for any reference to me, re-reading any sentence in which he might declare his love for me, send a greeting or express any concern for my welfare.

The last two letters were written when I was almost five years old, and were sent from Italy. Mum had removed the envelopes with his return address, something I didn't discover for many years. It was her way of humouring me, while at the same time thwarting any chance of me contacting him. She told me he went to Italy and didn't come back, and she knew nothing more about him. It was a devastating dead-end and I couldn't imagine how I could ever find him. I felt it was me who had been abandoned, even more so than my mother had been.

Mum tried to comfort me the only way she knew, spinning me a tale about him caring so much for me that he had left me a legacy. It was a pot of money to be kept safe for the day I would marry, because my father wanted me to have a fine wedding and live happily ever after.

When I returned home to nurse Mum, I decided it was time to ask her for my inheritance. It caused yet another disagreement between Steve and me.

'Any dough Mum has is her retirement fund. It should be left intact as far as possible – what's so hard to understand about that?' He made it sound as though I was trying to rob my mother and leave her destitute.

I was in tears. 'So,' I sobbed, 'would you rather we get married in a registry office?'

It all felt so unfair. No one had stopped him enjoying his own inheritance. Steve had squandered his father's money on a car, nothing as important as a wedding. I was too hysterical to recognise there was no inheritance. I didn't understand then that it was another of Mum's flights of fancy, a fabrication dressed up to look like a fairy-tale movie ending. A lie that she repeated several times. Sometimes when Mum made up a story, the line between truth and fiction blurred so much even she herself no longer knew the difference.

Sometimes it is easier to live in a make-believe land than it is to live in the harsh light of reality.

In truth, I wasn't sure myself whether I wanted to get married or not. I felt I should, and Colin wanted to, but I wasn't looking forward to it. There was the 'right thing to do', and there was my secret inner feeling something was wrong, and I was stuck between the two. Mum said nothing, and as I was a minor, I would need her permission. All Steve was interested in was striking a bargain. His relationship with his girlfriend of two years had blossomed, and wedding plans were in full swing.

'I won't come to your wedding – and I won't invite you to mine – okay?'

Long-suffering Steve had no desire to have an unmarried sister with a round belly complicating the biggest day of his life. By the time he would marry in a few months' time in May, I would be well down the track, and there would be no hiding my condition.

Procrastination and indecision led to one week after another with no wedding plans being made, until my condition was far too obvious for any self-respecting minister to marry us. At least, that's what I told myself – and Colin. In fact, I hadn't asked any ministers, self-respecting or otherwise. I just knew I didn't want to stand before one with my fat belly in front, people sniggering at my back and Colin standing beside me. Somehow I was still hoping for a miracle alternative, and using a potentially reluctant minister as the excuse bought me time.

PART TWO

Childless Mother

1972–1974

27

I returned to the house at Old Guildford, co-existing with Mum in the same remote manner as years of habit had bred, and living in an uneasy truce with Steve.

He took control of the hospital bills and my appendix operation expenses, taking me to see the social worker at Parramatta Hospital and helping me explain the truth. Eventually all doctors waived their fee. It was Steve who took me to the maternity hospital to book in for my delivery and made sure appropriate arrangements were in place for my baby's birth.

I continued to work and continued to see Colin on a daily basis. Little by little, I began to adapt more to his family than mine, and in the process I gradually severed all the invisible links with those who had been my support network during my growing years. The van den Avoorts were a distant memory, the Hawkins were in Melbourne, Vicki and her family were moving to Adelaide. I rarely saw my aunts and uncle any more, and my cousins were busy with careers, marriages and families. The Spearmans and Kulpie were pushed into the background. My relationship with Steve's girlfriend, which had started out like big sister, little sister: her fussing over my hair and me testing out my fledgling cooking skills on her, was floundering. I had eyes only for Colin, and if you did not like him, it meant you did not like me either. He so monopolised my attention, I had little time for anything else beyond him and work. I even stopped writing to Barry.

My job was going well. It was clerical work, which I found mentally stimulating and easy on my body. Every day I was handed several sets of architect's plans and asked to work out how much Gyprock plasterboard was required for the wall linings. The most economical length of board was eighteen feet long, so the challenge was to use that length as much as possible, and then there were the other materials: board for the wet areas, cornices, and ceiling roses from time to time. It was a responsible job for a school leaver, but one I grasped immediately. Every time I opened a new set of plans it was as if my internal eye snapped on to the patterns laid in front of me, and the process of calculating the job-site materials, using only a slide rule and a calculator, absorbed me for the next hour or two. It was like being given a set of puzzles and told to go play to your heart's content and pick up a pay packet for your trouble.

I knew I was a doing a good job because the estimators would soon let you know if you had miscalculated or ordered the wrong materials, and I rarely made that mistake. I could keep pace with the older, more experienced clerks, and my costing of materials was equal to or better than theirs – not that they were happy about that.

The tension between the other clerks and me started rising. I had made the disappointing discovery that adults in the workplace could be just as petty and spiteful as teenage girls in the schoolyard. Rather than a world of mature and reasonable grown-ups, I had stepped into a minefield of gossip and too much interest in other people's business. I had been wary of being drawn into conversation around the lunch table, scared in case I let slip something that could be held against me, so in desperation I gathered up my grease-proof-paper-wrapped sandwich and took refuge with the older workmen in the backroom.

I knew the other office staff didn't like me, but as my desk was the first of six lined up along a blank brick wall, I couldn't see the secret language behind my back, or the rolled eyes and silently mouthed obscenities.

One morning, the oldest of the women confronted me at my desk. Her body language was aggressive; her legs were spread wide, her hips thrust forward.

'The boss wants to see ya. His office . . . *Now*.'

Her face was smug with a self-satisfied smirk around the corners of her mouth. She thrust her breasts up and out, as if they were the authority on some secret I did not share, flounced back to her desk and with a superior smile at the other clerks, she dropped heavily into her swivel chair.

Suddenly I was very apprehensive. In full view of the other staff, the boss had often stopped by my desk to encourage me in my work. Until now, nothing he had to say to me had been private. If he wanted to speak to me behind closed doors, it was not a good sign.

I prepared myself for something unpleasant, however what he said came as a complete shock. A *shock*. The word is a noise, and the noise is physical. *Sh-o-c-k-k-k*. It hits you like a slap in the face and vibrates through your body.

He looked embarrassed, squirmed in his chair a little, looked me straight in the eye and launched into his speech. 'The ladies have reported to me their suspicion you are pregnant. Is that correct?'

I heard my gasp of breath as if it came from someone else, outside me. I was tempted to lie – but how could I? I could only mumble my assent. Gossips those women might be, but in this case their scandal mongering was spot on.

He was sad, genuinely sad and disappointed. I could see that from the droop of his shoulders and the way he spread his hands wide in a gesture of defeat.

'I'm sorry. So, so, sorry. You're one of the most promising on the team. But I'm going to have to let you go. I wish it could be different. Really, I do. But you have to see my position. The ladies have made it quite clear they refuse to work with you. I can't have five people down tools over a silly young girl who's got herself in trouble.'

I wanted to argue with him – but on what grounds? It had really been too naïve of me to imagine I would be immune from their gossip. I blamed myself for not trying harder to win them over. If I had been friendly towards the other women it might have been different. Perhaps they would have supported me, rather than rounding on me in such a way, savaging me like a pack of wolves turning on the wounded one among them. Deep inside, I knew my boss was in an impossible situation. I had withheld the information of my pregnancy from the beginning. If I had told him at the interview he wouldn't have hired me. I was grateful he had encouraged me and treated me so well, and paid me regularly, and I knew he was genuinely sorry to let me go. I was given a glowing reference and a friendly, regretful, fatherly hug as he saw me off the premises.

It didn't change the fact that half an hour later I was standing alone on the station platform, forlornly contemplating my future. Six months' pregnant, single, broke, alienated and confused – what was my future from here?

•

For the previous six months, I had lived in a turmoil of mixed feelings, some negative and some positive, most of them contradictory. I felt shame and pride, regret and anticipation, humility and defiance, depression and excitement, anger and happiness, insecurity and love. So much was happening around me, to me. At the same time, something was happening inside me.

Another life was growing within me, within my being. At first I had mistaken the bubbly feelings in my stomach as gas from the appendix operation. But then I recognised the butterfly fluttering as the sign of my baby's awakening. He or she was there, calling for my attention, reminding me the first battle had been fought and won. We grew slowly at first, so it was months before we revealed ourselves to the world. I felt protective and frightened for the baby's wellbeing, feelings which intensified when I started losing blood regularly. Not much – just enough to need attention and regular medical check-ups at the public hospital outpatient clinic. On two occasions I had spent all day at the hospital having blood and urine tests every couple of hours. I became so drained, the nurses resorted to running taps to stimulate me to pee. I bled all the way through my pregnancy, without ever knowing the cause or significance. Sometimes I would sit for hours on a wooden bench in the clinic waiting room for what seemed like a ten-minute examination. The doctor was rarely the same, so we didn't develop any rapport. They didn't consult me, they examined me, and they never shared with me any diagnosis, or information on how I was progressing. If ever the doctor left the room, I would scramble for my file and try to understand what was recorded there. I might as well have been trying to read a foreign language.

The blood loss and disinterest of the doctors was another battle we fought and won, and with each victory came the growing conviction I was carrying a baby who was meant to be born, that there was no accident in why we were together. I didn't know whether I was carrying a boy or girl, but in my mind it was a boy. Something ancient, some remnant knowledge flowing in my life-blood compelled me to believe my first-born should be male. A protective shepherd who would guide and safeguard the siblings, who would take the lead in times of need – it was an irrational belief, but one of which I was convinced. We were two people sharing one face to the world. What I did, how I felt, affected my baby, and he communicated with me.

Like the silkworm moths of my childhood, my baby would emerge from my womb in the beauty of new birth, and one day he would spread his wings and fly away from me to take his place in the world. What was the legacy with which I would send him forth? My gift to him would be illegitimacy; he would be a poor bastard kid, a second-rate citizen. If there was a God, I couldn't understand why he had chosen me to mother this child: such were the depths of my feelings of inadequacy. Yet he *had* chosen me, and there must be a reason for that. I believe in fate. Everything in life has a reason.

Now we stood on this station platform, the two of us entwined, facing the latest crisis and stressing about what lay ahead. I placed my hands protectively around my tummy. 'It's just you and me against the world,' I whispered.

Baby rolled over. A long, lazy, slow roll, bulging out my stomach and snagging my dress, dragging one foot behind him. The foot jutted out several centimetres at an angle just below my navel. I traced the line of his heel with my palm. 'We're okay. We're okay. Rest easy my little one,' I whispered to him as I rubbed my belly and pushed gently. He gave a little wiggle and pulled his foot back into a place that was comfortable for both of us.

The train arrived and I entered an empty carriage. I sang my favourite lullaby to him as we travelled home, crooning over and over:

Lullaby and good night, thy mother's delight
Guardian angels are near
So sleep on with no fear
They will keep thee from harm, till you wake in my arms
They will keep thee from harm, till you wake in my arms

He lay there, making quiet movements as if listening to the sound of my voice through his watery nursery. After a while he became still, and I imagined him sleeping peacefully, quiet and secure in his safe haven.

It was what awaited him in another few months' time that preoccupied my thoughts.

28

'What's that in the warmer, love?'

'Beef Bourguignon,' I quipped.

'Beef – what?'

'Give over, Sheila,' his mate chimed in, 'it's just plain old stew with a bloody tarted-up name.'

'Yeah, well . . . sausages and mash'll do me any day. Lots of gravy on that, girlie.'

Yep. The clientele of the Family Hotel had no airs and graces. They were just decent salt-of-the-earth blokes in blue singlets and dusty work boots. They didn't care that I had a fat stomach and no wedding ring. Just as long as the food was hot, the beer was cold – and I wasn't *their* daughter.

It had been hard for me to get another job; I certainly couldn't pick and choose now. I was glad to be taken on by the pub, even though it was heavier work and I was on my feet all the time. The focus was the counter lunches, a frantic few hours that kept us busy serving cooked meals to local workmen. Before lunch, I worked hard, cleaning rooms and lugging out laundry, and afterwards, I scrubbed the kitchen then mopped the tiled floors, dragging a heavy metal bucket with me. Sometimes a function would mean I had to set up the dining room, and I used a little ingenuity to make it attractive and festive. The work took a physical toll, especially for a young girl reaching the end of her pregnancy, but the upside was these people weren't judgmental. My body may have been worn out but my mind was at peace.

By the time Steve married and moved out of home in May 1972, I was up to weekly hospital visits. I wasn't close to my due date, but my condition was being monitored regularly. If one doctor couldn't find a heartbeat, I would steel myself to be told it was all over, then the next doctor would find two, re-measure my abdomen and mutter about twins. Not one of the doctors told me what was going on, until around the middle of June, when one said the birth was 'imminent'. I left my job at the pub, only to find myself dragging around the house, going into a cleaning frenzy and imagining every twinge to be the first sign of labour. The only notable event was my seventeenth birthday. My baby had held on tenaciously through x-rays, operations, bleeding, passionate arguments – even a fall down the back stairs – and now he was holding on tenaciously to his life within the cocoon. That was what I understood was happening.

The doctor had it wrong, very wrong. I know that now, because I have tracked down my medical records. I may have convinced myself I was carrying a special child, but even I knew I was not the Virgin Mary, and that is the only way I could have been due to give birth in the middle of June 1972.

The records show that each week a different doctor measured my belly, and since ultrasounds did not exist, each doctor estimated my progress from those measurements. The records are scant, a single page, barely more than a list of examination dates, fundus height, estimated pregnancy weeks, blood pressure and weight. I flicked over it at first, until something odd jumped out at me. My pregnancy moved along faster than the weeks ticking away. I ran my finger down the list, making pencil notations as I went. In late March I was twenty-two weeks. Four weeks later, on 24 April, I was twenty-six weeks. So far, so good. After that, it goes completely awry. Over the course of the next six calendar weeks, according to the doctors' scratchy estimates, I advanced a full twelve weeks.

Why subsequent doctors didn't query or correct this anomaly is unclear; they simply gave up and added a question mark each week. At the beginning of July, several weeks ahead of my correct time, but with the understanding I was overdue, one doctor scheduled me for an induction the next day. They all seem to have overlooked that my original due date had been clearly recorded as the first week in August.

•

In 1972, most single girls in my situation were either hustled down the aisle or bundled into an unmarried mothers' home. The mother's wishes were ignored, and if the father was still around but they hadn't married, then the girl's parents usually told her to end the relationship. The term 'confinement' came to mean *just that* for the women sent into these homes. Thousands of unwed women entered their doors with a baby in utero, only to leave months later with empty arms and empty hearts. It was a system of baby farming, sanctioned and upheld by state, church and society. Many women tell heartbreaking stories of their treatment in these institutions, and they frequently refer to the persuasion, coercion and even force that was used to get them to give up their babies and sign adoption papers. Some weren't told there was a revocation clause – a thirty-day 'cooling-off' period – during which a mother could change her mind about the adoption.

There was only one message for these girls: if they kept their baby they were being selfish – to the baby and to the adopting parents, who desperately wanted to have a child. The best thing they could do for their baby was to give it up to a loving home where it would be cherished, provided for and nurtured in a way that no single mother could ever hope to achieve.

'Your child will be a bastard. How could you do that to your baby? How can you punish your child for your sin? No child deserves to carry that stigma. And how can you care for him? You think you will love him, but mark my words, you will find it so hard you will soon realise you have put a noose around your neck. Better to give him up straight away before you come to resent him. There are so many people of good home and background with so much love to give – give your baby every chance to grow strong and stable. Let your baby have a right to grow up free of shame. Don't blight him with your mistake.'

When the time came to give birth, these mothers were transferred to the adjoining hospital for the final stages of labour. Drugged and incoherent, few ever saw their baby or heard its first cry, and many gave birth with a sheet held up at their waists, so they couldn't see their newborn. Even though their babies were just down the hall in the nursery, they weren't allowed access, nor were they allowed to feed them. Discharged shortly after their delivery, sometimes girls returned within the thirty-day revocation period to be told their baby had died. It may have been a social experiment born of good intentions, but it was administered with cruel and flawed acts of punishment and biased judgments. Women were made to feel that they were unworthy to carry the name of mother.

The outcome of these adoptions was a lottery. I know of many successful adoptions and some disasters, and plenty more that are neither one nor the other. I know of adoptees who are eternally grateful they were the ones to be adopted after meeting siblings who were raised in appalling conditions by their birth parent. The opposite is also true. The debate of nature versus nurture rages forever without any clear-cut answers.

Each story of adoption is as unique as the person telling it. None is identical – but there are similarities. Something many adoptees share is the drive to overachieve, born of a need to prove their worth. There is a roiling within them to overcome the sense of loss and inadequacy stemming from what they feel was abandonment by their mother. If the mother had died in childbirth, there would be sadness and grief and a longing for what might have been, but there would also be the knowledge and acceptance that the separation was out of the mother's hands. It's different when a mother gives up her child for adoption. An adoptee carries the feeling that the mother *chose* to end the relationship. It becomes a personal thing – 'my mother didn't want me – because . . .' and in trying to work out the truth for themselves, many blame themselves: that they weren't good enough, cute enough or loveable enough. They doubt and lose the sense of their own value as a person.

For a mother, there may come a time when she has to reassure her child he or she *was* loved and *was* wanted. How can you not love a being who is such an intrinsic part of you? Who grew within you for so many months, who moved within you and communicated with you in the secret language that takes place between a mother and her unborn child?

The cutting of the umbilical cord and the removal of the baby is the primal wound, a rending of the bond between mother and child that no manner of reconciliation can ever hope to mend. In its place is born pain, a pain like that of childbirth. It will recede but never leave, and with each trigger the pain will return – and the memory of the pain will pass from one generation to the next.

•

From time to time I still wonder why I wasn't sent to a home. Was it because we weren't regular churchgoers and fell outside the circle of influence of the ministry? Or did Mum still have memories of her time in an institution, and enough unspoken empathy to spare me the same experience? Or was she too ill, and too distant, to make any decisions on my behalf? Or, was it a selfish desire to keep me close, to ensure I was on hand to look after her?

Did Steve keep his counsel out of respect for Mum or because it was outside his authority, given he was my brother, not my father? Or, had Colin and I made our point strongly enough that we convinced the decisionmakers we intended to become a married family? If that was true, why was no one demanding we tie the knot with all haste?

Perhaps it was much simpler. Proverbially, I had made my own bed, and now it was my responsibility to lie in it. Everyone else held off and left me to work it out for myself.

•

Jason was born in a last-minute burst of instructions from the hospital's resident medical doctor who had been called about fifteen minutes earlier when trouble was looming.

'Grab him under the chin and pull him out.'

'No chin!' was the panicked response from the midwife groping around my no-longer-private parts.

'Then under the arm. *Pull him out.*'

My baby was born blue with the cord wrapped around his neck. The midwives whisked him to a little crib and clamped on a tiny oxygen mask before I had a chance to touch him. Waiting to hear your baby breathing independently is one of the most tense moments of your life. I lay there terrified that after all our struggles we were to fail at the last hurdle. It may have been less than a minute, and yet it seemed such a long, long minute.

When he was stable, the doctor placed Jason on my chest, his warm body under the loose wrap still gooey and bloody, slippery and new. I shucked aside the shoulder of my gown, and gently wrapped my arms around him, pressing him close, feeling his skin against mine, his little hands opening and closing on my chest and his face nuzzling into my neck.

The doctor stared down at us for a while, sharing in the quiet companionship of our first moments together.

'Well, he's certainly not overdue,' his gentle voice broke our reverie.

'How can you tell?'

'Good skin, that one. No peeling or redness. In fact, look, he even still has down on his body.'

I pored over every feature of my newborn. He had taken on a healthy pink colour, right to the extremities of each perfectly formed finger and toe. His thick, dark hair was still matted. Long and lean, a healthy baby, just over three and a half kilos. I cradled him gently. I can't describe the feeling, the overwhelming rush of tenderness that overcame me. Jason squirmed to look up to me, his unfocused eyes opening and closing towards my face.

'Oh! He's got blue eyes. I thought they'd be brown.'

'Silly girl,' replied the doctor, laughing, '*all* babies are born with blue eyes.'

That was the first of many things I had yet to learn about babies and motherhood, but none of it mattered in that moment.

29

Our baby was born on 4 July at 9.06 pm, but Colin's visit had to wait until normal visiting hours the next day because he had no rights; he was the father, but he was not my husband. As far as the law was concerned, bastard children *have* no father. He had spent an anxious evening at the Coddingtons – our Guildford neighbours with telephone contact – and now they arrived as a group, Colin, Mum, Mrs Coddington and my former school friend Doreen.

'You look radiant!' exclaimed Doreen. She looked amazed, 'I expected to see you washed out and exhausted.'

I *felt* radiant, elated and uplifted – euphoric, even. I had lain awake on a high until just before dawn, reliving the experience and marvelling at the magic of bringing new life into the world. I woke from a light doze when Jason was brought in to try his first feed. The joy of his birth had exhilarated me, enlivening my thoughts and senses, and making every part of my body tingle with memory. Even being born on American Independence Day seemed significant in my mind, and my thoughts were darting from place to place, going over and over each moment of the last twenty-four hours.

Healthy mothers and babies with no birth complications had the option to go to the annexe, an historic pre-Federation two-storey house where babies stayed with their mothers full-time in a home-like environment, an innovative concept in post-natal care then. It seemed my delivery wasn't routine enough, though, so Jason was taken to the nursery shortly after birth and I was sent on to a hospital ward.

The maternity ward was much like the surgical ward at Parramatta Hospital, multi-bedded shared rooms opening off a long corridor. My stretcher trundled along the corridor, passing one doorway after another, until we reached the end, a small room in the bottom corner, just big enough for two beds. It looked as if it had been designed for something else, a storeroom or linen room perhaps, although it contained all the basics of hospital accommodation.

Sometime after midnight another bed was wheeled into the room. Its occupant was unconscious, and stayed that way until well after sunrise.

'Ohhh,' I heard a groan from my companion when she woke up. 'Ohhhhhhh,' she groaned louder this time.

'Are you okay?' I asked.

'Ohhhhhh . . . I'm never doing that again.' It was an agonised cry.

'What happened?'

'Caesarean. Oh my god! The pain. You've got no idea. I've been cut in two.'

Therese and I shared the same birthday, same year. Her daughter had been born just after midnight, and my son a few hours before. Their dates of birth were different, but only by one or two ticks of the clock. We made jokes that our coming together in this way meant they should marry when they grew up. Star-crossed mothers.

Her mother visited later that afternoon. 'Fate has nothing to do with it,' she said bluntly. 'You're here together because neither of you are married. The other women don't want to mix with you.'

Therese's mother was a rough egg, and her youngest was a three-year-old who could swear like a trooper and had obviously learned this from her. A no-nonsense woman who was standing firmly by her daughter, she was indignant for us, but we were both so hardened to society's prejudices by this time that we didn't actually mind at all. We were served our meals after the others and assigned different shower times in the common bathroom. We weren't allowed in the nursery when the married women were tending to their babies. We never met another soul besides hospital staff in the week we stayed there, but every one of those people accepted we were keeping our babies, and that was the important thing.

'If you name the father on the birth certificate and you later marry him, your child will become legitimised.' The social worker was sitting next to my bed helping me complete the birth registration form. She had no way of knowing how intensely I felt about illegitimacy, but then she didn't need to. Everyone knew the impact on a child of being born out of wedlock. 'Of course, you'll have to get the father's signature on the form.'

Not for the first time, I was relieved Colin and I were still together after so many upheavals. Our rollercoaster relationship had threatened to derail many times, our fights could be physical or petulant and sulky and we never had two coins to rub together or any sense or structure to our future. Nevertheless, we had stayed together, despite latent family opposition, despite my doubts and uncertainties, despite society's prejudice, despite it all – or because of it all. I was too emotionally entangled and dependent to discern the difference.

I made sure Colin signed the form that night. He had no objections. It was one more weapon in his armoury. Another item of proof, as if I needed any more, that our destiny was entwined. Any idea I could rise myself above what Colin had to offer was a flight of fancy on my part, and the sooner I accepted that, the sooner we could all get on with being a family. Couldn't I see how thrilled he was to be a father and how he was going to be the best father on earth? Sure, he could make an Olympic sport of being hired and fired – but so what? He always found another job, didn't he? There's no way we'd starve. What did I take him for? A man who didn't want to support his family?

'It's not about what work you do or how much money you have, honey. It's about the love, and I love you more than you'll ever realise. You know that don't you? Don't listen to other people. Just because they think I'm a no-hoper doesn't make me one. I know I've treated you pretty bad at times, honey. I am truly very sorry, you know that, honey, all those horrible things I've said and done – you know I didn't mean any of it. None of that matters now. It won't ever happen again. We're a family now, honey, and we need to stick together. That's what families do, honey. They stick together through thick and thin.'

30

Cousin Esther's bassinet had served her three babies well, and she was glad to lend it to me. I often set it up on the enclosed veranda when the day was at its warmest. The worst of winter had passed, and the air outside was fresh and clear. I would swaddle Jason in his checked bunny rug, with only his head peeking out, crowned in soft, dark hair. I would stroke his face and marvel at this beautiful being, tracing my finger against the soft skin of his cheek, and the tip-tilt of his nose, before tucking him in and draping a net over the bassinet. He would sleep peacefully until the next feed.

Aunty Myra came down from Tascott to help. On the first day of her stay she watched me wring the nappies from the bucket where they'd been soaking in disinfectant. I dropped them into the washing machine, into the water I had heated earlier. 'Is that it?' she asked. I nodded.

'Gwenny-love. Use the copper.' She pointed to it in the corner of the laundry. 'You need to boil them good and proper. If Jason gets an infection, he could be dead within a month.'

I didn't want to listen. How could she suggest I would kill my baby? 'I'm doing what they told me in hospital,' I said, my voice sullen. 'Things have changed since your time.'

Aunty Myra bit her tongue. She had come to help. She knew Mum had nothing to offer. Occasionally Mum would show passing interest in Jason, but I was always jumpy when she lifted him from the bassinet, scared she might drop him. She was so awkward with him that it was hard to believe she had two children of her own. She didn't make the effort very often. Sometimes she would stop by his bassinet and look down at him sleeping. Most of the time, though, she stayed in her room and slept herself.

Soon Aunty Myra started voicing her concern about Colin again. The more my family criticised him, though, the more I felt bound to stand up for him. It was as if they were calling my judgment into question, and I needed to defend my choices, as well as defend Colin. It was a matter of loyalty.

'What will you do when the money stops?' Aunty Myra quizzed me. She knew the government had given me a pension for six weeks.

'Colin will get work soon,' I told her brusquely.

'Perhaps, Gwenny, if you went to work too, the two of you could get on your feet?'

'Are you joking?' I turned on her. 'My place is with my baby.'

Aunty Myra bit her tongue again. She wanted to help, but I didn't give her a chance. She returned to Tascott after a few days.

Cousin Esther also lent me a baby bath, which fitted into the stand for the bassinet. I bathed Jason lovingly every morning, encircling his neck and head with one arm and rubbing lotion on his skin with my free hand, splashing the water over him and swishing a face washer around. Then I'd lay him back and let the water drift through his hair as I swayed him gently from side to side. He delighted in the feeling, gurgling and lifting his knees up to his chin and down again. Water splashed around, but there was never much in there and the tub was deep enough so it didn't slosh on the floor. One day I found

Mum giving him a bath, and when I walked into the room she looked guilty and dropped him. Jason slid under the water. I grabbed him and lifted him out, my heart thumping in fright. He was crying from the shock, maybe more because I grabbed him than because Mum had let him slip, but that didn't stop me turning angrily on her. Fear was in her face, too, whether because she understood what had nearly happened or because I had frightened her, I don't know, but it was the last time she touched him. From day one, she never nursed Jason or changed a nappy, but then I didn't ask for her help either. There was never an expectation on my part that her help would be on offer. I was convinced Mum was incapable of caring for a baby; she was so often distracted, in her own world and withdrawn.

To begin with I had plenty of milk and Jason fed every four hours, even more at times, but I wasn't comfortable and he seemed to be hungry and colicky. I found breastfeeding agony. I had to swap sides every few minutes as I couldn't stand the excruciating tickling sensation. I would clench my teeth and force myself to endure it, my body tense. I made constant visits to the baby health clinic in Granville, pushing Jason to the bus stop in the pram which again Cousin Esther had lent me, and when the bus pulled up it was a job to get the pram folded while balancing the baby in my arms. By the time we reached the clinic I'd be frazzled and anxious, but the nurses told me I was doing fine and nothing was wrong. I didn't know what was right and what was wrong. I had to believe what they told me. They were the experts, even if some of them weren't mothers themselves.

I was still anxious about whether he was thriving, and so the clinic nurses agreed to 'test-feed' me. They weighed Jason, then watched as I fed him, and weighed him afterwards. They were satisfied with the result, but they also noticed he was irritable. 'Perhaps your quality is inadequate,' one offered. They told me I could top him up with bottled milk and vitamin drops, just to make sure he was no longer hungry, and showed me how to sterilise the empty bottle in boiling water. I stopped at the chemist shop and used some of my pension money to buy bottles and teats. Jason had no trouble switching between breast and bottle and back again, and finally I was reassured he was getting enough to eat.

Two weeks later Jason was crying his hungry cry, calling for his two am feed. I carried him to Steve's old bedroom, changed his nappy, and settled on the bed for his feed. He nuzzled for a moment, then pulled away impatiently and started crying again. I felt around both breasts. Something was odd; they were slack when they were usually full and straining. Turning on the light, I inspected myself closely. When I pressed against my breasts no milk gushed out; there was barely a dribble. Five-week-old Jason was screaming mightily by then, but I had nothing to offer, for it seemed I had suddenly lost my milk.

There was nothing for it but to prepare a bottle. I was shaken and in a hurry as I boiled the empty bottle in one pan and the milk in another. Jason was screaming frantically now, and his cries rattled my nerves. I strained the milk into the bottle, but it was too hot. I ran it under the cold water tap, but the sound of running water made me want to go to the toilet, which was way down in the backyard. By the time I returned the milk was too cool. I put the filled bottle back into the saucepan and brought the water back to the boil. Within moments the milk was too hot and again I had to run it under the tap. Jason was crying so hard now he was hiccupping and gulping air, and I was feeling flustered and in need of the toilet again. I'd developed this problem since the urine tests in the hospital and now it had come to haunt me. I could feel myself starting to panic. I had to concentrate on Jason's needs; otherwise I would be running up and down the back steps all night, with Jason screaming himself unconscious. Finally, we settled down with the bottle, but my milk never returned, and that was the end of my proud ambition to breastfeed my baby for the first year of his life.

•

Soon afterwards, Colin moved in to the house at Old Guildford. We were breaking another of society's taboos, living together outside of marriage. I didn't know anyone else who dared and I felt very brazen, but went ahead and did it anyway. Mum didn't stop us. She didn't voice her opinion – she had no opinion as far as I was aware. We squashed together in my single bed, with Jason in the bassinet beside us. When Jason slept at night, I slept too, but I heard his breath in every moment of my sleep. If he snuffled or stopped breathing for a moment, I woke immediately, terrified something bad would happen. Colin could sleep through anything. I'd never had a man live with me, so I didn't know whether to be exasperated or grateful.

We liked reading to each other in bed, and the lull of our voices seemed to help Jason sleep contentedly. At other times, though, he was restless and colicky even though I burped and burped him until he fell asleep on my shoulder. I tried putting him on his back and rotating his legs in bicycle movements. 'It doesn't matter which end the wind comes out,' was the advice from the woman who showed me how to do it. It didn't often work, and I felt helpless not knowing how else to comfort my baby when he seemed in so much pain.

Colin never stirred when Jason woke for his two am feed. He could have helped with the nappy, but there seemed little sense in us both being awake. I was never sure what to do about the nappy, whether it should be changed before or after a feed. I decided it must be more comfortable for him to feed in a clean nappy, and yet he regularly dirtied it again before we were finished. I erred on the side of caution, and changed him twice every time. We had been given two dozen nappies as a baby gift, and they were constantly in the wash. I fretted about how long they might last, and how we might afford replacements. Colin was working on and off – he even worked a few weeks at Luna Park, just as I had only two years before – but fatherhood hadn't inspired him to stick at one job.

•

I knew Rachel was still living down the street, with her husband and in-laws. It was just a few doors up from the Nixons, but her Aboriginal family had gone cool on her. They thought she had 'gone white', and were shunning her, so Kulpie said. It seemed to suit Rachel's mother-in-law; it wasn't as if Mrs F would be inviting *them* around to tea anytime soon. I had no idea how Rachel was coping – we hadn't spoken for almost two years.

Jason was about seven weeks old when she came to see me. I had no warning of her visit. I spied her from the kitchen window, pushing her toddler in his pram, leaning hard into it to get him up the hill. When she turned the corner into my street, I imagined she was on her way to the shops, but I moved to another room so I could see where she was going. Her son had shiny blond hair and dusky skin, and he was a solid little chap.

Then I realised she was walking through my front gate. I waited inside until I heard her knock at the door – just to be sure she really would.

'Hello, Gwen,' she said gently, a soft look on her face, 'I've come to make peace.' I went soft too when I looked at her. I couldn't be hard, I was just so glad to have my friend back in my life. I welcomed her in.

'Gwen, I'm so, so, sorry about what happened. I know Mrs F was making trouble. I shouldn't have listened to a word she said.'

'I'm sorry, too,' I said, 'I should have stuck up for you more. And I know I should have come to see you when you had the baby. I was just scared you'd tell me to go to hell.'

'Oh, Gwen. You know my temper. Sometimes the words are out before I know what I'm saying,' I was nodding vigorously. Rachel giggled. 'Boy! I was so *angry* to think you'd been talking about me behind my back . . . but I know now it was Mrs F's doing. She practically confessed as much to me.'

'Did she? Huh. That's something. But, I should have come and explained. Let you hear my side of the story . . . You know, I get so hung up on getting hurt. So damned proud and defensive . . .'

'I wished you'd come.' Her eyes wavered. 'I could have done with you on my side.'

'Oh yeah,' I sighed – I knew exactly what she meant. 'I should have known you'd calmed down by then. God, I'm so sorry, Rachel.'

We looked at each other ruefully. 'Friends again?' I asked tentatively.

'Gwen, we'll always be friends. You know that. But that's why I've come now. I didn't want to go away without telling you that.'

'Go away?'

'Yes, Dave is joining the Air Force. We're being sent interstate for his training.'

'Oh Rachel! How will you manage?'

'I want this, Gwen. I made him enlist. He's been in and out of work and won't stick at anything regular. I'm so sick of it all. He doesn't pull his weight, and Mrs F thinks the sun shines out of him. I'm going to work every day in the factory, and it's hard work, and when I get home, all Mrs F does is tell me how wonderful her son is. She never misses a chance to put me down.'

'You're working in a factory? I thought you wanted to work in a laboratory?'

'Yes, it's not what we dreamed, is it?'

'But, doesn't it make it easier – living with his parents? Doesn't that help?'

'What? Oh come on, Gwen! You know better than that!' Rachel laughed, 'Oh, Mr F's a sweetie, but he doesn't get a look-in with Mrs F around. That dragon. She's always carping at me, telling me I don't know how to look after my own son. And she pushes me aside. I can hardly get any time to myself with him. Much more of this and he won't even know I'm his mother. No, Gwen, I'm looking forward to getting away from them. Time for Dave to grow up and be a man. Time for us to be our own family.'

A family. That was what Colin was always saying. 'Stop procrastinating, honey. Time for us to be our own family.'

Rachel noticed the thoughtful look on my face. 'What about you, Gwen? How are you coping?'

'Well, okay, I guess. You know Colin's moved in?' Rachel nodded. 'It should work, shouldn't it?' I appealed to her. 'I mean, Colin could work, and Mum still has her pension. We don't pay rent, just buy the groceries. I could look after Jason and Mum both. If Mum gets better, when Jason's older I could get work too.'

'That sounds like a good plan. How is your Mum?'

'Like usual. You know she had another breakdown?' Rachel nodded again. I wiped a hand across my forehead, tried to gather my thoughts. I let out my breath with a long sigh. All I ever seemed to do these days was sigh. I felt under so much pressure, tied up tight, knotted inside. 'Well, it's like before. She keeps to herself mostly. But she's got a bee in her bonnet about my housekeeping. She complains to me whenever Colin is not around. *Then* she's talkative.'

'What about?'

'The food, mainly. You should see how petulant she can get. First she glares, and then she sulks like a child who hasn't got its way.' I sighed again. My voice was a laboured monotone.

'What do you cook?'

'Oh, you know. Casseroles, rissoles – things that can be made from cheap meat. It's the Irish stew that gets her really ratty. Spits at me that I'm serving poor man's food. She wants rump steak back on the menu, but we can't afford it. I've got no idea how she ever managed it, but of course, we never ate fruit and vegetables. She says the problem is that there are two more mouths in the house. She's really starting to harp on that.'

We looked at each other. It was a repeat of our old lament: which of us was worse off? Rachel stayed for a while, we talked about other things over coffee and biscuits, and then she left. Although our paths did not cross again for another ten years, I never felt disconnected from her again.

Colin had moved in to support me, that was the idea, but it suited him also. He and his family had been angry with their father ever since he'd started courting Betty soon after their mother died. When their dad and Betty rushed off to get married only a couple of months later, the family was livid. They thought it was too soon after their mother's death, that the hasty marriage dishonoured her memory, and that Betty did not hold a candle to their mother. I tried to be angry about it too, because I wanted to support Colin in everything, but in truth, it really didn't bother me at all. I was happy his father had someone to share his home and life, and Betty was a nice enough woman. Tougher than Colin's mother, but there was no malice in her. Sometimes it seemed as if she was staring right through me. It was because of her glass eye. It was fixed to the one direction and shone a bright clear blue in artificial light. It was unsettling the first time I met her, but I soon got used to it.

Colin's father decided to re-paint his house, making it fresh and bright for Betty, but his kids grumbled that he never made such an effort for *their* mother and they didn't want to help, so even though he was getting old and his hips were troubling him, he did it all himself.

When we saw how nice it looked, Colin and I thought that we could do the same for Old Guildford. Mum wasn't keen on the idea and Steve thought it was just a trick to get money from her. Steve had been the man in our household for so many years, it was natural for him to continue making decisions on her behalf, and he held her power of attorney. She was not capable of making decisions herself, at least, none that were outside of her routine habits. It was beyond her to envisage how we could paint the house, and Steve didn't trust us to finish the job anyway, so it stayed as run-down and sad as ever. Steve and I were barely communicating by this time, and the ill will between us was palpable. We avoided each other whenever he came to visit Mum, and I never visited him and his wife. They were living kilometres away, so there was no chance that we would bump into each other when we were out and about either.

Sometimes when I think back to those first months of motherhood, I wonder whether I was suffering post-natal depression, until a wiser voice reminds me how the odds were stacked. My weird upbringing had taught me so many survival skills that I didn't realise what a miracle it was that I was coping under those circumstances at all. I actually thought I was meant to be able to manage efficiently. One day, though, just for a moment, I let myself glimpse another world.

Jason was lying on the bed in Steve's old room. He had just had his bath, and I was letting him kick for a while. He liked the freedom and the chance to explore his hands and feet even though he was too young to coordinate them. Through the open window I heard the sound of a girl laughing and squealing. Doreen was racing down her drive with her boyfriend chasing her, both of them dressed as if they were off for a fun day out – looking very young and full of life. I turned away from Jason as I focused on Doreen and her man jumping in his car.

That should be me. It was a stray thought that came unbidden. Carefree youth. No worries or responsibilities, only lots of laughter. That's what seventeen should be. My spirits plummeted. I felt as if the life had drained out of me.

Jason gurgled. I turned back to him. His face was split with a wide toothless grin; as he looked up at me his eyes shone, and his arms and legs waved and kicked like the sails on a windmill. It was as if he had read my thoughts and was saying, 'Look at me – I'm fun too!' My heart filled with warmth. Why would I yearn for anything else in life? I gathered his naked body into my arms, hugging, and laughing, and crying, all at the same time. I was so happy to have this little person to love, and to love me in return.

Meanwhile, Colin was still pushing for us to marry and I supposed that's what we were expected to do. I was meant to be so grateful that he had stood by me, rather than deserting me when he knew I was pregnant. Lots of men did that, but not mine. I could be proud of him. I loved him, I told myself so, and I desperately wanted the legitimacy for Jason. When we talked to Mum about it, she unexpectedly came to life.

'I won't give my permission.'

Where did this sudden resolve come from? She had never talked to me about not marrying, or offered me any alternative. No one had talked to me about an alternative. I didn't know Aunty Myra had wanted to step in, have me and Jason with her, but other family members had scotched that idea. All I knew was that if I lost Colin, I had no way of supporting Jason, and besides, he had the right to have a father. I of all people should understand the impact of growing up without a father. Illegitimate and fatherless. No, not that, not for Jason – not for *my* son. Together we wheedled her around.

'Well, I won't give my permission. Not until Colin has a job.' She was obstinate.

Colin got a job within the week. Inside my head, there was still a niggling doubt. Again the feeling I was being pushed and pulled, my head and my heart in conflict, my loyalties divided. I was being manipulated, but I was too naïve to recognise that.

'He has to hold the job for a month before I will sign the papers,' Mum said, placing a last-minute condition on her agreement.

The next day, Colin came home from work later than usual.

'I went to see the Anglican minister in Parramatta today.'

'What?' He had caught me off-guard.

'Uh-huh. He has a date free next month. He's holding it for us. We need to go see him for an interview tomorrow.'

'But . . .'

'No buts. I've already invited people including my aunt and uncle. They're really happy for us. My uncle is taking the photographs, no charge.'

Colin knew me too well. He knew I lacked the courage to tell his friends and relatives that we had never discussed this, that he had lied when he told them we agreed on the date and I was ecstatic our arrangement was to be official at last. After all, Jason was already more than two months old. We couldn't go on living together forever. People were only tolerating that because everyone expected us to marry. I didn't have the inner strength to lose even more face. I could hardly choose this moment to say, 'Stop! It's a mistake!'

The marriage arrangements were made within the month, gathering me up along with them. I was going through the motions, while wishing there was some way to make it stop, somewhere to run to, someone who would step in and rescue me. Colin borrowed his best man's suit; his best man borrowed someone else's. The best man's sister lent me a dress that she had worn as a bridesmaid: it was a sheath of yellow shantung silk, with matching gloves and an artificial bouquet. I'd stayed in touch with my primary school friend, Lilly Hawkins, and six months earlier, when I'd written that I was pregnant, she'd travelled up from Melbourne to visit me. She was shocked when I told her in the one breath, 'He has been violent towards me and I am marrying him', but she agreed to be my bridesmaid, thinking I would marry during her visit. 'Lilly,' I begged her now. 'Can you come back to Sydney please?'

She turned up with a beautiful silk chiffon-over-satin dress that her mother had paid for. I showed her mine. 'They make curtains out of my material,' I said with disgust.

'Let's swap,' she suggested. We tried, but Lilly was modelling part-time, and it was obvious that my post-baby figure would never fit into her dress. My look said it all, hopeless, haunted.

'Gwen, how do you feel . . . really . . . about all this? Marrying Colin. Is it really what you want?' Lilly asked.

I sighed again. Tried to think. Nothing was going right in my life. It was just one stumble after another. The day I met Colin I was digging in the garden, dreaming of a life filled with passion and happiness. Instead . . . 'Lilly. I'm frightened. I am so, so frightened.'

'Oh Gwen.' We looked at each other helplessly. She was still only sixteen herself – we were both too young to know how to get out of this desperate situation.

Colin's father and Betty hosted the reception at their home, boiling chickens, making salads and buying beer and soft drinks. Everything was done cheaply but it still used up two weeks of our precious income.

The night before, Betty led me to a discreet corner of the loungeroom.

'It's not too late to call it off,' she said quietly.

My heart tipped over. 'But everyone is invited.'

'They can be uninvited. You need to think about this. Only do it if you're really certain this is what you want.'

For a moment I was tempted to reach out, to seize this chance with both hands and let her drag me out of the quagmire that I felt was sucking me under. Then I remembered no one liked this woman. She wasn't part of the family, and couldn't speak on their behalf. My loyalty lay with Colin, and I owed it to Jason to give him a father.

Colin and I married at St John's Anglican Church in Parramatta on 23 September 1972. Colin was nineteen, I was seventeen and our son was twelve weeks old. The church was old, badly lit and with a haunted feel to it, a fitting parallel to my childhood home. For some reason I walked down the aisle with Lilly behind me, and some of the wedding guests mistook her for the bride, but when I stood in my place, a single shaft of daylight slanted towards the altar and the gold shantung dress shone in that beam of sunlight. I was so glad to have Lilly with me. Only a few of my family joined us. Uncle Jack gave me away, and Aunty Nan, Cousin Esther and her daughter were with him, but Mum only came to the reception afterwards. There was no sign of Kulpie or Aunty Myra, and Steve held fast to his decision, and refused to have any part in it.

Later that night, after we had collected Jason from the babysitter and were huddled in the single bed at Old Guildford, there was a tapping on the bedroom window.

'You coming out or what?' It was Colin's mates, Brett and Roy. The night was young and they were still in party mode. So was Colin.

Lilly was sleeping in Steve's old room, and heard him leave. She slipped into my bed and put her arms around me.

'Gwen, are you okay?'

'I think so.'

'It's just . . . when you were standing in front of the minister . . . you suddenly went so pale.'

'Yeah . . .' I felt tears building up. 'I thought I was going to faint.'

'So did I! I've never seen anyone go so white. You looked like a cartoon.' Lilly sounded incredulous. 'I've never seen anything like it. I didn't know what to do. I stood there wondering whether I should step forward and help you, or wait for you to fall.'

We were both crying now. We hugged each other some more.

'And Gwen. The way Colin was standing was weird. God, Gwen, he was so . . . I don't know . . . aggressive. That's it, he seemed hostile. Would he ever hurt you again, do you think? It's just, it seemed so strange.'

I paused, then confessed. 'I'm not sure.' I felt the shock run through Lilly's body. She looked at me, stunned. 'But he says it will never happen again.'

'Ohhhh Gwen . . . Where's he gone now?'

'I don't know . . . to the track maybe.' I felt annoyed, with his mates as well as Colin.

'The track? You mean the racetrack? Why – what for?'

I rolled my eyes and shrugged, hands upturned. 'No idea.' I had no explanation for what was happening to me. I had waited so long for a rescue, but it had never come.

Lilly sat talking with me for hours more, alternately hugging and crying with me until we both slept after Jason's night-time feed.

Dawn was breaking before Colin returned. Lilly was still huddled in the bed with me, trying to console someone whose problem was beyond her comprehension. Her sheltered upbringing hadn't prepared her for my world.

31

After that first time, in Mum's living room, before I fell pregnant, Colin had promised he would never hit me again. It was an empty promise. When did it start again? I can't remember. He didn't hit me when we lived at his father's house, I can be certain of that. He wouldn't have had the nerve to do that in front of him. His father would have flattened him.

He didn't hit me when I was pregnant. We argued often, raised voices and had sulking fits, but never a punch. I can be certain of that. Well, *almost certain*. Maybe a push or a shove – but never a punch. Surely not.

So, did it begin when he moved into Old Guildford? How could that be? In my mother's house, with the chance Steve might find out? No, it couldn't have been then, not when he was enticing me into marriage. Surely not.

No, it didn't start again until after we were married. It didn't start until he was sure I was tied to him, I'm certain of that. Well, *almost certain*. Surely, surely, if he was violent shortly before we married, I would have had the good sense to send him packing. Surely.

But as I've said, love born of insecurity is a twisted passion. Maybe I forgave him.

I cannot be certain exactly when the violence started again . . . only that it did . . . and that I stayed. Each fight was meant to be the last, and there was enough time between fights for me to believe that.

It wasn't as if he battered me. He didn't leave me smashed and crying in a pool of my own blood. It might have been a slap across the face, or a punch to the head or the upper body. Once, twice – maybe three times. Not a nonstop bashing. Enough to shake me up, but not enough to go to hospital. It seemed to take him as much by surprise as it did me. We both knew he had a short fuse. When he lost his temper it was in frustration, not something he planned to do. It was a quirk of his nature. This is what I told myself, anyway.

He begged me to forgive him, and I *did* forgive him.

We loved each other – didn't we?

Love born of insecurity *is* a twisted passion.

It seemed to me that when Colin came into my life it was like being hit by a meteor. In that moment when our paths collided I was flung off my trajectory, and now we were married I found myself in another universe altogether, and anything I had planned for myself was obsolete and forgotten. Every day was a new venture into the unknown, and where it would lead was anybody's guess.

•

I struggled along. We had no money. The pension had finished weeks before and the job Colin had used to secure Mum's signature to the marriage was already lost. When the colours ran in my best dress, the only going-out dress I owned, I shed a few tears of frustration. I had left it soaking and forgotten about it. I was trying so hard to be a good wife, just like Jane Wyatt in *Father Knows Best*. Jane was so fresh and welcoming when her husband came home from a hard day's work, and I modelled myself on her, changing my clothes, putting on makeup and tidying my hair. I overlooked the fact that the TV show was out of date and idealised. I had to use something as a guideline for happy family life. It had been months since I could afford to buy makeup, and I worried about how I'd manage when I ran out; and I hadn't had the money for a hairdresser since our wedding day. My hair was too long and falling in uncontrollable waves. Jane Wyatt made it look so effortless, but for me, my hair was just another anxiety.

Colin liked to have money, but he didn't make the connection between regular work and regular income. He earned in fits and starts, and liked to drip-feed money to the racetrack in the hope of a big win. My little pot of bursary money was long since gone, squandered on a secondhand car, which broke down constantly. Now I was preparing Colin's tax return in the hope of a few dollars' refund. The form didn't have enough space to list all his jobs, and I needed another foolscap page. The problem with changing jobs so often was employers held back the first three days' pay. They said it was insurance in case you weren't suitable. Colin had many jobs that never brought a dollar into the household.

His sister was allocated a brand-new house in the brand-new government housing estate of Mount Druitt. She and her husband and two daughters had been waiting for years, and finally the day had come. Colin and I also had our name down with the Housing Commission, but I didn't hold any hope we'd be offered anything in the near future: we were too far down the list.

We couldn't stay here at Old Guildford, though. Things were bad between Mum and me, and even though Steve and I never spoke anymore I knew he was not keen on us living there. He had wanted me back when Mum came home from hospital, no doubt picturing me caring for her when he left home to get married in May. Then Jason had come along in July, followed by Colin the next month. Steve didn't approve of the package deal and was convinced we were taking advantage of Mum. Colin's behaviour did little to reassure anyone, and Mum was suspicious of both of us, too. Soon we had our marching orders.

We found two rooms in the back of a house owned by a Yugoslav family. I found it harder to keep such a small place clean and tidy, especially with nappies soaking in buckets wherever there was space, but my main regret was we two families were separated by language and custom and hardly mixed at all. I would have liked to know them better, especially the wife, who admired Jason whenever I was about, cooing to him in her own language until he rewarded her with a smile, but she never intruded into our space even though she knew we were often alone. We may have been a 'proper' family now, but Colin still preferred to spend his free time with his mates, especially when a weekend shooting party was on offer.

He had wanted me to learn to shoot, too. He started by getting me to lie in the scrub on my stomach. 'Brace the butt into your shoulder and squeeze the trigger,' he said. The recoil of his .303 nearly blew my shoulder out of its socket and I jerked the barrel upwards, firing aimlessly into the air. 'Squeeze the trigger. *Squeeze.* Let the rifle do the work.' After a few more failed attempts he left me in peace. I had enjoyed our occasional joint trips to the country, and was curious to know how to use a rifle, but I found no joy in killing rabbits and kangaroos, even if he told me we were doing the property owner a favour. Since Jason had been born, I didn't even ask if we could go along on these trips.

•

We'd been married six weeks and it was the first Tuesday of November 1972. Colin returned home beside himself with pride and excitement, scattering notes all over the kitchen table. 'I've *done* it, hon. I've hit the jackpot this time.'

I gathered the notes and counted them. Well over 300 dollars. Enough money to keep us for another six weeks – maybe even two months if we were very careful.

'How?' I wondered if he'd stolen it.

'C'mon, girl. Take that look off your face. I won it on the Cup of course! Whaddya think?'

He'd boxed several runners in the Melbourne Cup and included the outsider Piping Lane. When it won, with Magnifique, Gunsynd and Scotch and Dry following behind, Colin's gambling habit was justified. Much as I hated seeing a portion of our meagre funds handed over to the TAB every week, even I had to admit this time we were in clover. My relief was short-lived.

Not long after, a man from the council turned up suddenly and demanded to inspect the house because a neighbour had complained it was overcrowded. A couple of days later my landlord came to me with a letter he couldn't understand. I had to explain that we were being evicted and he was not to re-let the premises. He was distressed because he needed the money. I was distressed because we had less than two weeks to find somewhere else to live. Neither of us understood what was wrong with the arrangement, and why it should be any business of the neighbour's, but we were powerless to argue with the authorities.

In a twist of fate, however, it seemed the council had done us a favour. We found a one-bedroom flat in half a house going cheaply because it was on a busy six-lane road. Our new home was vast. Our bedroom was at the front, with crumbling French doors leading onto a decaying wooden veranda at the side. The veranda ran the length of the house, and had been enclosed to make a small loungeroom and separate entrance. There was a kitchen–dining room, and a laundry–shower room. I felt as if I'd fallen into the lap of luxury. Everything was easier for me to manage at the new flat. One wall of the kitchen was lined with windows which opened onto the living room, so I could set up Jason's playpen there and keep an eye on him while I cooked, *and* I had an entire kitchen in which to do that, which was practically decadent in my view. It was just as well, as Jason was always hungry. I'd been feeding him rice cereal through his bottle, mixing a few grains in his milk, and then gradually increasing the mix until it looked like a slurry of wet cement. By twenty weeks or so, he was capable of taking food from a spoon, and I fed him vegetable mush. There was little other food in the house. Colin's father helped out by giving us corned beef from the factory where he worked. He 'acquired' it – just the same as he acquired electricity by rewiring directly into the street connection. I shredded the meat into fine fibres and mixed it with the vegetables. My son was being raised on potatoes and stolen corned beef, but I had no pride where his hunger was concerned.

Even though he was on solid food, Jason was still waking for a two am feed. I was exhausted, so I'd taken to going back to bed when he slept after his mid-morning bath and feed. I'd wheel the bassinet into the bedroom and the two of us would lie there in the dappled light cast through the half-closed venetians. I was used to the rhythm of his breathing and my chest rose and fell in time with his, even though every sense was alert to a snuffle or gasp. I could be deeply asleep at the same time as awake to him, and one day I didn't hear the click of the latch of the French door opening. I woke, startled, and found Mum standing at the foot of the bed, staring hard at me.

'What are you doing here?' My voice sounded harsher than I meant it to.

Mum recoiled as if struck. 'I thought it might be nice for us to be together. Have a cup of tea maybe.' She cast her face down, doubtful now. She had walked a long way to visit us. She'd never done it before, or mentioned any interest in a visit. I'd not been interested in visiting her either, and neither of us had a telephone. It had been weeks since we'd last had contact. Yet here she was, standing in my bedroom and looking hurt. I felt ashamed of myself.

'Sorry, Mum. It's just you gave me a fright. Come on then, I'll make you a cuppa.'

Mum glanced at Jason as I showed her the way to the kitchen, but she didn't ask after him. We sat at the table in uncomfortable silence. We had nothing to say to each other. After a while she got up to leave without telling me the purpose of her visit. Perhaps she woke up that morning with a sense of clarity and remembered she had a daughter and a grandson, but if it meant something to her, she had forgotten what it was by the time she arrived at my door.

•

The clinic sisters told me I should break Jason off his two am feed because I was walking around like a zombie and getting muddled in the head, and they were satisfied he was a healthy weight and eating plenty. They said he was waking for a cuddle rather than food and reminded me how long he'd been on solids. They told me to prepare boiled sugar water and give it to him instead of milk. The first night he rejected the bottle and cried until he fell asleep sobbing. The sisters told me to persist. Night after night for two weeks I repeated the routine, and each night he woke a little later until finally he was sleeping through to five am, which I thought was good enough. I may have broken him off an unnecessary feed, but listening to his frantic crying night after night was breaking my heart, and I felt as if I was betraying his trust in me. It felt like treachery, a deliberately deceitful act on my innocent baby. I did my best to make it up by lathering him with affection during the day.

Then I had a visit from a woman from the Child Welfare Department. She didn't explain why we came to her attention, but it couldn't have been good. I wondered who might have reported us. Had we been on her list ever since leaving hospital? That was months ago. Was it someone at the baby clinic? Did they think I was neglecting Jason? They knew his weight was good. They knew he was clean and well dressed. What was I doing wrong? Did they think he woke in the night because I didn't cuddle him enough in the day? If it was not them, then who had dobbed us in to Welfare, and why? Was it the couple who lived in the other half of the house? Did they think I was neglectful? What would they know? They didn't have a child themselves. Besides, they always seemed friendly with me. Or was it because they could hear Colin and me arguing through the thin

Gyprock wall? Maybe she thought we might harm Jason? Or was it one of Colin's relatives, but who? And why? The Welfare woman refused to say, and I never got to the bottom of it.

The woman wandered around the flat with the arrogant manner of one who had a right to be there. It was as if she was hell-bent on finding something wrong. She looked in the cupboards, checked my food, checked the refrigerator. She asked to see Jason, asked me how I bathed him and where he slept.

'Where is his cot?' she demanded.

'No cot,' I replied, 'he sleeps in the bassinet.'

'What! He's too big for that! Look how he's nearly touching each end!'

She left me with a written order to get Jason out of the bassinet, and with a veiled threat of what would happen if I did not.

We hunted the secondhand shops until we found a cheap used cot. It was layered in paint, the most recent coat a pale blue, which the shopkeeper thought would appeal to me. I knew from my time at the hardware store, and by the age of the cot, there was lead in the paint, so I whittled the price down. Colin and I then spent every spare moment stripping back layer after layer of paint – a painstaking job which needed to be cleaned up meticulously for fear of traces of paint stripper getting anywhere near Jason. The stripping was hard, but the sanding was torture. Eventually, I found it easier to wrap the sandpaper around a cake of soap so I could reach into every slat and crevice. The social worker's deadline hung over our heads, until finally we were back to bare wood, sanded as smooth as silk. We passed inspection this time, but I lived in dread of another visit.

Others were kinder. Friends of friends gave me their used baby clothes, most of them in near-new condition. When we left the house, I could be proud my baby was smartly dressed, which is more than I could say for myself. Our budget was so tightly stretched, even the power had been cut off twice. We had taken to going on visits to family members in the afternoon, and lingering until they had no choice but to ask us to stay to dinner. Most times it was mince on the menu, and I knew they must have been cautious spenders too, but I buried my sense of shame and reminded myself that at least Colin's brother kept a regular job. Surely on a manager's wages he could afford an extra meal or two.

Soon it was time for Jason's six-month inoculations. It was a hot December day and I dressed him in a sleeveless cotton top and shorts over his nappy, but even though the outfit was baby blue I knew people would still mistake him for a girl. He was such a beautiful baby, with a full head of auburn wavy hair and merry hazel eyes, and he had a loveable nature, welcoming attention and cuddles from everyone. On the bus to Parramatta he was in fine form, blowing raspberries and gurgling and smiling, keeping the matrons entertained for the twenty-minute ride.

He blabbered happily to the doctor at the health clinic until the moment the needle jabbed into his thigh. Then he fixed me with a look of stunned astonishment and confusion. *How could you let him do that?* it said. Again I had the feeling I had betrayed his trust, even though he reached up to me to be comforted and embraced. He was too stunned and shattered to howl like many of the other babies, and all the way home in the bus he cuddled his arms around my neck and buried his head into the hollow of my collarbone. His body felt soft and chubby and his warmth spread through me. Every so often he heaved one shuddering sigh, as if reliving that moment of assault, and he seemed so vulnerable, so delicate and fragile as he melded himself to me. I felt so protective of him, and so close, as if I was communicating with him, transferring comfort and understanding from my body to his.

Christmas Day arrived. We spent it with Colin's dad and Betty. Jason at twenty-five weeks spent much of the time contentedly perched in his baby bouncer, surveying the world and chortling at whatever took his fancy. The next week ushered in 1973, a new year, new beginnings. I hoped this year things might turn a corner. I was mistaken.

On a Monday morning a few weeks later, the alarm sounded at 6am. I tried to rouse Colin. He shrugged me away, muttered angrily and turned over.

'Come on. You'll be late again.'

'Not going,' he mumbled.

'What do you mean . . . are you sick?' When Colin got a migraine, he couldn't bear any light and vomited incessantly, but he had slept soundly all night.

'No job. Lost it.'

Oh no, not again. Dear God, how were we to keep going in this way? He hadn't had the guts to tell me when he came home from work on Friday. He let me go right through the weekend thinking everything was normal. He watched me wash and iron his work clothes and never said a bloody word.

Colin actually excelled himself on this occasion. He started one job on the Monday and lost it by Wednesday. Then he started another on Friday and lost it within two hours. Eventually I dragged the story out of him.

'So I was hired as a truck driver – right?'

'Yeah, right.'

'So they're moving coal. Small loads, one-tonne stuff. I turn up on the job and the truck's not loaded. I ask what's going on and this arsehole of a boss tells me the first thing I have to do is shovel the coal on the truck.'

'Mmmm?'

'Well, I'm a truck driver, right? I don't load the friggin' trucks. And I told the boss that.'

'What did he say?'

'He told me I load the truck or I don't have a job.'

'What did you do?'

'I punched him out. Hit him fair in the face. Knocked him down an' all.' Colin was grinning now. He was pleased with himself.

He wasn't so pleased when I nagged him to go to the employment office.

'Colin! You know we can't get any dole until you register.'

'What's the point? They'll make us wait six weeks anyway. I'll have another job by then.'

'But Colin, what if you don't? At least if you put the application in, any payment will count from now. Anyway, you can check the job board while you're there.'

In the beginning, Colin used to register as soon as he was out of work. I knew the real reason he resisted now was it was always the same woman on the front counter, and she knew him too well. He was embarrassed to face her.

'Lost your job again?' I could hear her voice sneering at him. 'What happened this time? S'pose the place burnt down?'

We all knew the only way to get the dole immediately was to show it wasn't your fault that you lost your job. Colin was running out of reasons for putting the blame anywhere but on himself. He knew we'd have to wait six weeks this time for sure.

What triggered our next fight? Was it the work, the money, the gambling? Was there a reason? I cannot remember. I can only remember the place – standing outside the shower with my back to him. Naked, one foot uplifted, stepping into the recess. We were yelling at each other. Why? Then the blow to the back of my head, the first one I didn't see coming. I fell forward, smashing against the glass. As I dropped, my forehead caught against the metal surround. Blood flowed from a cut above my eye. Seeing me crumpled at his feet, Colin hunkered down and held me, contrite, apologetic, begging for forgiveness.

When we argued I could never seem to keep my mouth shut. It took so little to spark an argument between us and I always tended to out-talk and out-reason Colin on any subject. I would go on and on, even though I knew when he ran out of words he spoke with his fists, and I knew his vocabulary was limited. I knew it – but I wouldn't learn. I resented being cowed out of speaking my mind because it felt as if I was betraying myself, downplaying my intelligence. I pushed on through the warning signs until it was too late to turn back. I never learned to duck, either. The blow always came sooner and faster than I expected, catching me mid-speech. My pride came before the fall. I should have learned that self-preservation was not cowardice. At the very least, I should have learned to duck sooner and faster.

Maybe we were fighting about his work when he knocked me down in the shower that day. The uncertainty was hard to bear. It wasn't as if he was lazy, or didn't want to support us. He tried his hand at any manner of things, using his charm to go door-to-door selling encyclopaedias, cookware, and other schemes lauded to us as the path to independence. For my part, I sold jewellery on party plans and pushed Jason in the stroller for kilometres around the district selling Avon. Despite all of Colin's best intentions, our financial weakness made us easy prey for pyramid schemers; and despite all the hype and projections of our sponsors, in the end we were cold-canvassing and only earning commission, and were always the poorer for having to outlay for the sales kits.

Colin's friends were constantly coming and going from the flat and every now and then they brought a toy for Jason. His favourite was a cloth teddy with a face on both sides. He would hold the teddy in both hands and chatter to it in a language I couldn't recognise, and whenever he turned it over he did a double-take when he saw the other face. He turned it back and forth in his hands and studied the two faces as if he was trying to analyse why it should be so, and when I came towards him he held it up for me to inspect too. I gathered him and teddy into my lap and we pored over the conundrum together, and when we played peek-a-boo with teddy, Jason laughed and chattered and cuddled us both.

Jason had mastered a look of pathetic helplessness, and when Colin's mates came through the front door he plastered it on his face and held up both arms, appealing for their attention. No one could resist scooping him up and carrying him around the flat as they talked to Colin or shared a coffee with us. I worried whether Jason was developing as he should, because although he rolled over and sat up well, he made no effort to crawl or move himself around. He didn't even hunch on his knees when he rolled on his stomach, although I sat behind him and tried to encourage him over and over. Sometimes I felt as if he would be permanently attached to my hip.

I didn't like to hold Jason while I was cooking, so I'd leave him on a rug in the living room surrounded with toys. He had no trouble reaching and handling them, and had enough control of his arms to fling them wherever he wanted, but he was accustomed to someone bringing them back to him. That was fine when Colin and his mates were around, but it had me on the run when I was home alone.

While busy cooking one day I was counting the toys as they hit the kitchen wall. The last one hit when I was chopping onions and I cursed under my breath. Any moment now Jason would raise up a wail that would persist until I came and gathered the toys back within his reach. I chopped away, willing him to wait a moment, until I realised all was quiet in the adjoining room. My curiosity was piqued and I crossed to the window. Jason was scrambling full pelt around the room, gathering up everything he had just thrown. So! The little man did know how to move. From then on I banned the mates from picking him up until he got the message that I had wised up to his game. I wondered how long it had been since he'd worked out he didn't have to crawl when company was around. This little guy was smarter than the adults who came to visit us.

We were nearing the end of our six month lease when Colin came home and let me know that his mate Brett wanted to leave home and they'd agreed to share a house together. Brett was willing to share the rent fifty-fifty on the condition I did his housekeeping: cleaning, washing, ironing and cooking. It was a generous offer since there were three of us, and the condition was no particular hardship as I was doing this work anyway. Colin and I had been struggling to meet our rent and the move would reduce that burden. It was a tempting proposition I couldn't afford to decline. We found a four-bedroom house in Bankstown, further away from Colin's family than was normal for us, but closer to the brother who'd been feeding us for so long, and the rent was cheap because the house was in a filthy condition.

It had to be thoroughly cleaned before we could move in. The major problem was the linoleum, which was ingrained with years of dirt. Someone told me I could cut through the grime with caustic soda, provided I wore protective gloves and a mask. We made arrangements for Jason for the day, and Colin dropped me and the cleaning gear at the house early in the morning. All day long I was on my knees scrubbing one room after another. I worked methodically, labelling the rooms in my mind. The bedroom on the right of the hallway would be ours; the one on the left would be Jason's. The loungeroom split the house in two. There was a bedroom off it, but it would be better to leave that as a spare room and give Brett the bedroom behind the dining room and kitchen. It was closer to the bathroom and he could come and go at will from the back door. He'd also be furthest away from Jason if he cried in the night, even though he rarely did that now. He still woke in the early hours sometimes, but no longer cried for a feed. He would sit up and talk to his toys until sleep overcame him again. I woke when he woke, but I didn't go into him until he fell asleep, and then I crept in and pulled his covers back over him. I always felt a rush of love and protection as I gazed at his sleeping form, so limp and placid and tiny in the big cot. A wave of emotion rushed through my body like a physical force.

These thoughts and more wove in and out of my head as I re-filled one bucket after another. The day wore on until long shadows were cast through the uncurtained windows. I was coughing from the vapours, the solution stung my eyes and my head felt woozy, and I began to wonder when Colin would return. I was so tired and dizzy I could have just about curled up on the floor and gone to sleep.

Day turned into dusk, dusk merged into night. The street lights came on and there was still no sign of Colin. I began to worry about Jason – had I left enough food, enough nappies? I began to worry about Colin – had there been an accident? I began to worry about me – had I been forgotten? Abandoned?

I left the house unlocked and went in search of a public phone. Colin's father accepted my reverse charge call and arrived an hour or so later to rescue me.

'Never, never do that again,' he told me sternly, 'Don't ever step out the door without money in your pocket again. You hear me, girl?'

I didn't like to tell him there was no money spare for me to have, and I was in shock that Colin had left me to find my own way home. He was angry that I'd called his dad. 'Oh for Chrissake! I just got caught up at Brett's. We had to talk about stuff for the move. Why'd you have to hit the panic button?'

'But Colin, it was dark. Late. I was worried about Jason.'

'Wha' for? He was right with my sister. Probably well and truly asleep. All you had to do was wait.'

'How did I know where you were? You might have had an accident.'

'Oh, you gimme the shits sometimes. Got a bollocking from Dad. Why'd you go and involve him? Jesus – I'm your husband! You should remember that. You're supposed to stick by me. Remember where your loyalty lies.'

From then on, I managed to squirrel away a coin here and there from the housekeeping, and when it was enough for a banknote I hid it away on my person, usually in my shoe. I nicknamed it my 'dump money'. After that experience, I never again left home without my dump money.

The neighbours across the road were a working couple with two young girls, and asked if I would be their babysitter. The girls were sweet and amiable, and the extra money was welcome. The neighbours helped me set up the spare room as a bedroom for the girls, two chubby blonde-haired, blue-eyed toddlers with fat bottoms and perpetually dirty faces. The eldest was out of nappies, but it seemed all her clothes still retained the saggy-baggy shape of where the nappies used to be. She was quite the chatterbox and liked to lead her sister into mischief. Whenever there was silence, trouble followed.

The girls liked nothing more than Vegemite or peanut butter sandwiches for lunch and I had arranged for the bread to be delivered. The baker left it on the front porch around mid-morning. The girls had become alert to the sound of his van.

One day I discovered the two of them sitting on the front porch, the remains of the loaf of bread strewn all around them. They had eaten through the soft middle and left the crusts. Most of the loaf was ruined. They'd been quick about it, catching their moment while I put Jason down for his morning nap.

'What on earth? Girls! What were you thinking? Now there's nothing left for lunch!' I roused on them sternly, perhaps too sternly. Their little faces collapsed into tears, but I still sent them off to their beds in the spare room to think over what they had done.

I opened the door a crack a little later and saw they were curled together on one bed, both asleep. It was a rare moment for all three children to be asleep at the same time and I grabbed the opportunity to do some laundry. Every appliance in the flat was rented except for the twin-tub washing machine, which their parents loaned to me through the week. On Sunday nights it was wheeled across the road to ours, and every Friday night it was wheeled back to theirs, and during the week I did all the girls' washing.

Time passed, the washing was billowing on the line and Jason was awake and playing on the loungeroom floor, and still the girls did not emerge.

I found them both sitting at the end of the bed, arms cuddling each other, and looking forlorn and lost. 'What are you doing here – why didn't you come out?' I was perplexed.

'You said we not getting any lunch and we had to stay here,' came the plaintive reply from the eldest. The girls' bottom lips dropped in unison.

I had to suppress a laugh – I couldn't believe they had taken me so literally. They looked so sad and sorry for themselves. I scooped up the two little mites with a hug and a giggle and rushed to reassure them I had worked out something else for their lunch. They were so ecstatic to know they could eat that day, and I reminded myself not to underestimate how much even the littlest child can absorb.

Then an Arabic neighbour heard I was child-minding and brought me her two-year-old son. He was a fine-looking boy with glossy straight, dark hair that hung almost to his eyes, which were as dark as his hair. She was insistent his only solid food should be boiled eggs and an occasional apple. He was still in nappies too, and the eggs were not kind to them, creating soft, foul-smelling poos that smeared his buttocks. The eldest girl – the only one of my brood who was toilet trained – had started to dirty her pants because she wanted to go back into nappies like all the others. She thought she'd get attention that way and I had to convince her she was the biggest and smartest of the children and had no need of them. The washing line was always full, and I was kept busy trying to account for who owned which nappies, although it was easy to distinguish Jason's, the thinnest of the lot.

The little boy was bored with his diet and was a finicky eater, pushing the chopped boiled eggs from one side of his bowl to the other without tasting them. Some lunchtimes I was hard pressed to get him to even take his bottle. Jason was big enough now for his high chair, and defended his right to feed himself, wasting no time about it, either. He was liable to cadge food off the girls, so I sat them at either end of the table.

Then I discovered if I put the two high chairs together, Jason would reach for the boiled eggs on the other plate. It had a territorial effect on the other boy, so he soon took up his spoon and rammed the eggs into his mouth before Jason could get to them. It wasn't pretty, but it was effective, and I could finish a lunch round in the certain knowledge everyone had had something to eat.

Despite the extra babysitting income, poverty ate away at us, and none of our efforts raised us up from its grip, yet Colin was as nonchalant as ever. Brett and he went more and more often on their shooting trips, and sometimes I suspected there were other girls involved, although I couldn't be certain. It wasn't Colin who dealt with the power being cut off, or who met the bailiff. There was nothing for the man to seize, because we owned nothing of our own, save a few sticks of second-hand furniture gifted to us on their way to the tip. Colin's solution for poverty was the racetrack, and many times when I paid for something by cheque, I later discovered our precious money had disappeared on a sure-fire tip.

•

Jason developed an attachment phobia to me. He started screaming whenever I left the room, even if it was only to make Colin and Brett a coffee. Colin tried to comfort him but Jason squirmed away and screamed harder for me, which Colin took *very* personally. Even though he had not been in the habit of spending time with Jason, Colin had been proud to boast of his son and show him off to friends and family, and to see him go so readily to all around him. He basked in the glory of their praise, but things were changing.

'Oh for Chrissake, take him with you. Brett an' I are talkin' here.' He'd lost patience with a son who rejected his consolation.

Colin was a rough diamond but he did have a kind heart. At least, that is what he showed to the world outside. It was one of the reasons I loved him so much in the first place, before I got to know him. He made friends easily and couldn't care less about their background. Black, white, brindle, able or disabled, Australian or foreign – it was all the same to him, and I was happy about that because it was my nature too. He was a city boy with a calling for the bush, and he had connections all over the place – down south at Jervis Bay, out west at Mudgee and even further west at Parkes. People responded to his happy-go-lucky way and his sense of humour, and if he came across a workmate who was new to the area and alone, like the German fitter and turner or the Moroccan labourer, he invited them to our place for a bit of Aussie working man's comfort and culture. I respected this aspect of his personality.

Once he brought home a real stray, an abandoned Labrador puppy which was too young to be away from the litter. She needed intensive nursing so I rigged up a snug box with cuddly bedding and a ticking clock I hoped she might mistake for her mother's heartbeat, although it didn't stop her whimpering for the first week. We named her Duchess.

Jason took her to his heart, just as Colin hoped he would. He would crawl to her bed and watch me feed her, and when she was stronger the two of them went around everywhere together. After a couple of weeks they worked out how to coordinate, so when I dressed Jason in the morning and put on the socks he despised, the next thing I would see was Jason sticking out his foot for Duchess to grab the toe in her teeth. I couldn't help watching them work it out together, Duchess backing up and Jason jerking his leg back, and in no time at all they had both socks off and Jason could wiggle his toes freely. Duchess would finish off with a thorough licking of each toe, while Jason chortled with laughter.

When I put Jason in his stroller in the backyard to get some fresh air, I left one with a rusk and the other with a bone. A couple of moments later, they had swapped. They wanted to share other food, too, so I had to separate them at meal times.

Jason couldn't say 'Mama' or 'Dada', but he was clearly saying 'Dutheth', and when he called, she came running.

One day, I heard a screech of tyres in the street outside, but it was a few minutes before I realised Duchess had burrowed under the front gate and wandered onto the road. She was breathing her last breath when I found her mangled and bloody body, her eyes already filmy. Such a tiny being, not even twelve weeks old, with her life ebbing away in front of my eyes. I knelt on the bitumen, helpless to know what to do, until a neighbour's husband came to my aid. I couldn't have faced it alone.

How could I explain to a tiny child their best mate was gone? Jason crawled around and around the house looking and calling everywhere for his Duchess. He turned to me for help – the look on his little face appealing for me to explain where she was hiding. It broke my heart to see his confusion, and I felt powerless to comfort him. He was only a ten-month-old baby, but that didn't diminish his sense of loss. We all missed Duchess – Colin was very broken up about it too – but Jason took it the hardest, and I felt devastated for him.

Perhaps it was to distract Jason that shortly after we joined in one of Colin's weekends away. We went to his favourite property, out the back of Lithgow on the road to Mudgee. His friends managed the place, but they didn't live in the big house we passed just after we turned in off the highway. Their house was a four-roomed fibro cottage, with a lean-to for a bathroom, further along the dirt track. Colin wanted to show off his shooting skills to me, so he, Brett and I left the house in the dead of night, rugged up and armed. Jason was snugly asleep, with the manager's wife keeping watch over him.

Soon a kangaroo was outlined in the light of the powerful spotlights mounted on the battered ute's roof. It was off at a distance and I couldn't make it out clearly, but I could see it was erect on its hind legs, ears twitched high and head turned towards us. Colin fired off shot after shot but failed to fell it, even though it must have been struck or it would have bounded away. Brett laughed.

'Leave it, mate, your aim must be off tonight. Plenty more in the bottom paddock.'

Colin swore – he didn't like being laughed at. I could feel the frustration rising in him, but I clamped my mouth shut and decided to stay close to the ute. His temper was flaring, and I thought if I strayed too far it might have been me he got in his sights. Like the time we were out in the paddocks after an argument and I heard the whizz of a bullet closer to my ear than I ever wanted to hear again. He said it was an accident, but I couldn't shake off the memory of it.

In the morning we wandered the paddocks. We came across a fallen tree trunk, its twisted branches crisscrossing horizontally, with one twiggy bough spiralling upwards. It was riddled with .303 bullets. Brett stepped back ten paces and squinted at it. 'That's your 'roo, mate!' He let out a hoot, slapped his hat against his thigh and started to laugh, a deep belly laugh that shook his body.

'No wonder the bloody thing wouldn't fall down!' He could barely catch his breath for the laughter. 'Look how many rounds you pumped into it. Oh God. The guys'll never believe this one!' He was clutching his hat against his ribs, gasping for air.

Brett's laughter was infectious so I started to join in, until I glanced at Colin. He was not laughing, and his face was getting darker by the moment. I stood frozen, too afraid to speak or move – doing nothing to bring his attention my way. This was between him and Brett.

Back in our own home, we were arguing again. We were in the loungeroom, facing off against each other. Behind me, the floor-height sash window was wide open. Colin lashed out with a punch to my face. When he connected, my head jerked back. I felt a sudden lash to my neck and I was knocked backwards. My momentum was fast and I was thrown straight out the open window, falling onto the gravel driveway below. I was badly shaken and bruised, with gravel rash and cuts all over one side of my body. Somewhere in my consciousness, I registered the hitting was becoming more frequent, and more dangerous.

Brett and the neighbours knew Colin hit me, but no one mentioned it. He was always regretful afterwards, and swore it would never happen again. I always believed him, and he always hit me again. It was a cycle of broken trust and fear, and I was being ground down. Nothing of my former life remained: no family, no friends, no education, no books, no letters. I was being swallowed up, consumed. Everything I tried seemed inadequate, and I concluded I was not worthy as wife or mother, and I deserved Colin's wrath – if it were not so, then someone would have put a stop to him slapping me around.

The nights were the worst. When Jason woke in the night I lay in the dark, staring at the ceiling and listening to him chatter to his toys while Colin snuffled beside me. The future seemed so hopeless I wished I could die, and I pondered how to make it happen. I used to think I felt so black it was not possible I would wake in the morning, but every day I did, so now the question was how to hasten my end. Cousin Ron took an overdose; another friend gassed himself in his car. How should I do it? Would it work if I put my head in the oven? Should I do it alone, or take Jason with me? How could I do that to Jason? But if I left him behind, what would happen to him? He was not even a year old. Who would look after him? But what was the alternative? What kind of parents were we? Where were we taking him? Where was *I* taking him?

The thoughts banged around and around in my head and there never seemed to be a solution. When Jason fell asleep I'd go to cover him, and as I stared down at his tiny, vulnerable body, I tried to cling to our invisible connection as if it were a fragile link to sanity.

32

In her Melbourne high school Lilly Hawkins had a long term on-again, off-again relationship with Shane, who was in the year above. When Shane had finished school at the end of the previous year he'd enlisted in the Navy and their relationship ended forever. When Lilly realised the Navy had sent him to Sydney for training, however, and that he was in danger of being alone and lonely, she put us in touch. Colin accepted him, as he did all people, and together with Brett, they went on one or two shooting trips until Shane realised killing furry animals wasn't suited to his temperament. Colin and Brett continued to go away, quite happy to leave Shane to continue visiting *me* in their absence, which he did regularly.

Shane was everything Colin was not. He was tall, well over six feet, and well built in a slim, muscular way, with soft, flaxen hair and close-set, probing eyes that could see into the soul. Moreover, he was highly intelligent, well educated and well read, with a bent for the spiritual aspects of life, and we could talk about all manner of things that were beyond Colin's scant store of knowledge or interest. I didn't recognise that when you are seventeen, lonely and isolated, the line between witty repartee and flirting is non-existent. I basked in his attention and conversation and fell over myself to demonstrate I was someone worthy of his bonhomie. When we were alone the flirting was outrageous; when there were others in the room we confined ourselves to snatching glances that transmitted secret thoughts and signals.

'You could leave him you know.' We were leaning against the kitchen bench, idly chatting over a cup of coffee. 'You *should* leave him.' Shane put it out so casually I didn't take in what he was offering. At first I took it as a rhetorical remark, but it was a subject that once broached had a way of creeping back into the conversation.

'Gwen, you're too good for him. You know that. You deserve something better . . .'

'What are you waiting for? Do you get a kick out of being knocked around?'

'C'mon, Gwen. Wake up. You've married beneath yourself. Get out before he drags you into oblivion.'

Shane was echoing thoughts I had been too loyal or too scared to voice. 'And how am I supposed to manage that?' I countered doubtfully.

'Well, I'll take you, of course. First lot of leave they give me, I'll have you out of here in a flash.'

'Where would I go?'

'I'll get you to Melbourne, explain it to my folks. Or Lilly. I can take you to Lilly. Her parents will back you up. And I'll stand by you. I'll be there to give you support.'

'But I can't leave Jason. What are you thinking?'

Shane looked offended. 'Did I say we'd leave him behind? *Of course* he'll come with us.'

'How will I support him?'

'Get one of those live-in housekeeping jobs. You're doing it now, anyway. Someone with kids who'll let you have Jason as well.'

'What about Colin? He'll tear me apart.'

Shane drew himself up full height. 'Not with me around. He won't dare lay a finger on you.'

I was the damsel in distress, and Shane was the knight in shining armour. He was going to gather us up on his white steed – or purple Monaro to be precise – and snatch us away from the ugly ogre. I could rely on him to protect us from any further harm, and all in the most chivalrous manner. At least, I told myself it would be chivalrous. The idea may have seemed unbelievable at first, but it was taking root.

Shane had brought mental stimulation into my life, and now he was offering me a glimmer of hope for the future. I thought less about suicide and more about how to extract Jason and myself from the marriage.

When I first broached the subject with Colin he raged and blustered, but backed down quickly when he saw I was resolute. Somehow it was easy to stand firm when I felt I had Shane in my corner. Colin then switched from intimidation to reconciliation, enlisting the help of our neighbours across the road, the ones whose daughters I was minding.

We sat with them at their kitchen table as they tried to mediate on his behalf. 'Colin is willing to talk to a doctor about how to control his temper. He might even go to a psychiatrist.' The woman's tone was sympathetic, encouraging.

That gave me a jolt. Colin was full of remorse and self-recrimination after our violent arguments, but he had never suggested he would consider professional help. That just wasn't the way we spoke in our family. I felt a little swayed, thinking guiltily that I should at least give him a chance to prove himself. I wondered who had come up with this idea. Would Colin see it through? And what if I said yes? Shane would have to drift out of my life, and I felt a pang at that thought. And if Shane left, and Colin was lying, then I would surely have lost my only chance at freedom.

'I think we need to separate first. Just a trial separation. When Colin has seen the doctors – I'll come back then,' I knew in my heart I was lying. My head was saying too little, too late, but I didn't have the heart to say that, and one part of me couldn't believe my marriage could end this easily. Now maybe I wasn't so sure myself that I wanted to end it.

I justified myself to her. 'It will be easier for us to see things more clearly if we just have some time apart.'

'Well, if it's just a short separation, then perhaps you should leave Jason behind? After all, you don't know where you're going, and Colin can get in a housekeeper. It's better to keep Jason in his own home – don't you think?' the woman pressed me.

Three pairs of eyes were boring into mine. I had talked myself into a corner this time.

'It's one thing for you to go off who-knows-where, but it's quite another thing to put a baby through that, don't you agree?' She smiled at me as if we were two intelligent women planning a day's outing.

'Shane says he's taking us to his parents' place.'

'And his parents? Have they agreed?'

'They don't know yet.'

'Well then . . .'

'But Colin doesn't even want Jason. Colin! Tell her! You know you said if I go, then he goes too. That you don't want a bar of him.'

Colin looked uncomfortable. 'It was anger. I just said that in anger, honey. Of course I want the little bugger. He's my flesh and blood.'

I looked around helplessly. It was true, Shane and I hadn't made any plans beyond getting in the car and driving to Melbourne. I was so desperate to make a break for freedom, I hadn't wanted to complicate the escape route with details. No one in Melbourne knew of this plan. No one was waiting to take in a woman and her baby.

'I'm going to get a live-in job. Jason will have a home. And he'll be with me. His mother.' I sounded unconvincing even to myself.

'Well, what about he stays with Colin until then. Colin can make arrangements to send Jason down when you have a place ready. You know he can put him on a plane if he pays for the hostess?'

Colin saw this moment to rush into the conversation, turning on the charm and the cheeky grin. 'Anyway, a week or two in Melbourne and you'll probably be glad to get back *here*.'

Everyone laughed, everyone except me. Nonetheless, I let myself be persuaded this was the best idea.

I joked that Colin was so glad to see the back of me, he helped me pack my bag. That's not quite the truth, but he did resign himself to my going, and when I had gathered my clothes and personal possessions, he did sit on the suitcase while I tied it shut. It occurred to me I was leaving my marriage with much less than I had brought into it. Nine months before I had walked in with my bursary money, some small savings, ornaments and keepsakes, some clothes and shoes and makeup – and now everything I owned could fit in one suitcase.

When Colin gave me another chance to change my mind, I comforted him again with the idea it was just a trial separation, and somewhere in my being I was beginning to believe that myself. When it was just Colin and me, face-to-face and calm, I still felt love and connection between us.

The timing of my departure with Shane was ruled by the timetable of the Navy, and as luck would have it, the date turned out to be Jason's first birthday. I changed and dressed him as usual in the morning, and as I lifted him from the cot I held him closely to me, breathing in his sweet smell and savouring our moment of intimacy as if there was no one but us two. He straightened himself in my arms and stared directly into my eyes, each of his little hands patting and cradling my face. It was as if he knew instinctively I was leaving. We cradled like that for a while, foreheads touching – and then it was time for me to go.

The material possessions I had brought into the marriage and lost weren't the issue in the end. When I left the house with twenty dollars and a suitcase, but not my son, I set off a series of events that ultimately led to us both losing custody of our precious child.

33

It was a long, anxious, mixed-up, emotional drive to Melbourne, a fourteen-hour journey we broke with an overnight stop at a motel. When that motel door closed behind us, the flirtation of the previous weeks met with my need for emotional comfort. There are no prizes for guessing what happened next.

If you can do *that*, then your marriage *must* be over, my naïve, unworldly voice spoke to me. I was only eighteen years old. I still imagined love and marriage in a black and white definition of loyalty versus unfaithfulness.

I rang Colin in the morning to check on how Jason had coped through the night. He demanded Shane come to the phone, and although I didn't find out until later, Colin blasted him with a string of abuse, calling him every name under the sun. We didn't need to tell him what we had done the night before. From Colin's point of view, it was enough to see his wife driving off with another man, to know where *that* would lead. Perhaps he hadn't really believed I would carry through with leaving him. Perhaps his calm and cooperation was part of his charm offensive to make me reconsider.

•

Shane's dad was underwhelmed with his son's tale of rescuing the fair maiden. He spoke with controlled anger. 'For a start – she's not a maiden. She's a married woman with a husband and a child and you've done her no favours by interfering. You'll piss off back to the Navy and leave her stranded. What's she supposed to do next? Grow up, Shane. This isn't a game! This is people's lives you're playing with here.'

My heart plummeted. I looked up to Shane as a man of action, my champion, and here was his father making him look like a silly boy. Maybe I had been wrong to have such faith in him. Was he going to leave me high and dry? What would I do then?

Shane saw my stricken look, read the fear and indecision in my eyes. 'Okay.' He addressed his dad, 'We'll book into the motel down the road then. I'll get this sorted.' Then turning to me, he put his arms around me and hugged me. 'Don't worry, Gwen. I'm on top of this.' Shane's dad gave me a hug too. He was infuriated with Shane, but sympathetic with me.

I burst into tears as soon as we were in the car, but at the motel Shane was able to comfort and reassure me. 'Dad's angry with me, Gwen – not you. I could see he likes you. He *will* help – you'll see. When he's calmed down.'

We jumped into the Monaro and drove to the nearby home of Lilly Hawkins, who had introduced me to Shane. I had not told her I was leaving Colin and her parents had no pre-warning I was about to descend on them. It was a huge relief, then, at the end of this long and emotional road, to be taken in by them. I really don't know what I would have done if I had been rejected. I hadn't thought that far ahead. There was no one in my own family I could run to, that was all I knew.

They welcomed me, dragged out a rollaway bed and set it up in

Lilly's room. If behind their bedroom door they whispered about the situation then they spared me their opinions.

The Mornington Peninsula of Victoria in the middle of winter was a misty place, and the house was set low and surrounded by trees and shrubbery. Outside, the morning air was crisp and cold, and the leaves of the trees dripped with moisture. It was peaceful. Any noise was enveloped and swallowed in the damp air, and only the occasional twittering of an unseen bird cut through the shroud. Inside, the house was cosy, with comforting puffs of warmth drifting upwards through the central heating floor grates. For a day or two I gave myself up to the peace, warmth, safety and caring support of a family who had known me since childhood. I had never forgotten it was Mrs Hawkins who guided me through that scary time when a girl becomes a woman.

Their support had its limits, however. They would provide me a temporary breathing space, but it was only until I found my feet, and it did not extend to getting involved in the breakdown of my marriage or how I was to care for my son. I needed work, and the work was to be found closer to the city centre.

I tracked down a job offer in well-heeled Toorak. These people could easily afford to give over a garage to accommodate their live-in housekeeper, and a nanny who came with a young child provided a ready-made playmate for their young son. It helped I was married; they would not have been so open-minded if I had been a single mother.

'I can start the job as soon as my son arrives in Melbourne. It will only take a day or two to organise a flight,' I told the woman confidently. I gave no thought as to how Colin would pay for it. He could borrow the money for all I cared. I rushed to share the good news with him.

'You want him. You come get him.' Colin's words were like a bullet zapping down the line.

'What do you mean?'

'What I said. If you want him with you – you have to come back here and get him yourself.'

'But, Colin. We had an arrangement. Like we talked about.'

'Well it's changed. Me and the little fella are getting on just fine. I'm not stickin' him on any plane.'

Colin had done a 360-degree turnabout in less than a fortnight, going from wanting no part of Jason's care to suddenly forming a paternal attachment. I was shocked to the core of my being. I had not seen this coming. I had naïvely expected that Colin would be so anxious to be done with the responsibility that he would have been impatiently awaiting my call.

I was cornered again. I had no way of getting back to Sydney even if I wanted to, and I wasn't sure I wanted to. Shane was back at his naval base, and I didn't have money for a train or a bus. Even if I did, would I go?

In my mind, if I walked back in that door, I was walking back into my old life. With Shane back in service, I didn't have another escape plan, and Colin would never let him back in my life. I had done my dash with my relatives, or so I thought. I still felt the shame of falling pregnant, and marriage had not erased that. My marriage had only increased the wedge between me and my family. With practically no money to my name and no one outside of Colin's family to turn to, I couldn't imagine where I would go in Sydney if it wasn't back to him.

I was in a quandary – go or stay – what should I do? I *should* go back, and the matter of money shouldn't be the reason to delay. I could hitchhike, couldn't I? Moreover, if I went back, it would have to be to Colin – for where else could Jason and I go? To my mother? Back to the house I had run away from once and been thrown out of the second time? Even if my mother was prepared to have me back, she would expect I had come to look after her. She would collapse at the first sign of trouble, and then Steve would be down on me like a ton of bricks. And there *would* be trouble, there was no doubt about that. She lived too close to Colin's family for comfort. Anywhere in Sydney was too close to Colin, in fact.

What if I hitchhiked back, grabbed Jason, and ran out of the house, ran back to Melbourne to take the job at Toorak? How would I manage that? I would have to stalk the house, waiting for a moment when Colin wasn't there. But if Colin wasn't there, where would Jason be? If he was with Colin's sister or sister-in-law, they would never hand him over to me. And how would I get back to Melbourne? I could hardly hitchhike with a baby. But how else would I get back to Melbourne?

No, I understood what Colin was saying. You come and get him, meant – you walk back in this door and I have you *right* where I want you. He had no intention of letting me walk away with Jason. If I returned to that house, then any hope of getting away again would be gone forever. I had told Colin I wanted a separation, not that I was leaving him for good. He had warned me it was a wild world out there, acting concerned that I was too innocent to appreciate what could happen when I left his protection. If I returned he would smother me with affection, and pat himself on the back that I had run back to him at the first opportunity. Then, bolstered with the confidence that I had tried to leave and had come back with my tail between my legs, little by little he would treat me even more badly. The part of me that said returning to Jason was the best thing I should do was surprised at the reluctance by the part of me that warned against walking back into the marriage.

Just a taste of what a peaceful home life felt like was already building in me a sense of horror at what I had just left. I had claimed a trial separation would give us both some thinking room, and even though I wasn't sincere when I said that, I was quickly discovering the truth of it. I had tasted freedom. I could think, speak and move without the pervasive fear of censure or retribution, and it wasn't until the restriction was lifted that I realised just how repressed I had become. To return would take more courage than it had to leave in the first place.

In the end, practicality won. When I calmed down, I realised Colin was using our son as a pawn to get me back, and if I wanted to avoid that, and to provide for Jason, then I needed a plan. In my rush to grab at the first opportunity to escape my miserable marriage, I had created a situation that was beyond my control to resolve unless I could build up some savings. To do that, I needed a job that went beyond a housekeeping position offering only a roof, food and bus fare, and there was certainly no point in taking the role if Jason wasn't with me.

I rang the Toorak woman and told her I wasn't going to accept her offer, even though I had left her with the impression I would start the next week. Then I set about looking for a clerical job in the city. In the meantime, I was living entirely on the good graces of the Hawkins family; they weren't only housing and feeding me, but paying my fares and expenses as well. My twenty dollars escape money had not gone far.

When Colin realised he had failed to coerce me into returning to Sydney he put Jason into the car and drove him all the way to Melbourne, two long days with an overnight stop. The Hawkinses agreed to him and Jason visiting.

Jason didn't seem to be any the worse for the long drive and was in happy spirits and well dressed. He was keen to share a new toy, a brightly coloured plastic fat roly-poly clown which couldn't be knocked over. We sat together on the floor and he showed me how whenever he pushed it downwards the happy face of the clown bobbed back up again, and every time it sprang up he chortled with glee. When I showed him it was the same for me he was so delighted he started clapping his hands. His joy was contagious, and he immediately won over all who came in contact with him. I had to acknowledge to myself he was being well cared for, even if it hurt me to recognise that. Colin was displaying a bond between them I had never seen before, and Jason seemed to be just as content to be in his company as mine. In his dealings with me, Colin had returned to the person who had wooed me at the outset, and the harsh thoughts and recriminations I had harboured over the last weeks were put aside and forgotten for the time being.

The crunch came the next day.

'So are you coming back with me?'

I shook my head. I couldn't trust myself to speak.

'Well, *he's* not staying.'

'What? I thought that's why you came!' I was genuinely confused. I had been wondering when Colin was going to leave, but it had never crossed my mind he was taking Jason with him.

'What gave you that idea?' Colin snorted out a reply. Any sign of the sweet man seeking my affection dropped away.

It was so sudden and unexpected I didn't know how to think. Would the outcome have been different if I had left the room, consulted with the Hawkinses and asked them to intervene on my behalf? Such calm and collected action belonged to an older, mature woman – a confident one who understood her rights so much better than my confused and downtrodden just-turned-eighteen-year-old self. The only reason I had been able to break away from Colin was because Shane had made himself a hero for a day. Now Shane was back at his naval base congratulating himself on a job well done, and I was facing up to Colin on my own, and I was not on strong ground.

I didn't *think*, I *felt*. Jumbled emotions of fear and guilt mixed with a warped impression of where I stood in this crisis. I could only react to what Colin threw at me. I had no well of reason from which to draw a coherent argument. He hadn't lost a job or bounced a cheque – it was me at fault this time. I had left the family home with another man – and I had left my baby behind. I had no moral high ground from which to launch a protest.

Colin didn't intend to leave the house without Jason, and I didn't feel in a position to beg Mr Hawkins to compel him. I was a married woman, and I could hardly bring in an outsider to speak against my husband. That's how my twisted loyalty felt. Besides, why would Mr

Hawkins even *want* to take my part? It had always been his wife who had sheltered and guided me, more so than her husband. For all I knew he was on Colin's side. And what if he did decide to stick up for me? Colin was just as liable to knock him out for his trouble. The sensation I could bring turmoil into this house of peace filled me with dread.

My choice was to get in the car with Colin and Jason or stay behind alone. If I agreed to go – then what? Back in Sydney, back in the house – there would be no chance to get away again. There was nowhere to go – no one to turn to.

In this, as in so many other situations involving Colin, I felt alone. I had no money: not a single zack, not a brass razoo. No money, no transport, no friends – certainly no family support. I would return to our rented house in Sydney defeated, and Colin would make the most of knowing I had tried to leave him and failed. The cycle of control and violence masked with care and love would start all over again. There was nowhere to turn, no such thing as a women's shelter, nowhere in Sydney for Jason and me to live while I looked for work, and no way of supporting us in the meantime.

All of this welled up inside me like a mountain of hopelessness. I was incapable of rational thoughts and reasoning – just a deep sense that this was my bleak reality.

Colin knew how to put the boot in and where to hit me at my weakest point. 'I know you shagged him, ya know.'

'What?' I tried to stop the guilt creeping into my face. I failed.

'Donkey Dick. Shane. I got it out of him when you two rang on the way to Melbourne. You can bet I gave him an earful. Hope it was *worth* it.'

'What do you mean?' I felt shame and panic. Colin was right. I *had* slept with Shane. I hadn't planned to – but I had. More than once since I'd left Sydney. But Shane hadn't told me Colin knew.

'Whaddya think I mean?' he exploded at me now, 'you're a friggin' adulteress! You should be bloody happy I'm even *prepared* to take you back. So quit stuffing around and get in the car.'

If I had any resolve, it was in shreds now. I pleaded, 'Colin, please. Please. Why would you want me now? Please, I am begging you. Just leave Jason here.'

'Well, you're whistling Dixie if you think that's goin' to happen. The law's on my side, you know. You walked out on me and you screwed another guy. Now *you're* screwed. Adultery! You think any court will give you custody? No way!'

When Colin left an hour later, he loaded Jason into the car, just as he had threatened to do. Back in control, he could afford to soften. He wound down the window. 'I'll still take you back. You know how much I love you. Give yourself a week or two here. Then you'll be missing us so much you'll be panting to come back.'

I should have laughed in his face. I should have screamed at him: 'In your dreams! The next time you see my face, we'll be in court. Don't think you can get away with this!'

But I didn't. I just stood shocked into silence as I watched him drive away with Jason. Labelled again as a slut and a sinner, not worthy to be called a mother. Marriage had not relieved me of that burden. Not one jot. If anything, it had only added to the low esteem in which society held me.

It was no idle threat Colin had made. This was a time in Australian society when it was still possible for a woman who had committed adultery to lose custody of her children. Deserting the child and husband only added fuel to the fire. It didn't matter that the husband may have driven the wife to it. A woman was expected to make a go of the marriage for the sake of her children, regardless of whether her husband was violent and a gambler.

34

I got a job in Melbourne's central business district, at the head office of Roger David's menswear, as a key punch operator inputting sales dockets onto reels of white tape. At the end of the day, each reel looked as if it was encrypted with Braille, and boiler-suited men carried them off to The Computer in dustproof bags.

Shane's dad, a builder, cajoled his English labourer into letting me sleep on the day–night couch of the tiny one-bedroom flat he shared with his wife. It was snug, but I didn't have much. All my things fitted on one shelf of the linen closet.

I hoped training would be my ticket to a better paying job, so I enrolled in a receptionist course and negotiated with the college to pay their course fee in instalments.

So, I had a job, a shelter and a chance to improve my skills. Little by little my 'plan' was taking shape, but on my current pay packet, financial independence and sole parenthood was still all a distant dream.

It was a pitiful amount of money. It wasn't even what I'd earnt at Luna Park in my school holidays. Forty dollars less tax – two-thirds of the average basic clerical wage – the standard discount for a female in the days before so-called equal pay.

'I spend more than that on alcohol,' Shane's father laughed when I showed him my first payslip.

Yeah, well, bully for you, I thought as I mentally totted up rent, food, fares and expenses and realised I would struggle to find a fiver a week to put away for savings. Someone had advised me single young ladies should be able to save a third of their weekly earnings, inferring if that weren't the case, they were spending too much on clothes and frivolities. Well – he wasn't living in my world, and I wasn't living under his roof.

A few days into the job, as I was concentrating on punching sales dockets, another clerk came up to me, a large brown envelope and a sheet of paper in hand.

'I need your stake,' she said as she shook the envelope at me.

'Pardon?'

'The footy. A dollar a week.'

'Ahh . . . footy?'

'Oh God,' she rolled her eyes, 'don't you play footy over the border? It's a dollar a week and you get it back if your team wins.'

'Oh . . . ah. I see. Betting. Yes, well, ahhh . . . thanks for asking me. I'm not, ah . . . well, umm . . . I don't follow footy, you see. So I'll give it a miss then, okay? But really – thanks for asking me,' I tried to look earnest and grateful.

She looked at me blankly, then blinked. 'Jesussss Christ! It's not a choice! If you work here, you go in the sweep. Just give me your dollar and I'll tell you when you win.'

Melbournians were footy fanatics, I discovered. Sports mad, in fact, happy to brace themselves against the cold Victorian winter, get out to a stadium, and scream their heads off while waving brightly coloured scarves in other people's faces. Personally, I preferred the lure of the cosy wine bars and cafes tucked into intimate alleys, but I couldn't afford that. I couldn't even afford the local food specialty

– fat sugared doughnuts bursting with jam. I certainly couldn't afford the dollar a week for the footy tipping, but I meekly handed it over every Monday when the envelope was shaken my way, even though my team – whoever that was – never won a game.

My job required speed, accuracy and concentration. My colleagues, all females, weren't interested in making friends with an outsider, and even if they had been, I couldn't afford to go out with them. My financial worries had increased. I was in need of expensive dental care, so now I was paying out for private health cover in addition to my other expenses.

I thought I was in the kind of job where I could fly under the radar and keep my head down; however, I was only a month in when I got into a passionate verbal argument with the senior girl. Under the lashing of her taunting tongue, I found myself reacting in precisely the same way I had been conditioned into with Colin – I slapped her full across the face. I couldn't believe what I'd done. I returned home that evening horrified with myself. All night I tossed and turned, eaten with anxiety about what the next day would bring. I didn't feel that I could return to the workplace. I was so ashamed and in fear of the reaction of both my employer and my colleagues, I felt physically sick. By dawn, reluctantly, I had to face the fact that if I didn't go back to work that day, then I would never be able to return again. Delaying facing the consequences wasn't going to make the situation mend itself.

All the way to work that morning the worry and sickness gnawed away at me, the revulsion at what I had done growing more enormous in my mind as I drew closer to the office. So I was dumbstruck to be greeted by all the girls getting to their feet and giving me a round of applause. One of them shared with me that they didn't think I would have the nerve to return; that I did so earned their respect and support, and also there was admiration for my having faced up to the office bully. That was all very well, but the incident had given my fragile self-respect an awful kick in the pants. I was mortified, and my bravado didn't mean that the girls rushed to make friends with me.

Things were awkward at the flat too. No one was pushing me to move out, but I knew I was an imposition. When my hosts had agreed to take me in, they would have been thinking it was for a week or two. But my wages were so meagre, I was stuck there.

Dragging my feet through the expanse of mist-shrouded Elsternwick Park every weekday morning on the way to the station, shivering for the lack of a winter coat, my thoughts were often glum. The cold and damp seeped through my body in the weak light of early morning. Melbourne in winter seemed a gloomy, miserable place; even the grand old buildings appeared grimy and drab, their imposing mass hiding any faint glimmer of sun. Their grubby facades heightened for me the feeling of dreariness, and emphasised my despair.

I was trudging through the cold, mist-shrouded, damp park and I was trudging through this life too. The future for Jason and me seemed as shrouded in mist as the trees in the park. I missed the feel of him, and the smell and sound. I missed Jason's first steps. I missed his first *everything* from twelve to sixteen months.

Telephone calls were difficult to arrange but at least Colin would write to me. Despite all that had gone before, we still thought of ourselves as a couple, separated, but hoping to resolve our difficulties. We wrote regularly, and sometimes I wondered if, after all, I should return. Maybe this time, things would be different.

There are no words to describe how miserable I felt. In one moment of loneliness and self-pity I wrote to Barry. In the eighteen months since our last letters, he'd married and a baby was on the way. 'Gwen,' he wrote. 'I'm a little at a loss as to what to say about Colin, Jason and yourself – you seem pleased that Colin and Jason are together – yet I detect a little sadness – perhaps you would rather have your son with you . . .'

•

It was about three months after our separation when I took a call at work.

'He's broken his collarbone. Fell out of his cot. Nothing serious, but you might want to come up.'

Colin wasn't as bombastic as usual. He was anxious to explain himself, repeating the story several times, explaining Jason had fallen out of his cot during the night. How it turned out the barrier wasn't secured correctly. Colin had a live-in housekeeper now, another woman like me, single with a young child, and it wasn't until the next day either of them realised something was wrong.

'He kept crying and seemed tender. We took him to hospital and turns out it's a broken bone. The doctors have strapped it up. He's pretty shaken up.'

This time I didn't hesitate, but in the course of arranging time off work and begging for an advance on my wages I had to confess the whole story to my boss. He was a youngish man with a modern outlook. I had expected him to sack me after the stoush with my work colleague, but he had actually been supportive. Now, despite his surprise at learning I had a child, he was sympathetic and reassuring. 'Of course you must go!' he said, as he signed the chit for the pay office to lend me the money. Then he helped me arrange the air ticket – three weeks' pay and my first plane flight. I was frightened being in the air, and frightened about what I would find at the destination. An inner voice nagged that the story of a fall was too neat, and I was kicking myself for imagining Jason was safe with Colin. I knew his temper – how could I have imagined it was only me he would hit? How could I have not seen this coming?

My baby boy was a pitiful sight. His shoulders were swathed in a figure-of-eight bandage that wrapped under his armpits and covered half his torso. He was sitting up in his cot when I arrived, motionless and ignoring his toys.

'Mum, Mum, Mum,' he tried to reach out to me, his expression one of appeal and bewilderment, as if he expected I could explain what was happening to him. I scooped him up as gently as possible. He leaned into me and let out a long, shuddering sigh, just as he had when he had been given his needles.

As I cuddled him, I examined him carefully, searching for any signs of violence, but found none. Behind me, the housekeeper was running over the story of what had happened and it was almost word for word what Colin had told me.

Both Colin and the woman were adamant it had been an accident, and nothing looked to be amiss. Everything was much as I had left it, except his cot had been moved to the spare room off the loungeroom. Jason looked well fed, and there were new clothes in a cupboard. He showed no fear of Colin or the woman, and I had to admit there was nothing untoward in him being a little subdued. I knew he had been given painkillers.

I chided myself for being paranoid.

•

It was clear the arrangement between Colin and the woman wasn't one of employer and housekeeper. What I found there was a family unit – mum, dad and two kids. I was hardly in a position to be critical; after all I had triggered the whole thing by running off, and with another man at that. If I was perfectly honest with myself, I recognised this woman and Colin were much better suited; they shared the same interests and way of speaking. They seemed comfortable together. Even more cutting to my sense of self-worth, I had to acknowledge our son was being cared for in a family environment, in living conditions that exceeded anything I was in a position to provide. It was a bitter pill to swallow, that I had been replaced so easily, that my place had been taken so quickly by another woman, not just in Colin's heart but in Jason's life. It was hard to comprehend this feeling of being displaced and on the outer, but I had brought it on myself, and I had to accept that fact.

For the past three years, Colin had been constantly in my life, and I had convinced myself I loved him, and yet it had taken only three months apart for me to regain perspective and realise I didn't love him at all. I didn't hate him, and I still felt connected to him – but I didn't love him. Maybe he had known all along and that's what had driven his erratic behaviour – loving and attentive one day, abusive and dismissive the next. It was only by dominating me, with fear, possessiveness and social isolation wrapped up in charm that he could maintain his hold on me, and once the chain was broken his power evaporated. I thought I should be jealous of the new woman but in truth I was relieved. Perhaps Colin was, too. We could now consider our marriage as finished, and any pretence of a trial separation could be revealed for the sham it always was.

My feelings about Jason were nowhere near as clear-cut. I felt he should be with me, and I wanted him with me, but I had nothing to offer. I was living on a couch for God's sake! How could I even contemplate uprooting him and dragging him off into the unknown? Colin was happy to let me walk out the door and out of his life, but he didn't intend to let Jason go with me. It was the strangest situation. It was only when I got out of the way that Colin had the opportunity to bond with Jason. He may have originally seen him as a pawn with which to win back my affection, but if that had ever been true, it wasn't now. There was no doubting his depth of feeling for his son.

•

I spent a precious few last hours with my son, talking, singing and comforting him, and feeding and dressing him as tenderly as I could manage. I was leaving him again, and it was heartbreaking, yet in my mind it was a temporary necessity. There was no place for me now in this house, and besides, I had told my boss I was only coming for the weekend. I had to get back to my job and work off my advance. If I was a different sort of person I may have left him in the lurch, but that wasn't my way. I couldn't let down his faith in me, and all my possessions were in Melbourne in any case. I was expecting that I would get my life sorted and get my son back with me. I didn't think I was leaving him forever. When I left, though, I left behind a cosy family scene, and I had boarded the flight alone, feeling completely bereft. On the return flight to Melbourne, I was as frightened of flying as I had been on the first, but the anxiety and trepidation I had felt on the outward flight was replaced now by a deep sorrow and sense of loss. My thoughts were a jumble, and I was struggling to make sense of my situation. In going to Melbourne with Shane I had left my marriage, but I was no longer with Shane. Colin had taken another woman into his life, permanently it seemed, although I knew in my heart if I just said the word, he'd dump her and take me back. Did I want that – or – did I want to grab this moment to sever us? Back at the house, it had seemed clear I was relieved to move on from him. Then, sitting alone in the plane without Jason in my arms, I wondered if I had made the wrong decision. On the other hand, if it was definite I was now a free agent, I could spread my wings and make another life for Jason and me. Exactly how was I to do that? I hadn't managed to save anything, I wasn't earning a living wage, and I was still only one step away from homelessness.

'Cheer up!' It was two Navy guys in the next seats. Sea-monkeys – that was Barry's scornful nickname for them, but then there always was friendly rivalry in the forces.

These two, Peter and Gary, *were* monkeys, chattering and jibing, cajoling me into laughter. They were being posted to Melbourne for a stint, and had just had a few days in Sydney with their families. We buddied up, and over the next six weeks, roamed around Melbourne together as if we were the Three Musketeers.

•

'I've got leave. I'm driving up to Sydney next week. How 'bout coming with me?' Peter popped the question as the three of us were driving back from a day out.

'Where would I go?'

'Well, to my place, of course. Mum'll love you. She's on her own. You know, you could stay on when my leave finishes.'

A chance to get back to Sydney. A place to stay. It was manna from heaven. I was making no headway in Melbourne. The emergency plane trip had consumed any savings and left me in debt for weeks. For nearly five months I had been in cold, wet Melbourne and had nothing to show for it. If I returned to Sydney, at least I could see Jason.

'You know,' Peter mused, 'I bet Mum would be all right about having your son with us.'

Again, my boss was supportive when I resigned. 'Yes, it's time you get back and sort your life out. Before this situation gets any worse,' he said.

My life *was* taking an upturn. Peter's mum *did* let me live there, just as he had promised. Doing the housework was a small way to show her my appreciation. The receptionist college arranged to transfer my course to Sydney and I completed it full-time within two weeks. The motel around the corner from Peter's home offered me a job. I was to start in the new year, on wages around double what I had earned in Melbourne, and that meant I could start paying board to Peter's mum. Then I could broach the subject of bringing Jason to live there. True, Colin hadn't actually let me near Jason yet, but as soon as I had the opportunity to bring him for a visit, I was sure she would fall for him straight away. Maybe she would even be his babysitter while I was at work.

Wrong. Wrong, wrong, wrong.

I was to discover that mothers who have brought up their only son single-handedly when their no-good husbands have run off and left them with nothing do not want that twenty-year-old son getting tied up with a separated woman who has a child. His mother's ambitions for Peter were much higher than that, and it was on Christmas Eve when she had had a gutful of grog that she chose to let me know just how little she thought of me. Peter was torn between choosing me or his mother. In the end, our tenuous new relationship was no match.

There was a catfight on a tremendous scale, with spiteful screaming words and clothes and possessions flying through the air. It finished with the front door slamming shut, and me on the wrong side of it.

I perched on my suitcase on the footpath outside the house, crying forlornly. Anyone passing by who noticed me outlined in the feeble light of the streetlamp would have thought me a godforsaken creature. But no one drove along the quiet back street. I wondered where the hell someone goes at eleven pm on Christmas Eve when they have no family and no money. Alone and homeless again.

Not for the first time, I issued up a silent prayer of thanks that Jason wasn't with me. I comforted myself that at least *he* had a roof over his head tonight.

There are times in my life when I can only put my salvation down to an unseen guiding force, and that night was one of them. How I came to be rescued was nothing short of a miracle. Several years before, when I was young and carefree and a regular at the Rivoli Dance Hall in Parramatta, I had met a cute-looking, dark-haired, freckle-faced young man called Alan, shy and newly arrived from the bush. We hit it off in a casual way, never dating, but looking out to dance with each other, until one or the other of us stopped going to the Rivoli and we lost contact.

Much later, on one of his many trucking jobs, Colin introduced me to Alan, the 'boss's son-in-law'. Alan and his wife, Susan, and Colin and I started doing social things together. Alan and I didn't recognise each other immediately – it took a few visits to narrow down why we seemed 'familiar' to each other. We couldn't shake off a sense of *déjà vu*. For my part it was the freckles in the open, smiling face, the caring manner and the last remaining touches of country shyness that triggered my memory. We shared a good laugh when we finally realised the connection.

It didn't take Colin long to lose that job, and I hadn't seen Alan and Sue for two years, but it was their names that came to me now through the fog of my distress.

I carried my case to the phone box at the end of the street. Thank goodness I could recall their surname. I scrabbled through the telephone book.

'Alan,' I cried down the phone, 'Do you remember me?'

One am Christmas morning, Alan and Sue dressed and drove forty minutes to fetch me, no questions, no prevarication. For the next two weeks they sheltered me, taking me into their modest Auburn home and helping me get my life back on track.

Then we drifted apart again. Not for any reason or dispute. Just because that's how angels work. They come into your life, bringing messages of hope in your weakest moments, until you are strong again, and they are called elsewhere.

35

My first impression of the Coogee boarding house was of a two-storey, cement-rendered, run-down building which may have once been a stately home. Its square shape and a turret sticking out of the flat roof gave the impression of a fort. A short, thick-set elderly man with swept-back thinning grey hair and a round, smiling face, answered my ring on the bell. He wore a pair of shorts and a short-sleeved cotton shirt that was buttoned chaotically.

I asked for Charles Bliss. 'As in heavenly bliss,' he'd sung down the phone in a heavy eastern European accent when I'd answered his ad for a room to rent.

'Ah, *ja*, *ja*. I am he. Kom, kom, I show you da room. Dis vay, kom now.'

When he raised his arm I noticed a tattoo at his wrist. *A survivor.* He shuffled in front of me, his slip-on sandals slapping softly against the socks he wore on his feet.

The room was on the ground floor in a back corner of the house – a long, spacious room with a single bed under a window at the far wall. Light poured in through another window onto the desk and chair beneath it. The shared kitchen and bathroom were nearby. The main street of Coogee was minutes away, and the beach was at the end of the road.

If I had to be a piece of driftwood, being buffeted here and there at the whim of the tides of life, then there were worse places than this to wash up. 'I'll take it,' I said, 'can I move in today?'

Charles K Bliss was *mad* in that marvellous, extraordinary way of the exceptionally brilliant and single-minded genius. Born Karl Kasiel Blitz, he was the inventor of a pictorial symbol language called Blissymbolics. I know now he is famous in the world of linguistics – and there has even been a movie made about him – but all I knew then was he was an eccentric survivor of the Holocaust, and my arrival at his house coincided with a time in which I was interested in twentieth-century Jewish history.

One afternoon, Charles was waiting for me, hanging around my door, and hopping from foot to foot. 'Forgiff me, my dear. Forgiff me. Today I haff cause to go to your room and I find all deze books by Jewish authors about Jewish people. You are Jewish – yes?'

His face was a mixture of mute appeal and excitement as he waited for my answer. I was caught off-guard and said the first thing that came in to my mind.

'No. I'm Catholic.'

Charles turned away and stomped off in a huff. He didn't speak to me for a week. For years, I felt guilty that I had offended him. I hadn't stopped to consider the role the Catholic Church had played in the death of the Jewish population of Germany and other European countries. It was only recently another Jewish friend put Charles's reaction into context, explaining that, in those years still so close to the end of the war, any hint there may be a surviving distant relative, or at least, any other Jew with whom they could connect, was a powerful emotional pull for him to reach out to me.

I can understand how he felt. I was struggling to reconnect myself.

I was sitting in my room a couple of weeks later when I heard the rustle of a note being pushed under my door, then Charles's slippers scuffling on the lino, heading away down the hallway. I unfolded the scrap of paper.

'This risky behaviour must stop. A single girl sitting alone in a room with a man is no good. You tell him to leave now. You make yourself get trouble.'

I looked around the room, I was definitely alone. Poor old Charles could get some strange ideas into his head, but I knew what had upset him. The night before I had visited one of the other residents of the boarding house. I had sat in his room for hours, listening dreamily to the sound of his clarinet playing. I sat up so close I could hear his breath travelling through the instrument. He caressed the music, letting it slide through the barrel in a reedy, husky tone, playing just for me, an audience of one. My neighbour was a member of a band with a regular spot at a Kings Cross nightclub. He was a sixty-something distinguished English gentleman who waxed his moustache and wore a bowtie. He was fond of telling me, 'I *love* children, but unfortunately I can't *bear* them!', then laughing at his own joke, but he didn't know I had a child of my own. Very few people did. Reading the note again, I laughed at the irony of it. Poor Charles, in his ignorance of my true circumstances, thought I had some honour worth saving – although exactly what danger an old homosexual clarinet player offered remained to be explored.

I was living in a decrepit boarding house with a deranged landlord, an ageing 'queen', a passing parade of men of varying ages and depravities and Bib and Bub, the two cockroaches who lived in our shared refrigerator. It was not an environment that would withstand an inspection visit from Child Welfare.

My problem, though, was even more fundamental. Almost from the moment Colin realised I was in Sydney he became transient, moving from place to place and taking Jason with him. There was no chance to sit down calmly and discuss access visits or custody. Nor did either of us seek legal advice – lawyers were a rich person's luxury.

Colin had me at a disadvantage. First I had to find him, and then I had to catch him. Without a telephone or a car or even a driver's licence, reaching across the stretch of Sydney suburbs before Colin scarpered was a challenge. He always seemed to be one step ahead of me.

At least I had a regular income – that was some leverage. The majority of it went on rent, food, transport and expenses, but I was able to squirrel a little away. I had moved into the boarding house in time to start my job as a motel receptionist at the Glensynd Motor Inn in Randwick. It was a haunt for racetrack sharks and underbelly gangsters, but that went over my head. I only knew that on race days, the room with a clear view of the finishing straight must be kept free for the high roller who was banned from the track.

The motel was run by a husband-and-wife team who had a single male friend with a very hot sportscar. I was flattered when he paid me attention. He was in his early thirties, smartly dressed, well spoken, darkly handsome, so suave – so sophisticated! I dared to think I was going to have a relationship with a rich, educated, fine man who would lift my life out of the gutter.

I was too silly and wide-eyed to realise that to him I was just a floozy who might turn into a bit of crumpet on the side. He never took me out in public. He would breeze into the motel at the dinner hour, skim past the reception desk barely acknowledging me, then take the lift to the top floor where he would wine and dine with my employers until my shift finished at around eleven pm. Then he would take me for a burn in his sportscar and show me the late-night lights of Sydney. Before too long he demanded his 'payback'. It was the early hours of the morning, we were sitting with the top down on the convertible, out in the backlands of Sydney's dock area, when he tried to force himself on me. I struggled out of his grasp and pushed him away. He sat back hard and sneered at me. 'Face it, honey – I'm the best thing that *ever happened* to you!'

'Well, at least you got the *tense* right,' I screamed back at him as I scrambled out of the car and slammed the door shut with a loud thunk. It was a damned long and footsore walk home, but at least I had my principles for company.

A couple of weeks later, my manageress came to me. 'We're going to have to let you go.' Oh no. 'But,' she looked at me brightly, 'the Zebra Motel down the road needs a receptionist. I put in a good word for you. Go see them after you finish this shift.'

Thank goodness the Zebra Motel hired me on the spot. My wages were intact, and I wasn't in danger of being homeless again. But I was still no closer to having regular access to Jason. I had no idea why Colin kept us apart. Whether a true paternal bond had developed and Colin was scared I would cut him out, I couldn't be sure. The only thing I knew for certain was that as long as Jason was with Colin, there behind them was a sympathetic woman. A single father with a beautiful young baby who had been abandoned by his evil mother was a magnet for every woman on the hunt. His relationships never lasted long, but Colin had no shortage of women willing to take him in and to indulge his tale of woe. At other times he would leave Jason with close friends and relatives. More than once I heard from them the story that he had left a bottle and a nappy and asked if they could babysit for two hours, only to then disappear for two days.

Once or twice, I managed to see Jason when Colin's dad and Betty had him. It was so tempting to think I could just take him away, but how? I felt I would be uprooting him from anything that looked like a home, taking him away from the family with whom he was familiar, the father to whom he was attached. And how would I care for him? Even if my small savings could stretch to childcare – just who would cope with my shifts? Seven am to three pm, and three pm to eleven pm, back to back, including weekends. Those were the standard hours for motel receptionists.

I felt so helpless, and was at a loss to know how to change my situation. On one side there was Colin – who always seemed to be in control. He earned more money, he could move around Sydney easily, he was usually living with someone who was home during the day, he had a father and a stepmother, two married siblings, and multiple friends – all of whom could step in at short notice.

And on the other side – there was me.

There was a story in all the newspapers of a father who had drowned himself and his baby son in a desperate act of murder–suicide. I was delirious with terror and scrabbling for details. Eventually the names were published – it wasn't Colin and Jason. My relief was indescribable.

The question still remained – so where were they this time?

•

The boarding house was a haven for single transient men, and the only females were Jean and me. Jean served in the British Army. She had two stints in Northern Ireland, and one of those was in the '69 uprising in Ulster. She was not about to take shit from anyone. Jean was a gift from the invisible angel who was hovering at my shoulder – sent to be in my corner in that moment when I was absolutely, conclusively, wretchedly, at the most alone point in my life.

'So where do you think he's at?' Jean asked me.

'Well. I don't know – but – I did have a dream. Maybe you don't go in for that. Just a hunch, really. But I have a feeling he's at Ilford.'

'Where?'

'Country place. Near Mudgee. He knows a bloke out there runs sheep for a Pitt Street farmer. Used to shoot there a lot.'

'He'd take a baby there?'

'Well, the three of us went together once or twice. The manager's married. I dunno. But the dream was pretty clear.'

'So are you going?'

'Well, that's the thing. I don't know how to get there. The train only goes as far as Lithgow.'

'How long by car?'

'About five hours.'

'Well. Seems like I'm driving you then.'

•

When Colin came out to see who was kicking up dust on the long road up to the manager's cottage, he got the shock of his life when he saw me climbing out of the car. Sure enough, he was there with Jason and his latest lady love. An insipid, scrawny woman with lanky blonde hair and a curled-up lip which gave her voice a nasal twang. She was juggling Jason on her hip, and that got my goat good and proper. The manager and his wife had to get involved, and when the dust settled, we arranged to meet back at a motel in Lithgow, which Jean had booked earlier in the day. Jean had rightly anticipated this would be a long trip.

When Colin brought Jason to the motel, the woman came too. All of us spent the afternoon together. The moment was immortalised in a few photos: Jason in Colin's arms in the car park; Colin and I looking down at Jason as he played with a toy truck; the woman and I sitting on my bed, Jason playing between us. What we discussed? Long since forgotten.

When Jean and I checked out the next morning, though, I was still empty-handed.

On a positive note, Jean and I took a lease on a two-bedroom flat in Bondi, and Jean started to teach me how to drive the brand-new Mazda 1300 her father in England had bought for her. I managed to get Jason for the occasional visit. I noticed he had become tentative and withdrawn. Something or someone had taught him to stay quiet and still. When I surrounded him with pot lids as a makeshift toy he didn't move – he made no attempt to reach for them or bang them together. When he abandoned himself to deep sleep, his breathing was wracked with shuddering sobs.

I worried about what we were doing to his psyche. Colin and I were engaged in a war of attrition, trying to wear each other down. We were driven by fear, immaturity and ignorance and Jason was becoming damaged in the process. I chafed at my inability to take control of the situation. I seemed incapable of coming up with a workable solution. I felt futile and useless, utterly at Colin's mercy. Day by day I felt I was becoming more of a stranger to Jason, just one of the multitude of women in his life, and wondered if he would ever bond with me again. I even worried that if I took him away, he might grieve for his father, after all this time.

Letters began to arrive.

'You slack slut.' It was from Colin's latest woman. 'What sort of a woman walks out on her baby? Don't think you'll get custody. You don't have the rite to call yourself a mother. [*sic*] Your just a slag. [*sic*] Get out of our lives. Me and Colin are a family now. Piss off to hell. Your not fit to have a baby. [*sic*]'

I wrote back, haughty and acerbic. 'I regret to note you have not been correctly informed of the circumstances leading to my leaving the family home last year . . . please allow me to elaborate . . .'

Another week, another letter – but already a different woman. Her words were almost the same – Colin must have fed a stock-standard story to these women.

'So you walked out on your baby and shagged another man and now you want to see that baby? You don't have the right to call yourself a mother. Don't think you'll get custody. They don't let sluts raise children. Whore. You never cared about Jason. I'm his mother now. Get out of our lives.'

I wanted to rant and rail against these bitches who claimed my baby as their own, but they were never around long enough.

Jean and I had been flatting together for more than a month and Colin was running out of places to hide, but one week ran into another and I was still no closer to having Jason with me. Almost a year had passed since I left my baby behind, and he was nearing his second birthday. It was so hard to believe I'd survived all that time without him.

36

The next time I found Jason, I found him in an *orphanage*.

Even today, I cannot fathom how it happened. Had I left Colin with the understanding that I didn't want custody of my child? Did Colin think he could just leave Jason there as another type of temporary child-minding? I do have a vague memory of something. Perhaps it was that Colin had left Jason with a temporary carer, and when he failed to return, that carer took Jason to the orphanage. Perhaps I am wrong to think it was Colin. Or perhaps it was Colin who told me *that* version.

My next memory is of the two of us arriving at the orphanage together. We were there to meet with the minister in charge of the institution.

The double-storey home was imposing: solid, with two symmetrical wings running left and right off a central tower. Colin and I stepped through an archway into the gloom of a front portico and rang the bell.

We were led down a long, gloomy hallway and ushered into a room dominated by a sturdy wooden table and chairs. This place was dark and solid, and the people who ran it were serious and stolid, the beacons of establishment and authority. Colin and I had been flying under the radar of Child Welfare for almost a year, playing at being grown-ups and pretending we knew how to parent a child. We were about to be set straight.

'You want the best for your child – surely?' The minister had been speaking for a long time, telling us all the reasons we were unsuitable parents, and why adoption was the best outcome for Jason. He didn't need to do much to convince me. My self-esteem and resilience were at such a low point by then. All my proud ambitions were in tatters, and I had lived up to the dire predictions of all who sought to judge me. They were right all along. It was true that I was a bad mother. I hadn't provided protection and nurturing, and I was way out of my depth in raising my child to be a healthy, happy adult. There were so many women out there who were better than me, of good morals, emotionally developed, and living in secure, loving, happy marriages. The minister had told me this, and much more, as if he could read the thoughts I had been secretly harbouring but had tried so hard to ignore.

Even if I could bring Jason home to the flat Jean and I were renting, how would I manage from there? Sure, I had a job with a living wage, enough to keep me off the street – but it wasn't going to support a growing child or pay for full-time childcare. There was no point in looking to Colin to provide any maintenance – he hadn't been able to support us when we were a family, so he wasn't about to start now. Colin had already told the orphanage he could no longer afford to look after Jason. Somewhere in the telling, I was written out of the picture. The official file stated I 'told my husband I no longer wanted to be married' and left them both when Jason was three months old, and then Colin had struggled to cope on his own ever since, as if there had been no contact from me until this moment. No one asked me for my side of the story. We hadn't even married until Jason was three months old, so what else did they overlook?

Three years earlier, when I had dodged the adoption treadmill, I was so determined I could raise my child. And yet here I was, sitting across the table from this softly spoken man of the cloth finding myself agreeing wholeheartedly I was making a complete hash of it. What he had to say wasn't so much coercion, as persuasion of the strongest kind, a gentle and logical browbeating.

'Adoption is really the best thing for him. Surely you see that?'

'I'm not sure . . .'

'Well, the alternative is that he becomes a state ward.'

'What?'

'He will have a guardianship order placed over him. The state will be responsible for his welfare. Is that what you want for Jason?'

I felt myself drowning in the pull of history. History repeating itself. What type of mother could mine have been if she hadn't spent her young life in an orphanage? Would I have been a better woman if she had been a normal mother? If she had married and I had had a father to guide me? If together they had insisted I stay home and study more? Would that have made me a better person – a better parent?

'Is that what you want for Jason?' the minister repeated.

What I wanted for my son was opportunity. The opportunity to grow to his full potential. It didn't matter to me if Jason grew to be a truck driver or an intellectual – I wanted him to have the room and opportunity to develop into whatever he was happy to be, and as far as his mind and his ambition extended. I didn't want external circumstances outside his control to have the power to impede or frustrate him. I wanted my child to grow wings and spread himself as far as he dared. To feel it was his *birth right* to be whoever he wanted to be – whatever that may be.

What did I have to offer? Only a legacy of insecurity and poverty.

What life might my child forge if he was brought up in a stable family environment, with security of housing, a good education and stimulation of the mind?

What if he became a state ward? Would he spend his life looking back on what person he could have been – if only, if only – he had been born to different parents or in different circumstances?

The minister's argument was a powerful one. It was time to break the chains on an inheritance of poverty and insecurity and allow Jason to make new links in an alternative world of stability and opportunity. The minister didn't mention the option of fostering, or outline any financial assistance that may have been due. History records that the single mother's benefit was introduced in 1973, albeit the recipient had to wait six months before receiving any money. I didn't know about this, and I didn't know anyone who was receiving such a payment. When I look back now, I wonder how I didn't – but the fact remains I *was* unaware: of any rights to assistance and of the existence of any support groups for women in my situation.

I was an eighteen-year-old girl who had reached this stage of adulthood without much guidance. The minister wasn't about to give me the benefit of his. At least, not any that might see me retain custody of Jason as a single mother.

When we stepped away from the table, Colin and I had agreed Jason was to be surrendered for adoption.

37

We were permitted to collect Jason from the orphanage and take him to Scarba House, where he would reside until he was adopted. We were so thoroughly cowed and chastened that they must have known we wouldn't try to run away; our immaturity had led us to this point, and it was useless to thumb our noses at the laws of society any longer. All we'd done was serve as an example of why they were right all along: we did not measure up to what was required of parents, and we'd been selfish to deny our child a better chance in life all this time.

Our mood in the car was sombre. We drove in silence, each absorbed in our thoughts, united in our unspoken grief. Jason rested in my lap, his eyes swinging from Colin's face to mine and back again, as if he had some understanding of the enormity of the moment. He was such a sensitive baby, often alert to the tensions between Colin and me, and he knew there was something wrong. My heart was breaking, but I dared not let him see tears fall.

I felt as if I was Sydney Carton in *A Tale of Two Cities* ascending the gallows, and his words skittered across my mind: *It is a far, far better thing I do than I have ever done.* All the way to Scarba it banged around and around in my head. This is the sacrifice I *must* make for my child. I must die, in order for him to have life and love. It is because I have failed him as a mother.

By agreeing to the adoption I knew I'd lost the opportunity to share myself with Jason – to be his guide in early life. It wouldn't be me preparing him for the world. That role would fall to others who were better equipped to introduce him to its vagaries gently and with loving shelter. They were the ones who had the means to introduce him to a different world, a kinder world, a world higher than any legacy I had for him. I convinced myself I had to stand resolute and see this thing through, even if it was tearing me into pieces. My only gift to my son was to set him free.

At Scarba we were ushered into a formal room at the left of the entrance hall. More dark furniture and a solid desk, and behind the desk, another solid figure of authority, the matron of the home. She made small talk with us as I held Jason in my arms, and then abruptly she reached for him.

'It's better this way. Don't drag it out.'

Jason was taken by surprise and squealed, looking back at us both in fright as she strode from the room and handed him to another staff member.

We were shown the front door.

It was done.

•

Of all the homes in Sydney, Child Welfare allocated Jason to Scarba House in Wellington Street, Bondi. They knew everything there was to know about me, so how could they have chosen this particular place? They knew I lived in Bondi, not even fifteen minutes' walk from Scarba. They knew I worked in Randwick, and they knew Wellington Street lay on the direct route between the two. I passed this point every morning and every night, but I wasn't allowed to visit or have any contact with Jason. Was their cruelty deliberate? The playground was hard up against the fence on Wellington Street – an open, iron fence with a clear view through to the sandpit and play equipment. Jason was frequently there, playing with other children, ignorant of my searching stares. I knew it would sear my heart every time I saw him, so close, and so unreachable, yet I could not make myself look away. I could have chosen a more roundabout route, but I could not bring myself to do that. I was torturing myself, but I was desperate for these last glimpses of my little boy. Try as I might, I found it impossible to turn my eyes away, yet even such a brief glimpse of my beautiful boy cut deep into my soul. My plea to the authorities to choose another home fell on deaf ears. They insisted this was where he would stay while he waited for his new family. I felt as if I was being punished even further.

38

The interview with the adoption agency was officious and probing. The Child Welfare Department allocated its head social worker to our case. She sat behind her desk looking like a stern schoolmistress and addressed us as if we were the naughty children. She and I stalled on the subject of religion. The Almighty had not comforted me with his grace, and I saw education as the way to improve one's lot in life, so I crossed out religion as a requirement of a prospective couple, but she persuaded me to recant. My signature littered pages of documents, and so did Colin's. We had given our official approval to proceed with adoption.

We were shown the door. Colin and I lingered outside the city office building for a moment, unsure what to do next, then, settling on an awkward embrace, walked off in different directions. Now our relationship was definitely at an end.

It was as if the authorities were not satisfied we were brought to this point but had to continue punishing and tormenting us at every turn. We had thirty days to change our minds, but they insisted we were not allowed contact with Jason in that time, even though I told them I could see him in the playground every day.

Then, another branch of the welfare department got its wires crossed. I began to receive child endowment cheques. It was a cruel slap in the face – now I no longer had access to my son, the government was finally prepared to pay me some small amount of money towards his upkeep. No matter how I tried to explain the situation the cheques kept coming, fortnight after fortnight, long after the revocation period had passed. Over the course of several telephone calls my distress turned to anger, anger to abuse – a remote voice on the other end of the line staying calm and disinterested throughout –

'There's no need to swear . . . Please don't swear . . . I can't help you if you keep swearing . . . I'm hanging up now . . .'

I collapsed on the floor of the telephone box in an agony of hurt and frustration and hysteria. My son was gone forever, and in his place was a slip of government paper.

•

I forced myself to be resilient for the thirty days, which was all the more poignant as both our birthdays fell during that time. I relived every moment of the day he was born two years before, just twelve days after my seventeenth birthday. We had been through so much together in that time that I could barely remember having ever been a child myself. I was determined to see this period of revocation through, all the while knowing that once the time expired there was no way either Colin or I would ever regain custody. At the end of the grace period I was in telephone contact with a social worker at Scarba House. What she had to say took my breath away.

'You do know, don't you, that most people only want babies? It's quite possible your son will not be adopted.'

No! I *did not* know this. It had never been my intention that he grow up in institutional care. That was my *greatest fear*.

She went on, 'But as it happens, there is a couple who are very keen. They have taken him out on short excursions and it's going well. He has taken to the husband and their little puppy immediately.'

It was unorthodox for her to be telling me any of this, but I suppose my situation must have challenged her ethical guidelines. Every so often she would accept a call from me and impart a morsel of vague information, or ask some advice of me in return. Mostly it was to clarify his reactions to new situations, places he might be familiar with, had he ever had a dog of his own – and, by the way, would I happen to know the name he was calling this one? 'Duchess,' I said. 'He'll be calling it Duchess.'

'It's all going well; it's very encouraging. They've started to take Jason home on the weekends. He seems to be settling in very quickly . . . The department is very satisfied with the progress. The woman is a bit like an older version of you. Sometimes when she comes to my office and I look up quickly, I mistake her for you for a moment.'

That comforted me. I was still smarting about how easily Jason had taken to his new father, but I had to admit I could hardly expect anything else.

'They are very keen to adopt Jason, but we have arranged for them to foster for two years.'

'What?' I was appalled. None of that was what I had understood or expected. I had been so focused on my inadequacy as a mother, and how every other woman was better than me, that I had never imagined adoptive parents would be anything less than perfect: equipped to give my child everything I couldn't, particularly emotional security. And if fostering to another family had been an option – why hadn't that been tabled as a viable alternative for us?

'Well, that way the Department maintains a level of control over the placement. We can monitor things and if we feel it necessary, we can take Jason back from that family.'

I felt as if my world was spinning out of control. At every turn, my son was being threatened with institutional life. The original sin of my grandmother, passed to my mother, and then to my son through me. All the dysfunction, separation and insecurity in my family's history. Would this chain never break?

As it happened, Jason settled in quickly to his new family, and soon it was no longer proper for me to maintain any contact with the social worker.

'You know,' she said, 'I'm not supposed to be speaking to you at all. You are not supposed to know anything about the other couple, or how he is progressing. You do know that, don't you? It's all supposed to be secret. It's just that, well, your case is a bit unusual, and our chats have been helpful to get Jason settled; but really, well, it's time for you to stop calling now. Time you put it behind you and get on with your own life.'

Right or wrong, better or worse, I had made a decision I was going to have to live with forever. There was no turning back now.

39

We know not what we are born into. Some are born into wealth; some are born into poverty. Some are born to nurturing; some are born to neglect. We know nothing of this in our first moments in the world. What we share in our moment of birth, all of us, is we are all born to the loss of the womb, the haven that has been our sole connection to another living being. In *that* moment of loss begins our search to belong, to be embraced and encircled by an invisible thread which connects us one to the other. But my thread was broken, and I belonged to no one, nowhere.

•

Another motel needed a receptionist and I grabbed the work. I was working for two motels at once, seven days straight week after week, eighty hours each week, but I could not fill the hole, stop the desperate thoughts. Sometimes I sat on Bondi Beach very late at night, listening to the surf creeping closer, staring into the dark distance as the incoming tide lapped higher and higher around my hunched body.

If I could just hold my nerve, a wave would wash me in, and the rip would carry me away . . .

I bought a teddy bear and fantasised I was giving it to Jason, that we were playing with it together.

When I got home from work I drank and drank until I was too confused and woozy to put myself to bed. Jean helped me up the hallway and into my pyjamas. She tucked the blanket around me and absently removed the teddy bear from the pillow, dropping it on the floor.

'No,' I screamed, 'No, don't take him. Don't take my baby! Give me my baby, my baby.' I was crying hysterically, too drunk and distraught to know it wasn't a child. Jean grabbed the teddy bear and pressed it to me. I cuddled and crooned to it until I dropped into a fitful sleep.

I was desperate. Desolate. Grabbing, clutching. I found myself stealing glances at every child in a stroller, or following the path of any curly-headed moppet from across a crowded department store floor.

I was like Jason, trawling the house for his missing 'Dutheth'. I looked for him everywhere, but I knew he was dead to me.

I felt the loss and the longing for my disconnected other so deeply within myself I thought I would go mad.

It was too hard to live in the same city and have no idea where Jason was, to have no right to visit occasionally.

I had to distance myself from this hurt and torment.

The loss and the longing would never leave me.

It was only the distance that would ebb and flow.

•

They told us mothers adoption was the best thing for our child, and the best thing for us. They told us to get on with our lives, to make a new start. They told us it was a second chance for both of us, for both mother and child, that we should be grateful for the opportunity, that we would go on to have other children when the time was right. No one explained that one child cannot replace the loss of another, no matter how many more children might come along. No one explained you may never bring yourself to have another child – for fear of losing that one also. It's too great a risk. No one explained you would carry a hole around inside for the rest of your life, and no one explained that by maintaining secrecy, there would be no opportunity to grieve the loss of your child. No one explained that you would be denied the comfort of a period of mourning, because our children *are not dead* – yet they were meant to be dead to us.

The spectre of our absent, living children would haunt us every day for the rest of our lives – but no one explained that. We were supposed to be able to walk away and forget it had ever happened. It was impossible.

•

Three months after I signed the adoption papers, our lease on the Bondi flat was nearing its end. Jean had been my rock for the past six months, but now she needed to relocate to Melbourne, and I decided to make a new life in Adelaide, far away from wherever I imagined Jason might be living.

I arrived to the dry heat of Adelaide towards the end of October 1974. It was time for me to start a new life, to take on a new identity, just as my mother had done before me. I passed myself off as a young, single girl, travelling around Australia for fun and experience. No one was supposed to guess I'd had a baby that I'd given up for adoption. I had to keep that inside me. There was only one family I confided my truth to, when I discovered their daughter was in the same situation.

It was hard to get a job and my money was running out. 'We don't like you Easterners coming over here, trying to get work,' said one recruiter. 'There's barely enough for our own people.' I finally landed a job as a dental nurse in a one-man surgery. I had no training for the role, but that didn't matter, as long as I took a cut in wages. The positive side was that the two of us were too busy to get drawn into personal conversations, and we rarely took a lunch break. My secret could stay locked away.

I was living at the YWCA temporarily, and when I got the job, I took a lease on a one-bedroom flat, and bought a second-hand FB Holden. I overstretched myself. I became so desperate financially that I swallowed my pride and wrote to my mother for a loan of around a week's wages. She sent me a cheque with a note asking me to repay it within eighteen months. 'So I can send it back to you for your 21st birthday,' she wrote.

I dropped into depression. I was functioning on the outside and hollow on the inside. My letter-writing dropped off. Jean mailed me a stunning writing set. Weeks later she mailed me a Parker pen. Finally she mailed me a note, 'Do you want me to write the letter, too?' She probably thought I was having too much fun to take the time to write. As if.

After a long, lonely year I met a man with whom I went on to have a torrid three-year live-in relationship. Now, I learned what it meant to be a victim of domestic violence. Now I knew what it meant to be left in a pool of blood, to have your head split open, your nose broken. I learned how difficult it was to break away. One time I left him and booked into a pub but he chased me down. Another time I left and went to a girlfriend's house but he chased me there too, and smashed her face and trashed her place for her trouble. I grew so desperate, I tried to drown myself in the bathtub, and one night I locked myself in a wardrobe all night. I huddled in there, frightened and so quiet I was barely breathing, thinking over and over: Thank God I am not dragging Jason through this.

At least I'd been smart enough not to combine our finances. My dental nursing job had finished when my boss sold his business, and I had managed to get a job as a receptionist/telephonist at a customs agency in Port Adelaide – the start of my career in shipping, as it turned out. After a few months, I became a waterfront clerk, looking after importers with particular customs clearance needs. I was the only female attending vessels and wandering around the port. All the others were office-bound, in the typing pool or bookkeeping. It was good money for a young girl, at least double that of dental nursing.

I managed to save in secret. I did lend my boyfriend some money for a car, which he never paid back, but after two years of careful saving I had enough, and I went to Europe, using Jean's mother's house in Kent as a base. Before Jean and I had vacated the flat in Bondi, her mother had flown out from England for a visit. I took to her immediately. Jean was the fourth of her six adult children, and she'd had a lifetime's practice at mothering. 'If you ever come to England you must come and stop with me,' she'd said. I took her at her word. I stayed in Europe for four years. Jean's mum and I got so close, she tried to adopt me, but her solicitor said I was too old. Even today I consider her children my siblings.

It was years later before I realised my choice in men stemmed from my childhood insecurities, exacerbated by the loss of my child. No one offered us mothers counselling. No one acknowledged our grief. We were supposed to forget about it. No one warned us about the trauma we'd feel. Some women became alcoholics. Some women became drug addicts. I became a victim of domestic abuse. When the hospital surgeon was treating my broken nose, he asked me why I stayed with my boyfriend. 'Next question?' I answered. I had no idea myself that my lifestyle was evidence of separation trauma.

The fourth of July was always the worst day of the year. Every birthday, imagining Jason, now three, four, five, six years old. What was he doing? Was he happy? Did he remember us?

At least when I got to England I could confide my distress to Jean's mother. I didn't have to pretend to be someone I was not. When I travelled to the continent, though, I didn't tell people. I played the role of the carefree Aussie backpacker, until finally one night, over a glass of wine in a youth hostel, I found myself confiding in a young man who'd also had a traumatic experience. Once I started to talk with strangers about my child and the adoption, I found relief for my pent-up emotions. There are so many women who still keep their experience a secret. I can only say that for me, the more often I spoke about it, the easier it became to find a place for my feelings, but still I was haunted by the ghost of my baby. Over time though, I built up the feeling that our story was not finished, and that somewhere, somehow, there would come the day our paths would cross. Our thread was broken, and I mourned his loss, yet I couldn't shake the feeling that our connection was not completely severed.

Epilogue

If the first part of my life was about disconnection, then the second has been about reconnection. Despite all, I managed to start a new, happy and comfortable life. I married a good, stable, hardworking man in 1986, when I was in my early thirties. Although Bill and I have no children together, his two from a previous marriage have provided us with four delightful grandchildren, and I imagine we will live to see their children in time. I had a successful career in shipping and logistics, something that suited my analytical and practical nature, and I was able to handle myself in a male-dominated field. I was well respected by my peers, frequently promoted, and highly paid. I achieved all that despite not having a university degree, although I have since obtained a Masters in Electronic Commerce. My large staff even liked my leadership style, and often told me I had the ability to see the world through other people's eyes. Bill and I are retired now to a brand-new apartment on a golf course beside the Pacific Ocean, and his practical household support enables me to spend my time writing.

I'm surrounded by family and friends, and even those who were once lost to me are back in my life: Rachel Nixon, Lilly Hawkins and

Vicki Hall, who all appear in this book. Cousins Esther, Phillip, Pat, Bruce and Chris – they are all in my life, too. Aunty Myra, Uncle Jack, Aunty Nan, Kulpie and Cousin Brian have all passed, but we were reunited long beforehand.

Steve and I settled our differences after some years, drawn together by Mum's deteriorating mental condition, and now we are close. In writing this book, it wasn't possible to document a lot of in-depth detail of my childhood. Some of this would have been about Steve, and the deep kindness and caring he showed towards me in our day-to-day lives back then. If this means he comes across as harsh and controlling in these pages, it wasn't intentional. He is, in fact, a gentle soul, and a good listener. He took care of me, but he was catapulted into the role of father at such a young age when he himself had no male role-model, no counterbalancing male influence. He tried hard. He was burdened with the responsibility of me, without having the experience of knowing how to deal with someone who was such a different personality to him. 'Why are you always so dramatic?' he would say, exasperated at my latest outburst. I was high maintenance, and we were raised in an era when corporal punishment was commonplace, so is it any wonder he imagined physical chastisement would curb my rebellious behaviour? It might be outdated and controversial now, but it was the norm when we were growing up. I know all he ever wanted was the best for me, and it galled him to see my life derailed by Colin.

In early 1982 when I returned from Europe Colin visited me once. He wanted to let me know he was re-marrying. Since then we have gone our separate ways. We went through tough times together when we were young – and we were so *very* young. I know I am older and wiser, and I imagine he is too. I don't bear him ill will. Just as I have gone on to build a happy life for myself, I hope the same for him.

On Mothers Day 1981, aged sixty-one, Mum gave up her struggle with life's reality, and re-entered Rydalmere Psychiatric Hospital. She was kept in the admission ward for some time before being transferred to the secure long stay ward. This signified a change in her treatment – from active rehabilitation back to the community to passive care for her mental disturbance. Mum never lived out of full-time care again. As a consequence of the Richmond Report, which was introduced in New South Wales in 1983 with the aim of de-institutionalisation, Mum was moved to a nursing home. This was the first of three in which she lived over the next thirty-one years. She died in December 2012, shortly after her ninety-third birthday.

There is no denying I felt bitter towards her when I was a teenager. I cannot escape thinking about how her mother and her sister stood by her. This enabled her to keep two children born of two different fathers and raised out of wedlock. Yet she failed to do the same for me. Thankfully, that only occurred to me through this writing, or I might have said some very cruel things to my mother, things I would live to regret saying. At the time, in 1971, I did not relate my mother's unplanned pregnancies to my own. I was too wrapped up in the social stigma of my time, and the fear of illegitimacy for my child. I didn't expect my mother to stand by me in this crisis because my life had been spent shielding her from crisis.

These days, I try to concentrate on what our mother did do for Steve and me, rather than what she did not – or *could* not do. I know I cannot blame my mother for not being able to come to my aid. Mum suffered a strange mixture of bipolar disorder (manic depression) and schizophrenia. I now realise that she spent most of her life debilitated and dominated by a cruel illness that masked her true personality, an illness that eventually consumed her personality entirely. In her autobiography *An Angel at My Table* Janet Frame hit the nail on the head when she referred to mental illness as suffering *a loneliness of the inner soul.*

I cannot name the drugs Mum was prescribed, but I do know they created her zombie-like condition. The drugs of the 1950s and 1960s were a fantastic breakthrough in the treatment of mental illness, but they were crude in comparison to what is available today, although lithium is still popular. These days, mentally ill persons are regularly prescribed selective serotonin re-uptake inhibitors (SSRIs), which means the medication can target specific brain chemicals. I think Mum's drugs were more like a weapon of mass destruction, to use a current analogy.

All I can feel for my mother is compassion, and relief I have not suffered her fate. If there is such a thing as an after-life, I hope for my mother that it is peaceful.

I met my father when I was twenty-five. I went to Italy to look for him, and discovered he was living in Sydney, not so far from where I grew up. He had always known where I was, and had even driven past once, but he explained that he imagined I was having a good life and making himself known would only disrupt it. If only! I didn't let that embitter me or occupy my mind too much, though. Just as Aunty Myra had taught me, I accepted things as they were, and my Dad and I connected well after a settling-in period. He was in his mid-fifties when we met, and used to being the authoritarian in the house, maintaining a serious façade and sheltering his wife and children. It made him seem stern, yet I could always drag a laugh out of him. I'd make a quip and he would go poker-faced. 'C'mon Dad,' I would say, 'you did think that was funny. I can see the corners of your mouth twitching.' Everyone would hold their breath, waiting for him to put me in my place, when sure enough, the smile would broaden, and the eyes twinkle. *Cheeky girl!* I could read in them, but I think it pleased him that I could see beyond his severe exterior. We reached out to each other in a curious and cautious manner, and spent hours at his kitchen table in conversation, just the two of us, with everyone else in bed. I cherished those moments, even if I was never sure where they would lead. He was a very intelligent and dignified man, and our conversations ranged far and wide. Although he never spoke much about his time with Mum, when he did wish to broach a delicate subject, he would lean forward and say conspiratorially: 'I can tell you this,' dropping his voice even lower, 'because you are a *woman of the world*.' Then he would launch into something he considered too risqué for his other daughters to hear, but was in reality quite innocuous.

The first time I met him, I went to an electronics and whitegoods store in Leichhardt, Sydney, which he owned. Dressed formally in a suit and tie, he was short and stocky, with a thick thatch of grey crinkly hair, hazel eyes, thick eyebrows and a nose on the large side. Not as large as mine – but recognisable all the same.

'Come out the back,' he said, 'and we'll have coffee. Do you drink coffee?' he asked as an afterthought.

'Yes, please.'

As he passed the mug to me, he said, 'Tell me what you've been doing these last twenty-five years. You don't mind if I keep one eye on the shop do you? There're thieves everywhere.'

He closed the shop at five pm, and a short time later the security grille rattled.

'Ah! That's your sister, Cynthia. She works at the florist up the road.'

My eighteen-year-old sister burst in, shy and excited at the same time. Dark-olive complexion, curly hair, big brown eyes, full lips and face.

'My!' she said, 'Don't you look like Rosa!'

'Who's Rosa?' I asked.

'Your other sister!' said Cynthia.

I thought I wanted to meet my father as a hello and goodbye, just to place him in my life, understand how much of my personality was his, and how much was my responsibility. Maybe find out if it was he who gave me hairy arms – that sort of thing. But you don't just walk in and out of an Italian family: their concept of kinfolk is wide and encompassing. My dad came as part of a package deal. In addition to my sisters Cynthia and Rosa, I had a new brother, Giancarlo, and a step-mother, Ida. Thirty years later the family has swelled with their descendants, and I still have one foot planted firmly in my Italian family.

I was confused and overwhelmed at first. I was used to thinking of myself as a lone-wolf orphan, and now a simple family picnic could mean thirty people filling up a local park.

Dad had a habit of ringing me every fortnight, and saying 'Do you know how long it's been since you called?' How can a man who has abandoned you manage to put you on a contact guilt trip? I used to complain to colleagues that I didn't know what I was supposed to ring about. It's not that I didn't want to speak to him; it was simply that I had seen him in person recently, and I didn't know what other news I could come up with every fortnight. 'What do families talk to each other about?' I asked them.

I played a role in home-nursing Dad when he was struck down with prostate cancer, and I was a member of the large family group who was at his bedside when he died, thirteen years after we had met. Although it was a heartbreaking moment, everyone present drew comfort in him being able to die in his own home in his own bed, surrounded by family, and we knew it was what he wanted too.

•

There are times when Steve and I muse our lives would have turned out differently if we were raised in another family. Theoretically, this means a form of adoption. However, when we talk about this, we approach it from the perspective of knowing the alternative. Knowing who our mother was, and the kind of life we lived with her, and convincing ourselves that there had to be greener grass on the other side.

There is a sense in my family history that the role of nurturing mother was lost long ago and, once broken, it could never be recovered. I was astonished when I discovered that the last legitimate birth on my maternal side was my great-grandmother in 1854. I was even more astounded when I learned that in 1892 her husband divorced her on the grounds of adultery and she lost custody of her two infant children. When I think how Colin threatened me with the very same thing . . . I have not expanded on the idea of an inherited legacy of disconnection in my book as it's not something I learned of until many years later. It does make one wonder, all the same, whether it's like a silent gene you carry in your bloodline.

Did the inability of my mother to function as a nurturing, guiding force play a role in my inability to be a successful mother – or did the two experiences stand apart? Can a child, starved of affection, ever give true mother-love, or must the circumstances of neglect repeat from one generation to the other? Or does it rest solely with the individual to look to role models outside the family, and – putting aside their personal inadequacies – lavish their children with all the stability and affection they never experienced themselves?

And what of the role of adoption in breaking the chain of insecurity and emotional instability? Does a new identity forge links to another history, stamp out this disruptive gene and create a pathway to a brighter future? Or, does the act of adoption create such insecurity in the adoptee that emotional stability is unachievable?

Certainly, those who were its greatest proponents believed it was beneficial. Until the mid-1970s it was a popular solution to the twin societal problems of single mothers and infertile couples, and a majority of people believed adoption was in the child's best interests. They also believed unwed mothers were undesirable role models, fallen women, lacking moral virtue.

It is well-nigh impossible to explain to any Australian born since the women's movement of the 1970s the dilemma caused by being sixteen, pregnant and unmarried in 1971. Social control of that era was based on a system of shame. To be homosexual, disabled, mentally ill, and even Aboriginal – or for that matter Asian – was a blight on the fabric of society, a barb against the rules and regulations that governed the way Australia saw itself. Being a single mother was way up there at the top of the list, in part because it was so difficult to cover up. I felt as if I had brought shame and degradation upon the whole family. I might joke now that I was only carrying out a fine family tradition, but in 1971 as a sixteen-year-old Australian girl, my situation was no laughing matter.

The system of shaming had miserable results for women, and there were few who envisaged the next few years would bring tumultuous change: social security for single mothers, the outlawing of the term 'illegitimate', the Family Planning Association changing its constitution to allow single women to be given contraception, the establishment of a pre-term abortion clinic, rape crisis centres and women's refuges. No-fault divorce and recognition of de facto relationships also liberated women. These rumblings were the domain of older, university-educated women fighting for the rights of the sisterhood. My working-class girlfriends and I had no idea these changes were in the wings. I could only deal with what I knew at the time. And what I knew was that I was a schoolgirl who was going to have a baby, and I couldn't think of one person in my world – maybe not even Colin – who was going to be happy to hear that news.

When I say something like that to a single mother today, the meaning and significance is lost on them. We are living in a different world today.

A single mother in 1972 wasn't permitted to rejoice in the knowledge that she was bringing a new life into the world, to anticipate the arrival, make plans for the future, daydream about the looks and personality of their connected being.

There's nothing I can do to change what is done. I cannot alter my core act of abandonment. However, through writing about my experience I have come to realise my agreement was obtained through manipulation and withholding of information. Informed consent it was not. I was deprived of legal and financial advice, care, and support, by church and welfare authorities who must have known that the winds of change were blowing through their bastions of moral indignation and righteousness. I was manipulated by the threat of what would happen to my child if I didn't agree to adoption.

I am saddened, not outraged, by this realisation. Whatever their motivation and advice, or lack of it, the fact is – the decision to relinquish my toddler was mine. It's *my* signature on those papers, and I have lived my life bearing responsibility for that action. Even if I had fully understood my rights and options, I may still have agreed to Jason's adoption. My ambition for him ran much higher than what I had to offer. I couldn't envisage the day when I would become an upright, participating member of society, just as deserving of respect as the next person, and just as capable of mothering. Quite the opposite, in fact. I had convinced myself I was not a capable mother. I had proved it to myself. I had tried, and I had made a hash of it.

One of the challenges for me in writing this book is reflecting on why I didn't fight harder to keep Jason. Everything looks so much more achievable in hindsight. Now that I'm financially secure, in a stable thirty-year relationship and with a track record of success in my work life, I have to remind myself that that woman did not exist forty years ago. I was so very young, uneducated, insecure, isolated and unaware of where to turn for help. Even people who might have stepped in, the Hawkins family, for example, were similarly uninformed about what my options were.

In fact, without support, I had few choices at that moment. As well, apart from the very basic consideration of how I was to afford his care, there was the knowledge that Jason's emotional wellbeing was already affected by the instability of his second year of life. It was easy for me to be convinced that I wasn't the best person to raise Jason, that it was in his interests to give him up. I saw myself treading in my mother's footsteps, and I didn't want that path for my child. I believed I was breaking the chain that had led to one family generation after another experiencing deprivation and destitution. In some unspoken, unformed way, that is why I have never had another child.

And, in this case, I do believe the chain was broken.

•

In April 1991, a new act of the New South Wales Parliament came into effect. It opened the lid on adoption secrecy, allowing adoptees who were over the age of eighteen to request their original birth certificate. Relinquishing parents could also request the adoption certificate. At the time the legislation was introduced, Jason was eighteen years old, and I was thirty-five.

Jason and I had a reunion twelve months later. I made the first move, by writing to his parents. Although they were open-minded, helpful, and kind, it was a rocky road to begin with and I wonder now if the approach should always be left to the child. When the parent makes the first move, it can be misinterpreted as an attempt to 'claim back' the child you abandoned when what you are really trying to do is 'reach out' to make yourself available and accountable.

The road to reunion started with an exchange of letters and photographs. Jason had grown into a young man who looked nothing like me apart from big hazel eyes. We could have walked past each other in the street without a second glance. He had a mop of dark curly hair and the thin face of a young man who is yet to flesh out into manhood.

We met on 15 March 1992.

I knew it wasn't going to be an easy get-together. It was certainly no joyous re-uniting and we did not fall into each other's arms like they show in television reconstructions. We were both wary after spending a lifetime protecting ourselves from the hurt and trauma of separation. Both of us were prepared for rejection.

Meeting your 'child' after so many years of separation is not something to be explained in a few paragraphs. I had a two-year-old toddler, on the brink of developing some independence, and meanwhile very dependent on me. A child I called my son. Seventeen years later, I met a young man, on the brink of being in charge of his own life, and I knew he was once connected to me, but I could not call him my son because I signed away that right, and because he told me very clearly he would be offended by that. Moreover, I knew nothing of how he made the transformation from baby to youth.

We were polite and formal with each other, but it was a tense afternoon. I felt like a wet dish-rag by the time I dropped myself into the passenger seat of my car. I went straight to bed and slept for twelve hours. I was certain there would be no further contact. At least I had been given the chance to explain the circumstances, hoping it would bring him perspective and perhaps some solace about having been adopted.

Then Jason followed up with another letter, this time with a softer tone.

Well, from this shaky beginning, and always with the full knowledge and encouragement of his parents, and later his parents-in-law, we have forged a connection. We have each found a place in the other's life. I know he is well established, secure, a devoted husband and father, and sought after in his chosen field of work. All the things you dream of for your own child.

Our reunion has had its stops and starts along the way, and many in the same position may also have experienced that. It's a credit to both of us, and our partners, that we have persevered, and that we have reached a level of accord and regular contact. Many reunions between adoptee and relinquishing parent fail over time. Mercifully, ours has endured. However, I cannot call him my son. Even Jason is not his real name. For the sake of his privacy, I Googled the most popular boy's name in 1972, and there you have it.

This is one of the core challenges for an adoptee, the issue of identity. The baby is born with one name and one family history, and then in the course of adoption, is given a new name and new family history. Now, with the stroke of a pen, I have bestowed yet a third identity. It is an absurd concept.

Therefore, one of the benefits of an adoption reunion, even if the reunion subsequently fails, is knowledge about the first family. Many adoptees seek medical history initially, but the longing for identity goes much deeper than that.

Many adoptees feel a sense of being unlovable, so worthless, that *even their own mother could not love them.* There are others who feel disconnected, lacking a sense of belonging genetically to another person. This need can sit side by side with a feeling of belonging and love in their adopted family. Or, the thought of genetics can terrify: do I have a 'bad' inherited trait which no amount of love from my adopted family can overcome? For others, not knowing the reason for their adoption can impede their ability to get on with their own lives; it becomes the focus of their attention. Concerns, both medical and emotional, can also arise when an adoptee starts their own family. When an adoptee holds their own child for the first time, many are overwhelmed by the concept of giving a baby away.

Reunions can be scary and painful and not always successful, but they do replace beliefs and imaginings with facts, and allow some perspective and clarity on both sides.

Ultimately, judgment on whether I made the right or wrong decision rests with Jason. My actions caused him pain, and yet he has turned the hurt around. Bill and I are welcomed into his family and home and always treated with care and consideration. We do not see each other frequently, and we do not confide in each other, but we do have contact, and that's more than many others in our situation enjoy.

I often dream that we will take a long, long walk along a solitary beach, unburden ourselves to each other, and settle our feelings once and for all. I know, however, it will never happen, so I just accept things as they are.

•

In March 2013, as I was writing this book, the then Prime Minister, the Hon Julia Gillard, said in Federal Parliament: 'Today, this Parliament, on behalf of the Australian people, takes responsibility and apologises for the policies and practices that forced the separation of mothers from their babies, which created a lifelong legacy of pain and suffering . . .' At last, the pain of thousands of mothers and their adopted children was recognised publicly and acknowledged.

As for me, well, I'm not a religious person, and yet somehow, there's an element within my core that some may recognise as a connection with a higher being. There is a sense of inevitability in my life, that the threads will intersect, and what is broken will once again be woven into its proper time and place. There have been so many times in my life when I could have descended into hell, and then, at that vital moment, some person or being has stepped in to gather me up and help me forward. For what reason, I wonder? And, I wonder, why did this collection of experiences happen to me? The only sense I can make of it is that there is a purpose, and the purpose is to bring a message of hope. I am a survivor, and I am a storyteller. My story is painful and personal, a story many might believe would be better left untold. Yet there are thousands out there who have a similar story, and who have a pain that festers within them, waiting to be recognised and understood. I hope by sharing my story, I help to speak for them, and that by speaking out, you may come to understand them better, and that they may draw comfort from knowing they are not alone.

Acknowledgements

My deep thanks go to 'Jason' and 'Steve' for supporting my decision to publish this book, despite the sensitive and revealing material.

There are so many other friends and relatives who have supported me through the many drafts of this book. Apologies to any of those I have overlooked! To Rachel, Lilly and Joanne, thank you for letting me stray into your personal stories. Without them, this book would have been empty. Then there are those who read even the early drafts and encouraged me to keep going: Cousin Phillip, Cousin Esther and husband Ray, and friends Janette and Jennifer (JR). Closely followed by those who read the ensuing drafts and assured me I was making progress: Kerri, Tim, Trevor, Christine, Bob and Marilyn. Sandra – thank you for your belief in me and unswerving passion! It was great to have you in my corner.

Special thanks to my dear friend, Helen Woolcott, who sweated over every word with me as we honed and honed the narrative into the 'almost-there' version. Also to Patti Miller of Life Stories Workshop, for her guidance in classes, and perceptive manuscript appraisal; and to Vicki Morrison of mothersmovingforward.com.au for spotting the title within the first ten minutes of looking at the manuscript.

My editor, Irina Dunn of the Australian Writers' Network, worked closely with me through another two drafts, got my work up to a publishable standard, and found me an agent. Of course, my deep thanks to Selwa Anthony; how amazing to think I stand up there alongside all her other illustrious Australian authors. Finally, I am grateful to *all* at Hachette Australia for taking on a debut, unknown author: with particular thanks to my publisher Vanessa Radnidge, and editors Karen Ward and Jacquie Brown.

Without the input of all these people and many more, this book would have been destined to lie in a bottom drawer, simply a collection of anecdotes, like an overly long letter to a trusted friend.